Perspectives on U.S. Energy Policy

edited by
Edward J. Mitchell

 Published in cooperation with the
American Enterprise Institute for
Public Policy Research

The Praeger Special Studies program—
utilizing the most modern and efficient book
production techniques and a selective
worldwide distribution network—makes
available to the academic, government, and
business communities significant, timely
research in U.S. and international economic, social, and political development.

Perspectives on U.S. Energy Policy
A Critique of Regulation

American Enterprise Institute Perspectives—III

Praeger Publishers   New York   Washington   London

PRAEGER SPECIAL STUDIES IN U.S. ECONOMIC, SOCIAL, AND POLITICAL ISSUES

Library of Congress Cataloging in Publication Data
Main entry under title:

Perspectives on U.S. energy policy.

(Praeger special studies in U.S. economic, social, and
political issues) (American Enterprise Institute perspectives ; 3)
    CONTENTS: Mitchell, E.J.   U.S. energy policy. —
MacAvoy, P.W. and Pindyck, R.S.   Price controls and the natural
gas shortage. —Mancke, R.B.   Performance of the Federal Energy
Office. [etc.]
    1. Energy policy—United States—Addresses, essays,
lectures.   2. Public utilities—United States—Addresses, essays,
lectures.   I. Mitchell, Edward John, 1937-   II. Series:
American Enterprise Institute perspectives ; 3.
HD9502.U52P47   333.7   76-23093
ISBN 0-275-23640-4

PRAEGER PUBLISHERS
111 Fourth Avenue, New York, N.Y. 10003, U.S.A.

Published in the United States of America in 1976
by Praeger Publishers, Inc.

Printed in the United States of America

In early 1974 the American Enterprise Institute established the National Energy Project to examine a broad spectrum of energy policy issues. To this end, the project has commissioned numerous studies and sponsored several conferences and television programs. So far, about fifteen volumes have been published while three major conferences and four, two-hour television programs have been produced. Another dozen studies are expected to be published during the remainder of 1976.

High on the list of policy areas under study is government regulation of the energy industry. Among the studies already published in this area are the four included in this volume. The first section, *U.S. Energy Policy: A Primer*, challenges the conventional wisdom on the "energy crisis." In this study, it is argued that Americans are not the victims of greedy corporations, of their own energy gluttony, or of dwindling energy resources. Instead, they are suffering from a "seesaw" policy of government intervention in the energy market. The development of federal and state energy policies since the end of World War II are traced, with a focus on the petroleum and natural gas industries. Through the 1950s, such government-enforced mechanisms as market-demand prorationing and import quotas caused artificially high U.S. energy prices, huge domestic petroleum surpluses, heavy consumer costs, and production inefficiencies. Then, in the 1960s and 1970s, the situation shifted from surplus to shortage with the gradual imposition of price controls. Energy prices were held far below competitive market levels—a policy that stimulated consumption, dried up supplies, and eventually led to the current crisis. Also considered are the various proposals being advanced to close the "energy gap" and, when found wanting, this suggestion: a return to the free market.

Price Controls and the Natural Gas Shortage, by Paul W. MacAvoy and Robert S. Pindyck, traces the effects of the current natural gas shortage

45640

through the various markets and geographical regions where gas is bought and sold. The authors find that consumers in the northeast, north central, and western regions of the United States have had to shoulder a larger share of the shortage burden than consumers in the southeast and south central regions. They also find that future gas shortages will be more severe than previously forecast.

On the basis of these and other findings, MacAvoy and Pindyck evaluate four major policy proposals for the alleviation of the gas shortage, concluding that phased decontrol of the natural gas industry would best serve the interest of consumers as a group. They find that, without such a policy, the shortage will grow worse, and the large population and industrial centers of the northeast and north central regions will continue to bear more than their share of hardship.

The findings presented in this study result from the authors' latest forecasts of U.S. natural gas production and consumption under different assumptions about U.S. government energy-related policies. The work builds on the authors' earlier modeling efforts, incorporating much new information. The economietric model used is described in an appendix.

Performance of the Federal Energy Office, by Richard B. Mancke, seeks to evaluate the role played by the Federal Energy Office (FEO) during the oil embargo imposed by the members of the Organization of Arab Petroleum Exporting Countries (OAPEC). The FEO was established after the start of the OAPEC embargo, and charged with the responsibility for initiating policies to alleviate the ill effects of the oil shortages that resulted from the OAPEC action. Initially, the most important task was to take steps to prevent the United States from running out of oil products. The FEO responded with several allocation measures aimed at closing the oil-supply gap by reducing U.S. demands in an equitable way. It also enforced price controls. The author concludes that, on balance, the FEO's allocation measures and price controls not only exacerbated U.S. oil-supply problems, but also failed to create a more equitable distribution of the embargo's costs. From this probe of the underlying causes of the FEO's policy failures, the most important lesson that emerges concerns planning. Prior to the OAPEC embargo, the United States government had only the vaguest plans for dealing with such a contingency. Thus, both Congress and the White House panicked when it occurred. Good decision making is at best difficult in a crisis atmosphere. It becomes nearly impossible when the organization responsible for making speedy decisions lacks adequate staff, administrative traditions, a well-defined decision-making hierarchy, and is subject to political pressures from a plethora of interest groups—as was the case with the FEO.

Toward Economy in Electric Power, by Peter R. Chaffetz and myself, addresses an issue that is popularly viewed as a contest between consumers who balk at soaring prices, and electric utilities who seek higher prices in order to attract the capital necessary to meet growing consumer demands. In this political tug-of-war, one side gains when the other side loses. Chaffetz and I argue, on the one hand, that the nation is not confined to a choice between lower prices and shortages or, on the other, higher prices and adequate supplies. There is a third option: to lower the cost of generating adequate power by allowing private industrial firms to enter the power generation business now reserved for regulated utilities.

Specifically discussed are the lower consumer prices and the lower capital and fuel requirements that could be achieved by private industrial generation of power from steam now used solely in industrial processes. According to our estimates, private power generation from such "waste" steam could lead by 1985 to household electric bills as much as $3.6 billion per year lower than if the current system were maintained, while reducing the nation's fuel consumption by the equivalent of 680 thousand barrels of oil per day and its capital requirements by $5 billion per year. The conclusions of this study are based on a large-scale technical, economic, and legal analysis prepared under a grant from the National Science Foundation.

The National Energy Project is chaired by Melvin R. Laird, former congressman, secretary of defense and domestic counsellor to the President, and now senior counsellor with *Reader's Digest*.

CONTENTS

LIST OF TABLES

U.S. Energy Policy: A Primer

Price Controls and the Natural Gas Shortage

Performance in the Federal Energy Office

Toward Economy in Electric Power

LIST OF FIGURES

U.S. Energy Policy: A Primer

Figure

THE AEI
NATIONAL ENERGY PROJECT

The American Enterprise Institute's
National Energy Project was established in early 1974
to examine the broad array of issues
affecting U.S. energy demands and supplies.
The project will commission research into all important
ramifications of the energy problem—economic
and political, domestic and international, private
and public—and will present the results
in studies such as this one.
In addition it will sponsor symposia, debates, conferences,
and workshops, some of which will be televised.

The project is chaired by Melvin R. Laird,
former congressman, secretary of defense,
and domestic counsellor to the President,
and now senior counsellor of *Reader's Digest*.
An advisory council, representing a wide range of
energy-related viewpoints, has been appointed.
The project director is Professor Edward J. Mitchell
of the University of Michigan.

Views expressed are those of the authors
and do not necessarily reflect the views of
either the advisory council and others associated with
the project or of the advisory panels,
staff, officers, and trustees of AEI.

U.S. ENERGY POLICY:
A PRIMER
Edward J. Mitchell

1

ENERGY POLICY
IN PERSPECTIVE

A false perception of the energy problem is common to many experts and the man-in-the-street. Ask Americans what the energy problem is about, and they will probably say it is about shortages: shortages of gasoline, of heating oil, of electricity, of natural gas. Ask a more sophisticated audience, such as oil company executives or government energy officials, and they will express concern about future energy "gaps" as well as current shortages. They will talk of future energy "requirements" or "needs," and how future supply must fall short.

A Shortage Is a Policy

The trouble with these views is that shortages and gaps are not acts of nature that "happen to us"; they are the creations of men, the consequences of deliberate policy choice. Neither smaller supplies nor larger demands imply shortages. In fact, if we never found another barrel of oil or cubic foot of natural gas, or never mined another ton of coal, there would be no necessity for shortages.

This observation follows from the fact that at some price the energy market will clear. As long as either less is demanded or more supplied as price increases, there is some price at which supply equals demand. The matter has been put succinctly by Professor Milton Friedman:

> Economists may not know much. But we do know one thing very well: how to produce shortages and surpluses. Do you want to produce a shortage of any product? Simply have government fix and enforce a legal *maximum* price on the product which is less than the price that would otherwise prevail. . . . Do you want to produce a surplus of any

product? Simply have government fix and enforce a legal *minimum* price above the price that would otherwise prevail.[1]

Thus government policy makers always have three options in any market: (1) a market-clearing price, (2) a lower price and shortages, or (3) a higher price and surpluses. There are free-market policies, shortage policies, and surplus policies. The government is now following shortage policies in the energy market. In the 1950s governments (state and federal) elected a surplus policy for oil. In the 1960s they elected a surplus policy for oil and, simultaneously, a shortage policy for natural gas. It will be shown below that in 1965 we had at least 25 percent surplus capacity for producing crude oil, while through the 1960s we had a shortage of natural gas reserve additions on the order of 30 to 60 percent. While these policies may present problems for some consumers and producers—namely, the consumers who are not allocated all they want of the limited supplies and the producers who must hold unwanted surplus capacity or inventories—they are not problems for the government. They are the policies of the government.

There is nothing necessarily irrational about choosing a shortage or a surplus policy over a free-market policy. Like any policy, they have consequences that benefit some and injure others. For example, shortages of gasoline clearly benefit those who receive under rationing all the gasoline they want at less than the free-market price. Those consumers who would like to purchase more gasoline at the free-market price, but cannot, are to that extent worse off. Gasoline suppliers are also worse off. If one is more favorably disposed toward the benefitted group than the injured group, the decision to have shortages is not hard to justify.

Significantly, one group *always* benefits from either a shortage or a surplus policy. A rationing procedure must always be established to allocate a shortage among consumers or a surplus among producers, and the power to influence these rationing decisions is of considerable value. Thus, politicians, bureaucrats, Washington lawyers, and the communications media are beneficiaries. As a practical matter, the benefits accruing to this group may dominate the decision-making process.

Sometimes rather broad-brush reasons are given for the choice of a shortage policy. For example, free-market prices are not being allowed in the gasoline market because, it is said, this would hurt

---

[1] Milton Friedman and Robert V. Roosa, *The Balance of Payments: Free Versus Fixed Exchange Rates* (Washington, D. C.: American Enterprise Institute, 1967), p. 1.

the poor. This implies that the shortage option is better for the poor. Yet there does not appear to be the same degree of support among self-professed supporters of the poor for bread or milk shortages. Such shortages, by this reasoning, favor the poor even more than gasoline shortages. Furthermore, the poor consume such a small proportion of energy supplies that it is rather odd to suggest choosing energy policies primarily for their benefit. Direct assistance to the poor to alleviate their poverty would be more sensible.

It is also argued that a low price, or energy shortage, policy will help reduce inflation. By fighting inflation one can only mean maintaining the purchasing power of the dollar. From our gasoline example it is clear that those allocated all they want at lower prices find their dollars enhanced in value, but those without all they want find their dollars worth less insofar as gasoline is concerned. In what sense can it be said that *the* purchasing power of money is maintained? Unfortunately, in these circumstances the consumer price index reflects only the values of the enhanced dollars. This is an important reason why politicians choose shortages during periods of inflation.

Surely the most remarkable aspect of shortage policies is that many who support the choice of a shortage policy also claim that the shortage is the problem. In particular, many politicians urge prices below the market-clearing level and then bemoan the resulting shortage.[2] If we take them at their word, this implies that they do not know the consequences of their actions. If we do not take them at their word we must concede deception. Whichever is the case, shortage policies are usually not long-lived. Consumers and voters seem to regard them as measures necessary in an emergency that become intolerable after awhile.

Surplus policies, such as the crude oil surplus of the 1950s and '60s, seem to be blessed with greater longevity. One reason is that it is much easier to calculate the distribution of benefits and injuries on the supply side. Businessmen can readily measure in dollars and cents the effects of different prices and different allocation formulas. The difficulties of calculating benefits and injuries of shortage policies to consumers cannot be understated. We know that if the price is set only a little below the market-clearing level the number of consumer beneficiaries will be large but the benefits to each will be small. As the price is lowered individual benefits increase but the number of beneficiaries shrinks as the supply decreases. With demand and supply shifting all the time it becomes very hard for a politician

---

[2] For example, the National Energy Emergency Act of 1973 (S. 2589) labels the shortage as the problem.

or bureaucrat to fine tune the price and allocation formula to his constituents' interest.[3] In the case of surplus policies he has unlimited technical assistance from the cartel he has created.

An important exception to the factors tending to cause shortage policies to be short-lived is the fact that there may be substantial benefits from a shortage policy to suppliers of competing products. If there are close substitutes for a particular product, a shortage policy for that product increases the demand for the substitutes. This is what has happened in the natural gas market. Prices far below the market-clearing level for natural gas are creating artificial demands for liquified natural gas (LNG) and synthetic gas from coal, both of which cost at least double the probable market-clearing price. Strong opposition to deregulation of natural gas prices in 1972 executive branch discussions came only from those associated with LNG interests. And the principal Senate advocate of stricter and more extensive price regulation of natural gas is from the state with the largest bituminous coal resources.

Thus, while there is little likelihood of a long-run shortage policy on energy, there is a good probability of deliberate shortage policies for specific forms of energy. Many new forms of energy, such as synthetic fuels from coal, have a chance for commercial success only if shortage policies are imposed on competing cheaper sources, such as conventional oil and natural gas.

Is Energy Scarcity Increasing?

Abandoning shortage policies will mean higher prices. For awhile these prices will be higher than would have existed had free-market policies been chosen all along and higher than the level that will prevail in the long run. Supply in today's market is geared to the prices expected under a shortage policy. And, unfortunately, it takes several years for energy supplies to respond to price. In a free market everyone can have all he wants at the market price. There are no gaps or shortages. The true measure of scarcity, therefore, is price, and the measure of long-run scarcity is long-run price. The prices we will observe immediately when the free market is reinstated will overstate the long-run scarcity of energy.

The question that seems to concern many is whether energy is getting so scarce that severe adjustments will have to be made in the

---

[3] The problem of creating and sustaining consumer coalitions is discussed in Sam Peltzman, "Pricing in Public and Private Enterprises: Electric Utilities in the United States," *The Journal of Law and Economics*, vol. 14, no. 1 (April 1971).

way we live. This concern is not focused on the scarcity of oil-refining or electric-power-generating capacity, both of which have been giving us problems recently. We know these are basically manufacturing activities and are subject to no more scarcity in the long run than plants that produce automobiles or sewing machines. The concern is about the raw materials for these plants—oil, natural gas, coal, and uranium. Are we depleting these natural resources so fast that we will run out before long? Many think so.

If the age of an idea contributes to its validity then the doomsday thesis has a lot going for it. However, the doomsayers have not only been consistently vocal, they have also been consistently wrong. America has had less than a dozen years' supply of oil left for a hundred years. In 1866 the United States Revenue Commission was concerned about having synthetics available when crude oil production ended; in 1891 the U.S. Geological Survey assured us there was little chance of oil in Texas; and in 1914 the Bureau of Mines estimated total future U.S. production at 6 billion barrels—we have produced that much oil every twenty months for years. Perhaps the most curious thing about these forecasts is a tendency for remaining resources to grow as we deplete existing resources. Thus, a geologist for the world's largest oil company estimated potential U.S. reserves at 110 to 165 billion barrels in 1948. In 1959, after we had consumed almost 30 billion of those barrels, he estimated 391 billion were left.[4]

There are two reasons why these forecasts have been so wrong in the past and why they are so irrelevant today. First, there is the popular tendency to focus on proved reserves, which always appear frighteningly small. Proved reserves in the oil- and gas-producing industry are essentially the same as what are called inventories in other businesses. The fact that oil men hold only ten or fifteen years' supply of oil under the ground should be of as much concern to us as the fact that shoe stores keep only thirty days' supply of shoes on the shelf. To hold more would be unprofitable for the businessman and uneconomical for society. When we do find places, such as the Middle East and North Africa, holding fifty years' supply we are witnessing an error in business judgment, or an expectation of enormous growth of deliveries, or an extremely low cost of holding inventories, or some combination of the three.

When policy makers go beyond proved reserves to estimates of potentially recoverable reserves they often misinterpret the figures.

---

[4] DeGolyer and MacNaughton, "Report on National Energy Policy," privately circulated report, 1971, Table 20.

When geologists say that the United States has 300 or 400 billion barrels of potentially recoverable crude oil—about fifty to seventy years' consumption at current rates—they are assuming *present technology* and *present price levels*.[5] These quantities, as rough as they are, have meaning only if they have a price tag placed on them. But one of the few certainties in an uncertain world is that future technology and future prices will be different. The ultimate quantity of oil under the ground is (as Professor M. A. Adelman tells us) unknown, unknowable, and, most important, uninteresting. The pertinent questions are, How much do we have to give up to get an extra barrel (or billion barrels) of oil? How much is that barrel worth to us? If it is worth more than it costs, and it costs less than alternative energy sources, we should use it; if not, we should leave it in the ground. When we decide to stop using oil it makes no difference whether we have left in the ground an infinite amount, a trillion barrels, or a barrel and a half.

The focus on the very long run by the doomsayers is good strategy. Bad forecasting is rarely dismissed because it is bad; instead, people demand a better forecast. But economists and businessmen understand that no one knows what lies ahead fifty years and that the costs of searching for highly uncertain answers greatly exceeds their value.

Even forecasts of only the next ten to twenty years are of little value. To illustrate this point, consider the forecasts made of 1980 energy consumption in 1962 and in 1971, halfway to the target date. In 1962 the Committee on Interior and Insular Affairs of the United States Senate offered a consensus of eleven forecasts of 1980 energy consumption. Actual 1962 energy consumption, the 1980 consensus forecast, and the increase over 1962 implied by that forecast are shown in Table 1. For comparison, figures for representative 1971 studies are also shown. Table 2 gives the same comparison for projected oil consumption using the same sources.

The more recent forecasts predict an increment in energy consumption 60 to 80 percent larger than earlier forecasts. In the case of oil the more recent forecasts predict increments 70 to 120 percent higher. For perspective, the *difference* between the 1962 Senate Interior Committee consensus forecast of energy consumption and the 1971 Department of the Interior forecast is considerably greater than 1973 U.S. oil production and more than double 1973 U.S. oil

---

[5] Ibid.

Table 1

ENERGY CONSUMPTION FORECASTS, 1962–1980
(quadrillions of British thermal units)

Source	Forecast Date	Actual Consumption 1962	Forecast Consumption 1980	Forecast Increment 1962–1980
Senate Interior Committee[a] (consensus of eleven forecasts)	1962	47.4	82.0	34.6
National Petroleum Council[b]	1971	47.4	102.6	55.2
Department of the Interior[c]	1971	47.4	108.7[d]	61.3

Source:
[a] U.S. Congress, Senate, Committee on Interior and Insular Affairs, *Report of the National Fuels and Energy Study Group on Assessment of Available Information on Energy in the United States*, 87th Congress, 2d session, September 1962.

[b] National Petroleum Council, *U.S. Energy Outlook: An Initial Appraisal, 1971–1985*, vol. 1 (Washington, D.C.: National Petroleum Council, 1971), pp. 13-14.

[c] U.S. Department of the Interior, *United States Energy: A Summary Review* (Washington, D.C.: Government Printing Office, 1972), p. 12.

[d] Interpolated from 1975 and 1980 forecasts assuming constant rate of growth.

Table 2

OIL CONSUMPTION FORECASTS, 1962–1980
(millions of barrels per day)

Source	Forecast Date	Actual Consumption 1962	Forecast Consumption 1980	Forecast Increment 1962–1980
Senate Interior Committee[a]	1962	10.6	16.4	5.8
National Petroleum Council[b]	1971	10.6	23.5	12.9
Department of the Interior[c]	1971	10.6	20.6[d]	10.0

Source: Same as Table 1.

imports. One might also note that the rate of oil consumption forecast by the Interior Committee for 1980 was already achieved in 1972.[6]

[6] For a survey of earlier forecasts see Pacific Northwest Laboratories, *A Review and Comparison of Selected United States Energy Forecasts* (Washington, D. C.: Government Printing Office, 1969).

This kind of forecasting performance is clearly uninspiring. More important, there is no reason to believe that we can significantly improve our forecasting accuracy in the future. Changes in tastes, technology, and resource discoveries are so unpredictable as to make ten- or twenty-year forecasts little more than crystal-ball gazing.

Apart from undercutting the doomsday thesis, the inaccuracy of forecasts has great significance for public policy. The notion that government can successfully plan to meet specific future energy "needs" or "requirements" by blueprinting supply programs for oil, coal, and other energy sources over the next decade is pure illusion. *Almost certainly such programs would result in large surpluses or shortages and unnecessary costs.*[7] What *is* called for are institutions that are self-adjusting and responsive to change. The market is one such institution. The political and bureaucratic processes as we know them today are not.

What little we do know about the intermediate future, say 1985 or 1990, does *not* suggest significantly increased energy costs. The world energy market is, of course, dominated by Middle East oil. Adelman, using very conservative figures, sums up the world oil market this way:

> For at least fifteen years we can count on, and must learn to live with, an abundance of oil that can be brought forth from fields now operated in the Persian Gulf at something between 10 and 20 cents per barrel at 1968 prices and in some other provinces at costs even lower when account is taken of transport.[8]

When we turn to the United States, matters are not so simple. We have already mentioned the 300-400 billion barrels estimated, but the "supply curve" of U.S. oil and natural gas is not nearly as flat as the Persian Gulf curve. At any one time a great deal of oil is being produced in the United States at costs of twenty cents per barrel and at costs of $4.00 per barrel. The high-cost barrels must, of course, set the market price. Nevertheless, knowledge of what the average or "typical" barrel might cost does give us a point on the supply curve, and if the "tilt" of that curve does not change greatly, it can tell us something about likely future costs at the margin.

In the early 1930s the average cost (excluding bonuses, royalties, taxes, and other rents) of producing a barrel of U.S. crude oil was

---

[7] One must recognize that surpluses can be just as costly as shortages. Indeed, because of their longevity surpluses might be presumed to be more costly.

[8] M. A. Adelman, *The World Petroleum Market* (Baltimore: Johns Hopkins University Press, 1972), p. 77.

eighty cents.[9] In the early 1960s the cost has been estimated to have been $1.22,[10] and in 1972 another source gives $1.58 for onshore production and $1.51 for offshore Gulf of Mexico production.[11] Since the wholesale price index tripled between the early 1930s and the early 1960s average *real* costs appear to have declined.

We know that most future U.S. production will be offshore or in Alaska. One estimate of future average costs on the outer continental shelf is $1.61 per barrel.[12] The costs of Prudhoe Bay (Alaskan North Slope) crude run about twenty-five cents at the wellhead and no more than $1.25 delivered to the West Coast.[13] Some other Alaskan crude could run higher at the wellhead, but generally it would be closer to market.

Most of the still unproven future reserves appear to be on federal lands. This has an important bearing on whether the costs mentioned above will tend to determine market prices, or whether more marginal sources, say from secondary or tertiary recovery projects, will do so.

The federal government has been extremely reluctant to permit exploitation of petroleum resources on its lands. Naval Petroleum Reserve Number Four, which contains the geological extension of the Prudhoe Bay field, has sat untapped for half a century. The director of Naval Petroleum Reserves believes the U.S. Geological Survey estimate that Reserve Number Four holds 33 billion barrels of crude oil reserves—an amount greater than present "Lower 48" reserves—may prove conservative.[14] Sitting untapped, outside Los Angeles, is the nation's third largest proved oil field—Naval Petroleum Reserve Number Three, the Elk Hills field.

There seems to be no rational explanation for leaving these vast reserves untapped. The House Armed Services Committee, which oversees the naval petroleum reserves, simply has shown no inclination to allow Americans to make use of them. And when an official of the Defense Department recently endorsed exploitation of "Pet 4" by opening it up for competitive bidding, a major television network

9 U.S. Department of the Interior, *Report on the Cost of Producing Crude Petroleum* (Washington, D. C.: Government Printing Office, 1935), and Adelman, *World Petroleum Market*.

10 Adelman, *World Petroleum Market*, p. 76.

11 U.S. Department of the Interior, "Questions and Policy Issues Related to Oversight Hearings on the Administration of the Outer Continental Shelf Lands Act," mimeographed, March 1972, pp. 86-87.

12 Ibid., p. 88.

13 Calculations by the author, 1971.

14 *Oil and Gas Journal*, 17 September 1973, pp. 38-39.

saw it as a potential scandal rivalling Teapot Dome because the official held stock in an oil company!

When we turn to natural gas the picture is clearer by virtue of a more extensive cost study, and the picture is bright. We will have much more to say about this later.[15]

The upshot of these cost estimates, plus other supply studies, is that there is an abundance of petroleum likely to be available at moderate costs. The quantity of coal available at near-current real costs is well known.[16] And the long-run supply curve of uranium consistently embarrasses supporters of breeder reactors.[17]

This is not to say that real energy costs will not rise. Rather it suggests that the incremental barrel of oil might cost double what it has been costing—but *not* five times today's cost. In terms of consumer prices a doubling of the price of oil from the $3.50 per barrel level prevalent in early 1973 to $7.00 per barrel means a little more than eight cents added to the price per gallon of gasoline and heating oil. That implies a roughly 20 percent increase in gasoline price using August 1973 prices as a base. Twenty percent is hardly the kind of change in price that drastically alters lifestyles. In 1964 gasoline consumers in Cheyenne, Wyoming, paid average gasoline prices which were almost 25 percent higher than those paid by consumers in Wichita, Boston, Detroit, and St. Louis.[18] This did not seem to dramatically affect the way they lived.

Indeed much larger differences in energy prices seem to have little recognizable effect on people's lives. It is not uncommon for electric rates to be 50 or 100 percent different from one town to another in the same state. A 250 kilowatt hour electric bill in Pleasantville, New York, is three times that of Plattsburgh, New York, yet does not seem to have resulted in profound differences in living patterns.[19]

This is not to say that energy consumers don't alter energy consumption in response to price changes. The evidence suggests that the consumption response to price changes is substantial. A recent study indicates that a 30 percent change in gasoline consumption could be induced by only a 40 percent change (in the opposite

---

[15] See pages 23-24 and 66-69 below.

[16] U.S. Geological Survey, *Coal Resources of the United States, January 1, 1967* (Washington, D. C.: Government Printing Office, 1969).

[17] National Petroleum Council, *Report of the Nuclear Task Group* (Washington, D. C.: Government Printing Office, 1972), pp. 21-27.

[18] *Platt's Oilgram Price Service* (daily publication by McGraw-Hill), various issues.

[19] Federal Power Commission, *Typical Electric Bills* (Washington, D. C.: Government Printing Office, 1970).

direction) in price. Electricity consumption seems to respond almost proportionately to changes in electric rates.[20] The point is that these adjustments in consumption are not catastrophic. They do not alter noticeably the way people live.

Why an Energy Crisis?

While costs of producing energy have changed over the years, there is no evidence that they have changed so quickly or so dramatically as to bring about the current scarcity. If the supply side is not to blame, what about the demand side? Statistics developed in Appendix A show a significant acceleration in the growth of energy consumption between 1965 and 1970 as compared with the periods 1960 to 1965 and 1955 to 1965. This suggests that a rapidly rising demand for energy might have caused the crisis.

However, the evidence does not support this thesis. For consumption growth to have caused the crisis, its acceleration must have been induced by an exogenous increase in demand. Three pieces of evidence make this unlikely. First, the gross national product actually grew at a slower rate (3.4 percent per annum) from 1965 to 1970 than it did from 1960 to 1965 (5.3 percent) and from 1955 to 1965 (4.1 percent). Since the economy would have to provide the main stimulus for demand growth, how can we explain an acceleration in energy consumption growth alongside a deceleration in economic growth? Second, if we go beyond overall economic growth to search for exogenous factors we do not find them. One serious attempt to attribute accelerating consumption to factors such as declining efficiency of electric plants and the growth of air conditioning—if these could indeed be considered exogenous factors—concedes that only a modest portion of energy consumption growth can be explained in this way.[21]

But most important, an exogenous increase in the rate of demand growth implies rising prices or, at least, less rapidly falling prices. The fact is that real energy prices were falling throughout the 1950s, and the decline accelerated continuously through the 1960s and early '70s right up to the middle of 1973. Real energy prices

---

[20] H. S. Houthakker and P. K. Verleger, "Dynamic Demand Analyses of Selected Energy Resources," a paper delivered to the American Economic Association, December 1973.

[21] National Economic Research Associates, "Energy Consumption and Gross National Product in the United States: An Examination of Recent Changes in the Relationship," privately circulated, March 1971.

Table 3

ENERGY CONSUMPTION, ECONOMIC GROWTH, AND ENERGY PRICES, 1950–1973

	Average Annual Rate of Change				
	1950–55	1955–60	1960–65	1965–70	1970–mid-1973
Energy consumption: heat index	3.4	2.5	3.9	5.3	n.a.
Energy consumption: value-weighted index	7.7	4.6	4.9	6.2	n.a.
Real gross national product	4.7	2.3	5.3	3.4	n.a.
Index of energy prices	−.62	−.8	−1.3	−1.7	−1.9 [a]

a Preliminary estimate.
Source: Appendix A.

fell 3.1 percent from 1950 to 1955, 3.7 percent from 1955 to 1960, 6.5 percent from 1960 to 1965, and 8.1 percent from 1965 to 1970. The fall from 1970 to June 1973 extrapolates to a five-year rate of 9.4 percent. Overall, real energy prices fell by about one-fourth between 1950 and the middle of 1973. The figures on energy consumption and prices and economic growth are shown in Table 3. Details may be found in Appendix A.

This price pattern implies that it was not so much exogenous shifts in demand that spurred consumption, but rapidly falling prices inducing consumers to purchase more energy. In short, energy was becoming more and more of a bargain compared to other consumer products—and so consumers bought more.

Everyone knows that since the summer of 1973 many energy prices, particularly for petroleum products, have soared. What we have experienced is an accelerating decline in prices over two decades followed by a sharp upward thrust in the past year. It is clear that changes in energy costs or in the demand for energy cannot account for what has happened. There is only one source of explanation: changes in government policies that have artificially manipulated scarcities in the marketplace.

In the world oil market, prices fell during the 1950s and 1960s, the decline being interrupted only by occasional Middle East crises. This decline was not the result of falling oil production costs but of the weakening ability of exporters to sustain prices above costs.

By 1971 the cartel of producing nations had strengthened its ability to control production and prices. This is the major cause of oil scarcity outside the United States and clearly not the consequence of increased costs or scarcity of supplies. Middle East oil is at least as abundant relative to demand now as it was in 1950.[22]

In the U.S. oil market, state production restrictions, federal import quotas, and a tight federal leasing policy kept oil prices high in the 1950s and mid-1960s. As surplus crude oil capacity declined in the late 1960s, the natural response of a cartel would have been to raise prices. Instead, quotas were liberalized and prices held down, first by informal pressures and the rising quotas, and then by mandatory price controls. The real price of U.S. crude oil fell from 1967 to 1972. While domestic spare capacity was shrinking, public policy shifts dictated more imports and lower prices, stimulating demand and increasing dependence on foreign supplies.

In the United States natural gas prices rose through most of the 1950s. The installation of price ceilings in 1960 kept wellhead prices from rising further. The low ceiling prices increased demand as well as stimulating production out of existing reserves—it was hardly worthwhile to hold reserves for production at a later date if prices were not going to rise. But low gas prices meant declining exploration for new reserves since this was becoming more costly. A shortage of natural gas to consumers was inevitable, although this was hidden for a time by the use of huge reserves accumulated in earlier periods. By 1970 available gas supplies were falling short of demand.

The real cost of generating electric power fell through the 1950s and most of the 1960s. Real prices also fell stimulating consumption. By the late 1960s, however, the decline in production costs was reversed by a slowing in the growth of generating plant efficiency and the added costs of meeting environmental standards. These were not reflected immediately in electric rates, and the prospects for investment in the electric utility industry soured: the rate of return to a stockholder (including dividends and price appreciation) of a typical electrical utility fell to only 1.4 percent over the 1967-1972 period.[23] Capital became difficult to raise, and capacity could not be expanded to meet demand.

---

[22] The ratio of reserves to production in the Middle East and North Africa has been around 50 for the past two decades.

[23] See J. Hass, E. Mitchell, and B. Stone, *Financing the Energy Industry* (Cambridge, Mass.: Ballinger Publishing Co., forthcoming 1974), pp. IV-18-20, and B. Seligman, "What Others Think: The Declining Return on Electric Utility Investment," *Public Utilities Fortnightly*, 9 November 1972, p. 45.

Americans have been induced by changes in public policy to consume more energy. But the domestic public policies that stimulated consumption in the short run discouraged investment in the long run. The year of reckoning was 1973. Almost simultaneously the cartel of oil-producing countries that had previously failed to keep prices up and production down turned things around and raised prices with astounding success.

To the extent that U.S. international policies might have avoided this turnaround, part of the blame must be laid at the door of our policy makers. But even if U.S. policies are not responsible for the success of the oil cartel's price increases, they *can* be blamed for permitting us to become dependent upon the cartel. In 1972 the United States imported 500,000 barrels of crude and oil products per day from Arab countries. The shortfall in natural gas supplies alone—caused by severe Federal Power Commission (FPC) price restrictions—is estimated at the equivalent of 1,800,000 barrels of oil per day in 1972,[24] or three and a half times oil imports from Arab nations. While not all unmet gas demand was converted into additional oil imports, much of it was, since the Persian Gulf producers were the residual energy suppliers to this nation.

The energy crisis is a crisis of public policy. It is the consequence of shortage policies adopted without reference to the public interest. *There is no evidence that in a free energy market anything resembling a crisis, or even a problem, would have occurred.* The notion that these artificial scarcities are due to private conspiracies has no foundation. In spite of decades of investigation by the U.S. Federal Trade Commission and of unending charges by small businessmen, congressmen, and "public interest" law firms, nothing that would have had any significant bearing on market trends in the past couple of decades has been uncovered, the popularity of conspiratorial themes notwithstanding. The petroleum industry in particular has exhibited the major characteristics of a competitive industry.[25] To be sure, inefficiencies in market structure have existed, but these have invariably been the consequence of government policies and laws, not private conspiracies.

---

[24] Paul W. MacAvoy and Robert S. Pindyck, "Alternative Regulatory Policies for Dealing with the Natural Gas Shortage," *Bell Journal of Economics and Management Science*, vol. 4, no. 2 (Autumn 1973), pp. 489-492.

[25] Obviously this is not the kind of issue that can be dealt with adequately here. Nor is there a useful literature on the subject to refer to. For an attempt to expose some of the mythology of "big oil" monopolies see Appendix B. Also see Richard B. Mancke, "Petroleum Conspiracy: A Costly Myth," *Public Policy*, vol. 22, no. 1 (Winter 1974).

The list of government laws, programs, policies, and institutions determining the course of the energy market is long, but only a handful have been crucial. They are: the Mandatory Oil Import Program, the Texas Railroad Commission and market-demand prorationing, the Natural Gas Act and FPC regulation of natural gas prices, the Organization of Petroleum Exporting Countries (particularly certain Arab members), the U.S. Cost of Living Council and price controls, the U.S. Department of the Interior's minerals leasing policy, and the Environmental Protection Agency and the laws it is required to enforce. While other policies have had enormous impact on our pocketbooks—for example, the Atomic Energy Commission's multi-billion dollar research and development efforts in conventional and breeder reactors—they have had negligible effect on the energy market itself. Most of the remainder of this monograph is devoted to certain of the above mentioned government actions.

2

POLICIES WITHOUT
CRITERIA: GAPOLOGY

Central to an understanding of the political economy of energy is the knowledge that most publicly oriented energy discussions do not deal seriously with energy markets. To appreciate how the energy debate actually takes place, we must repress our knowledge of how markets work and adopt an approach that might be called "gapology," the theory or science of gaps.

The term derives from the procedure of setting out separately the prospective future demand for energy at *current* prices and comparing this to the estimated future supply of energy at *current* prices. In recent years, this comparison always ends up in a gap, or shortage. In this approach, the jargon of economics is used: "demand," "supply," "consumption," "production," and, in more sophisticated attempts, sometimes even "inventories."

The gap approach is so common that it is doubtful that there is anyone who has looked seriously at the energy question without coming across several gap analyses. Most energy companies follow this approach, but do not leave the gap unfilled—they almost always fill it with imports of overseas oil and liquified natural gas. (With recent Arab cutoffs, it is not clear how this will be handled.)

Government agencies, such as the FPC, usually leave the gap unfilled and forecast a shortage. A good example of the gap approach is to be found in the Department of the Interior's *United States Energy: A Summary Review*.[1] It forecasts energy "requirements" to the year 2000, breaking this down among different fuels. While these estimat take into account such factors as economic activity, population growth, and environmental controls, the only reference to price as a variable determining demand or supply is an analysis

[1] Washington, D. C.: Government Printing Office, January 1972.

of the effects of *relative* costs of different fuels on consumption and a comment to the effect that demand is "relatively insensitive to price."[2] The final chapter in the report goes on to consider the various options for filling the gap. In the case of natural gas, the traditional line chart is drawn showing total demand exceeding domestic and Canadian supply after 1975. In the gap on the chart is a series of question marks referring to the various options for filling the gap: liquified natural gas, Canadian gas, Arctic gas, and synthetic gas. While the importance of price in determining future domestic natural gas supplies is clearly noted in the report,[3] no statement is made regarding the price assumed in the projections, nor is there any suggestion that the gap might be closed merely by freeing the price.[4]

Gapological reasoning may also be found in everyday newspaper reports of the energy problem. On 2 December 1973 the *New York Times* ran this headline: "Oil Independence—U.S. Self-sufficiency by 1980 Is Unfeasible," followed by the statement that "most experts feel that, despite our best efforts, the United States is likely to remain dependent upon oil imports to make up the gap between domestic supplies and sharply rising demand."[5] Actually the United States could be self-sufficient tomorrow simply by abolishing all import rights and letting the domestic market clear. All domestic demand would then be met by domestic supply. The United States imports foreign oil not because self-sufficiency is infeasible but because it would be too costly. Whether we will be self-sufficient in the future should be dependent upon the relative costs and risks of foreign and domestic supplies.

Concerning ways to fill the gap the same article notes that "the United States has the world's largest coal resources, which will come increasingly into use as environmentally sound ways to use coal are found." This illustrates a principal feature of gap analysis: the emphasis on the *quantity* of potentially gap-filling resources rather than their *cost*. The quantity of U.S. coal resources is not a great deal more relevant than the quantity of energy emitted by distant stars (which I presume is much greater than that contained in our coal reserves). It is possible that we now consume more coal than we

---

[2] Ibid., pp. 6 and 13.

[3] Ibid., p. 22.

[4] A representative sample of gap analyses would also include the National Petroleum Council's *U.S. Energy Outlook: An Initial Appraisal, 1971-1985*, vols. 1 and 2, and Federal Power Commission, Bureau of Natural Gas, *Natural Gas Supply and Demand, 1971-1990: Staff Report No. 2* (Washington, D. C.: Government Printing Office, February 1972).

[5] *New York Times*, Section 3, p. 1.

ought to taking into account harmful effects on air quality. But finding "environmentally sound" ways to burn coal is not the issue either. The real question is whether it is less costly to burn coal than oil or gas, where cost includes not only the resources used in production but also the injury to people exposed to harmful emissions.

Here is another statement from the same *Times* article: "Many economists would add that projections of demand . . . are based on the assumption that there will be an adequate supply of energy." This statement has meaning only if "demand" means "consumption" and demand and supply are completely insensitive to price. But energy demand and supply are certainly sensitive to price, and therefore the statement is meaningless. If this *Times* article is an accurate representation of how a significant number of energy experts and economists think about energy issues, is it really surprising that there is trouble in the energy markets?

Filling the Gap

Once a gap or shortage has been revealed, the question that inevitably arises is: How do we fill the gap? This becomes the central question of public policy. Clearly, the gap-reducing or eliminating measures fall neatly into two categories: those that reduce demand and those that increase supply. At this point, serious divisions break out in the gapologist camp. Some are very much for reducing demand, for example, environmentalists. Others, such as energy producers, urgently want to increase supply. Thus, when it comes to specific policy recommendations, there is great conflict in the camp—what unites all gapological factions, however, is a similar perception of the problem.

There are several remedies offered to fill the energy gap. On the supply side there is usually talk of government R&D to develop new energy technologies—some even suggest crash programs on the order of the Apollo moon project. Also proposed are tax incentives and laws to remove obstacles to the siting of facilities, new leasing programs for federal lands and even direct federal exploitation of federally controlled resources. The value of each proposal is seen as the extent to which it increases supply.

On the demand side there is talk of eliminating "unnecessary" consumption, of requiring greater insulation in homes, of imposing changes in transportation methods, and of requiring more efficient energy-using equipment. The value of each suggested measure is, of course, the extent to which it reduces consumption.

Now it is obvious that there are numerous combinations of supply-augmenting and demand-reducing measures that will do the job. Each gapologist can choose his own set. Politically this is one of the great virtues of the approach. Each interested party can rank the measures in terms of his own self-interest and choose a unique combination that will do the job while maximizing his own well-being. Of course, one has to be careful to meet the constraints imposed by the game. If all the measures that benefit one personally, or corporately, do not fill the gap, one must go beyond them and choose further measures to close the gap, even though they may not involve personal gain. One must have a complete solution. This is why some parties are willing to back remedies that obviously do not benefit them. (For example, gasoline suppliers sometimes back gasoline taxes.)

The Role of Prices

It is also necessary to show balance. One cannot simply choose from one side of the ledger. Balance shows wisdom and enhances credibility. The President's energy message of April 1973 was widely criticized as unbalanced, favoring the supply over the demand side of the menu.

But what is wrong with this approach? Do we not want to fill the energy gap? Do we prefer shortages? The answer, as explained earlier, lies in the arbitrary assumptions of the analysis. Inevitably, the gapologist assumes that prices will remain at current or near-current levels. Current prices are prices that prevail today. They did not prevail yesterday and will not prevail tomorrow (unless, for some peculiar reason, we force them to).

Why should we project future demand and supply at current prices? Suppose instead we project them at prices three times as high as current prices. We will almost certainly then show a reversal of the gap—a surplus. Gapologists would then have to figure out ways of reducing supply and increasing demand. Indeed, this is the principal activity of gapologists in markets characterized by surplus policies. It was the preoccupation of U.S. oil men, and particularly oil state conservation agencies, until very recently.

A clever gapologist might see that we can create not only shortages and surpluses, we can even find prices that eliminate any gap—that is, that clear the market. And from simply observing markets, he will note that left alone they clear by themselves every day.

One can only conjecture that many gapologists do not really appreciate the fact that at higher prices consumers really do buy less and producers offer more, or that they believe these tendencies are so weak that only astronomical prices will eliminate gaps. This, of course, contradicts all experience in the energy market and numerous economic studies of energy markets. To cite a recent example, in 1970, during the period of severe scarcity of tankers and sharply rising demand for low-sulfur heavy oil, many consumers claimed that they could not find supplies. There was no low-sulfur heavy oil available—there was a shortage or gap, or so the claims went. Actually the government's policy of letting the market operate freely, allowing Americans to compete with foreigners for scarce supplies, permitted the market to clear. Prices did rise sharply. But investigations by the Office of Emergency Preparedness found *none* of over fifty claims of shortage to be valid. Lack of availability turned out to mean lack of availability at the price desired. Furthermore, the new higher prices turned out to be much closer to the long-run trend than the old prices. (The price of low-sulfur heavy oil rose from $2.00 per barrel to a seemingly outrageous $3.50. It is now $10.00 to $13.00.)

This fear of gaps often leads to hysterical and extreme policy positions. Because of the linearity of the analysis we hear talk of "needs" and "requirements" rather than "wants" and "desires." Needs, by definition, must be met, *or else*. This conception of necessity leads to exaggerated metaphors. Oil is no longer a commodity traded in a market; it is the "lifeblood of the nation." The oil shortage means "dramatic changes in lifestyles." Gapologists of all persuasions constantly speak in such urgent phrases.

If one adopts a market-oriented economic approach the problem immediately becomes two-dimensional: at some price the market will clear. We may not like the price at which the market clears, but we know that under different policies the market will clear at different levels. We must then analyze each policy to see what it actually does in the marketplace. A policy will injure some parties and benefit others; it will move the market price higher or lower; it will have a net benefit or cost to the nation and a specific distribution of costs and benefits among individual citizens. Whether we want a particular policy is a matter of preference and values, once we know the costs and benefits and their distribution. This takes us into the world of public choice and preference and out of the realm of necessity and compulsion.

This is not to suggest that energy policy decisions are unimportant. They are extremely important, because the differences in benefits and costs among alternative policies are enormous. But the gap approach to energy policy does not deal with costs and benefits. And many policies that would substantially curtail demand or augment supply—fill the gap—do not have desirable cost-benefit characteristics. Indeed, they may have almost no benefits at all, as the following concrete example illustrates.

Gap-Filling with R&D

To contrast approaches to policy choice, let us consider S. 1283, unanimously passed by the Senate in December 1973 "to establish a national program for research, development, and demonstration in fuels and energy." For a taxpayer cost of $20 billion the bill would establish federal energy corporations to demonstrate technologies for shale oil, coal gasification, advanced cycle power, geothermal steam, and coal liquification. As stated in the bill, its supporters are motivated by the findings that "the Nation is currently suffering a critical shortage of environmentally acceptable forms of energy," the "major reason for this energy shortage is our past and present failure to formulate an aggressive research and development strategy," and "the Nation's critical energy problems can be solved by 1983 if a national commitment is made now to accord the proper priority, to dedicate the necessary financial resources, and to enlist our unequalled scientific and technological capabilities to develop new options and new management systems to serve national needs, conserve vital resources, and protect the environment."

It is evident from the provisions of the bill that "shortage" is seen as the problem. The intellectual rationale for the bill, contained in the Senate Interior Committee's *A Study of Energy Research and Development Prospects and Shortages*,[6] although rather sophisticated, is still just one more argument in favor of filling gaps or shortages as the goal of policy.[7]

The policy criterion of the gap approach is simply that research and development result in the production of energy (which will, of course, help fill the gap). Note that this is a purely technical question, a subject for engineers, not economists or policy analysts. The National Academy of Engineering has doubts about the feasibility of certain coal gasification processes. "Formidable engineering and operating

---

[6] Washington, D. C.: Government Printing Office, 1973.

[7] The Senate study does discuss energy prices and costs of R&D-stimulated supplies but gives no evidence as to whether the energy prices assumed clear the market, or yield surpluses, or yield shortages.

problems must be solved" and "a high element of risk is involved."[8] But we will assume that everything the bill anticipates doing can be done, and at a cost no greater than that envisioned in the Senate study. This is a generous assumption in favor of the bill, but a critic of the bill can afford to be generous.

Insofar as policy choice is to be based on the policy's consequences for people—as opposed to gaps—much more than the technical feasibility of production must be considered. We must consider first what would happen if we did not assume a shortage policy. At higher prices supply and demand would tend to equate. In this case any production of fuel from newly developed processes would have to sell at a price sufficiently low to cause consumers to shift away from other fuels. This would cause a fall in fuel prices, a clear benefit to the consumer whether he consumes the old or the newly developed energy sources. On the cost side, however, the taxpayer will have to pay the costs of the R&D (unless it is passed on as part of the consumer price of the new sources). This cost must be weighed against the consumer benefit, particular attention being paid to the fact that the costs will be paid long before the benefits are received. There will, of course, be other beneficiaries. There will be a greater demand for the talents of certain scientists and engineers and for certain kinds of government bureaucrats to run the new programs. These people will find their influence and their incomes enhanced. There are also injured parties other than the taxpayer. The wealth of those who own shares in the energy companies whose products are displaced will decline, and employees of these companies will experience a drop in the demand for their services.

To deal with some specific numbers, let us focus on the case of coal gasification R&D, a project that looms large in both S. 1283 and recent presidential energy messages. If successful, and this is not a certainty, coal gasification R&D would offer us synthetic gas at a cost of roughly $1.20-$1.60 per thousand cubic feet (mcf) at the plant.[9] (There is almost an inevitability about these matters that

---

[8] *Evaluation of Coal Gasification Technology, Part I, Pipeline Quality Gas*, a report of the National Academy of Engineers to the Department of Interior, Washington, D. C., 1974, p. iv.

[9] The Senate study gives figures of $1.25 to $1.40 in 1977 and $1.00 to $1.15 in 1980 and thereafter (Senate Interior Committee, *Energy Research and Development Prospects and Shortages*, Table 10-2, p. 92). But a task force of the National Gas Survey suggests the possibility of much higher prices. See the *Final Report of the Supply-Technical Advisory Task Force-Synthetic Gas-Coal*, National Gas Survey, Federal Power Commission (Washington, D. C.: Government Printing Office, April 1973).

makes final costs much higher than initial estimates, but let us stick with these figures.) When would the supply of synthetic gas at $1.20 per mcf cause a reduction in consumer prices of gas? To come up with a rough answer, let us look at the studies of potentially recoverable natural gas in the United States and its likely cost. The Potential Gas Agency estimates undiscovered recoverable gas at 1,200 trillion cubic feet.[10] The U.S. Geological Survey estimates the figure to be 2,100 trillion cubic feet.[11] To be conservative, we will focus on the smaller number. A separate study by Ralph Garrett of Exxon Corporation[12] estimates that this 1,200 trillion cubic feet of gas could be recovered at a cost of seventy cents per mcf or less. This is consistent with Paul MacAvoy's estimate of a 1980 market-clearing price of sixty-five cents per mcf.[13]

But the Potential Gas Agency estimate does not include gas which may be available below 30,000 feet inland and 1,500 feet of water offshore. Presumably there are large quantities of natural gas available in these regions at costs lower than $1.20 per mcf. Furthermore, with technical progress in finding and producing natural gas, costs should fall in coming decades.

Even if we exclude these potential resources at prices between seventy cents and $1.20 per mcf, we are left with over fifty years' supply of natural gas at current rates of consumption. It is true that the demand for gas will tend to grow, but remember that current demand reflects the extremely low prices set by the FPC. The average 1972 price at the wellhead was 18.4 cents per mcf, a little more than a fourth of the estimated free-market competitive price. If the wellhead price ever rises to $1.20 per mcf, the minimum break-even point for synthetic gas from coal, a substantial reduction in demand can be safely assumed.

As suggested earlier, we have little idea of energy costs and prices even twenty years from now. There is no reason to spend billions on applied research to develop supplies that may or may not

---

[10] Potential Gas Agency, Minerals Resources Institute, Colorado School of Mines, *Potential Supply of Natural Gas in the United States*, October 1971. (The latest report, just issued in December 1973 but not yet seen by the author, gives 1,146 trillion cubic feet.)

[11] U.S. Geological Survey, Circular 650. A more recent publication, "U.S. Mineral Resources," Professional Paper 820, states that the range of estimates is between 1,178 and 6,600 trillion cubic feet.

[12] "The Effect of Prices on Future Natural Gas Supplies," a paper delivered to the Potential Gas Agency meeting, Colorado Springs, 28 October 1970. This paper, representing a large research effort, has not received the attention it deserves.

[13] See MacAvoy and Pindyck, "Alternative Regulatory Policies," p. 489.

be demanded half a century from now. The only sure beneficiaries of federal coal gasification research would be the bureaucrats, politicians, scientists, and engineers associated with the research program.

Another specific example of the gap-filling approach is the plan of the Michigan-Wisconsin Pipeline Company of Detroit and the People's Natural Gas Company of Chicago to convert North Dakota coal to synthetic gas and transport it to Michigan consumers. The delivered cost of the gas in Michigan would be $1.75 per thousand cubic feet, "or roughly three and one-half times the current cost of gas in the state to the companies."[14] Unquestionably there is a gap between supply and demand for gas in Michigan. But the gap is at a price less than a third of the cost of the gas to be delivered.

Is there a gap to be filled at a price three and a half times current prices? Almost certainly not. Then how can the project succeed? Simply because the high-priced synthetic gas will be "rolled-in" with the cheap natural gas and a moderate average price will result.

But why do the pipelines want the project? Because it will increase the rate base and thus the profits of the companies, something that does not happen when higher natural gas prices are passed on to the consumer.

But why do regulatory authorities permit this to happen? Because they are basically gap-fillers and do not understand the economics of energy markets.

The coal gasification case is just one example. The Atomic Energy Commission's nuclear breeder reactor program could be cited as another dubious case. Billions have already been spent on the project, but a recent study concludes "it is *impossible* now to demonstrate a definitive *economic* advantage to society from breeder introduction,"[15] a conclusion shared by earlier Office of Management and Budget studies.

This is not to condemn all energy R&D programs. (For example, further research on oil shale would appear promising. But it is doubtful whether the government should do it.) The purpose of these remarks is to issue a warning about energy programs intended to fill gaps rather than to generate benefits in excess of costs. The original endorsement of accelerated coal gasification R&D in the President's June 1971 energy message had no basis in cost-benefit analysis. Indeed no serious attempt was made by its supporters to

---

[14] *New York Times*, 23 December 1973.

[15] I. Bupp and J. Derian, "Another Look at the Economics of the Breeder Reactor," mimeographed, November 1973, p. 18. Italics in original.

carry out such an analysis, probably in recognition of what the outcome would be. Senate Bill 1283 suffers from the same fault. No serious evidence has been presented to suggest that the $20 billion to be expended will benefit anyone beyond those directly participating in the program.

3

THE OIL MARKET:
FROM SURPLUS POLICY TO
SHORTAGE POLICY

Uses and Sources

Crude oil can be burned directly just as it comes from the ground, but it is more economical to refine it into a number of products, each suited to particular uses. In the United States gasoline is by far the largest component of refined product consumption, accounting for 49 percent by volume of 1968 total domestic consumption. In the same year, distillate fuel oil, which is used primarily for home heating, accounted for 21 percent; heavy fuel oil, which is used by electric power plants, industry, and larger commercial and residential buildings, represented another 7 percent; and jet fuel took up 3 percent. Other products included liquified gases (such as propane), kerosene, lubricating oils, asphalt, and coke. Almost 4 percent was used as feedstock to petrochemical plants.[1] This non-energy, raw material use results in products ranging from plastics, synthetic rubber, and textiles to detergents, insecticides, and fertilizers.

Another way of looking at oil product consumption is to examine the sectors of the economy that use oil. Taking 1968 again, we can see from Table 4 that the transportation sector used more than half of all oil consumed, while the industrial and residential and commercial sectors each represented less than one-fourth of the total. Consumption by electrical utilities was minor, although more recent data show it growing rapidly.

Oil competes directly with natural gas in the home heating market and with coal and natural gas in the "boiler-fuel" portions of the commercial, industrial and electric utility market. Any of these fuels can be used to provide space heating or steam for industrial

---

[1] American Petroleum Institute, *Petroleum Facts and Figures*, 1971 ed., p. 156.

Table 4

SHARES OF TOTAL PETROLEUM PRODUCTS
CONSUMPTION, 1968

Energy Market	Share
Residential and commercial	24%
Industrial	17
Transportation	54
Utilities	4
Miscellaneous and unaccounted for	1
Total	100%

Source: Stanford Research Institute, "Pattern of Energy Consumption in the United States," mimeographed, November 1971, Appendix B, p. 14.

processes or for the generation of electricity. The boiler-fuel market, in which oil has at least one competitor, accounts for only about 35 percent of total oil product consumption. There are no close substitutes for the remaining 65 percent, primarily gasoline, jet fuel, and petrochemical feedstocks.[2] In this respect oil differs from coal and natural gas which compete with other fuels in virtually every market.

This division of the oil market into competing and noncompeting segments has been of some significance for public policy. In 1959 a mandatory oil import program was instituted that placed strict quantitative limitations on the importation of crude oil and oil products. By 1966, however, one product, heavy fuel oil, was admitted freely (although only along the East Coast). In view of the fact that this product competes with natural gas and coal in almost all its markets, it was one of the least important products to the industry and, therefore, the likeliest candidate for exemption from quotas. In fact, in earlier political struggles, it was the domestic coal industry that fought hardest for quotas on heavy fuel oil—the oil industry was relatively passive.[3] In 1972 heavy fuel oil represented 89 percent of all petroleum product imports and 46 percent of all oil and oil product imports, including crude.

The major source of crude oil used in the United States is, of course, domestic production, but imports have grown rapidly in the past few years. In 1959, when mandatory import quotas were

---

[2] We are including natural gas liquids under the heading of "oil" or "liquid petroleum." These are commonly used as petrochemical feedstocks.

[3] See Raymond Bauer, Ithiel D. Pool, and N. C. Dexter, *American Business and Public Policy*, 2d ed. (Chicago: Aldine, 1972), pp. 363-372.

established, imports represented 19 percent of domestic consumption. By 1968 this had risen to just 22 percent. Only four years later 29 percent was imported.[4]

This pattern of relative stability then sudden growth in the share of imports has little to do with the relative scarcities of domestic and foreign oil. Rather it is the outcome of shifts in public policy from surplus toward shortage worked out through the institutions of import quotas and producing-state production controls during the late 1960s.

Market-Demand Prorationing

Oil is found in underground pools or reservoirs. Property rights to mineral resources are defined in terms of boundaries projected downward from the surface. Commonly, numerous property owners hold mineral rights over a single pool. Oil is mobile underground, and raising oil to the surface in one place tends to draw it from other parts of the pool. The effective law with regard to property rights to oil is the rule of capture. Prior to the 1930s holders of the mineral rights were permitted to take as much oil as they could get by drilling on their surface property, whether or not they drew oil from under other properties. This led to competitive drilling, with each party attempting to get as much of the common pool as he could before the others got it.

Now it happens that rates of production beyond certain levels lead to lower ultimate recovery of oil. Thus, more oil could be recovered if the co-owners of the pool cooperated and produced the pool at a more moderate rate. Obviously this would be in the self-interest of the co-owners. Voluntary agreement could be reached that the pool would be operated efficiently as one unit with each co-owner receiving a share of what would have to be a larger total quantity of oil. But clearly there will tend to be considerable disagreement over what the shares should be, smaller owners frequently holding out for larger shares. In other words, the bargaining costs involved in voluntarily "unitizing" a field could be high.

In the 1930s several large discoveries were made, such as the Oklahoma City and East Texas oil fields, and large quantities of oil began to be produced, apparently in competition, as described above. Oil prices fell precipitously. Whether or not voluntary unitization would have resolved this problem eventually we shall never know

---

[4] U.S. Bureau of Mines, *Crude Petroleum, Petroleum Products, and Gas Liquids*, annual and December 1972 issues.

because state agencies stepped in and imposed mandatory prorating systems that allocated production among resource owners.[5] In some cases, besides assigning shares to resource owners, these agencies established a system for controlling the total production level for the state.[6] Thus, market-demand prorationing, as it is now called, consists of two separate aspects: an allocation of production among holders of common property—prorationing proper—and the restriction of total production to the market demand for oil at some particular price. The former aspect serves the purpose of conservation by eliminating the waste associated with competitive production from a common pool. The latter aspect is a mechanism for controlling market prices.

It is not usually recognized that the market-demand aspect of prorationing is a necessary consequence of prorationing itself. If allowable production were always set at the "maximum efficient rate of production," or MER, every producer would choose to produce at that rate. If one producer did not he would lose part of his share of the pool to other producers. Thus, even if prices fell to absurdly low levels, production at MER would continue. This is not what would happen with unitized fields. If prices fell below the expected long-run level, output from the unitized field could be cut back below MER and held in inventory for periods of higher prices. This response would be socially desirable in that production would be stimulated during periods of scarcity and inventories accumulated during periods of abundance. Prorationing continuously at MER would not have this feature and would result in a socially inefficient time pattern of production and consumption. However, the power to reduce allowables below MER so as to smooth out price fluctuations can also be used to keep prices above the levels that would exist if all fields were unitized. And it was.

---

[5] Some states have statutes permitting compulsory unitization of a field by the regulatory commission. This would be a far more efficient alternative than prorating. While Oklahoma and Louisiana now authorize compulsory unitization, it remains a controversial political issue in Texas.

[6] Major producing states with statutes authorizing the limitation of production to market demand are Kansas, New Mexico, Louisiana, Oklahoma, and Texas. Wyoming and California are the only states with production in excess of 100,000 barrels per day and do not have a "market demand" statute. But California authorizes a committee of private oil companies to carry out prorationing with similar results. See Interstate Oil Compact Commission, *A Study of Conservation of Oil and Gas* (Oklahoma City, 1964). For an extensive discussion of prorationing by an economist, see Stephen MacDonald, *Petroleum Conservation in the United States* (Baltimore: The Johns Hopkins University Press, 1971).

The rationale for prorationing has been presented so well by William J. Murray, Jr., a former chairman of the Texas Railroad Commission (TRC), that the reader deserves his exposition:

Assume a return to the date of the unfenced, open range. Also assume the absence of cattle brands and that the "rule of capture" which the courts have applied to the oil industry was applicable to ranching. Each rancher would turn his cattle loose on the range and would recover from the open range not that number which had initially belonged to him but the number which he could capture, slaughter and sell. Human nature being what it is, each rancher would be forced to immediately round up and slaughter all the cattle he could, selling meat anywhere he could for any price he could get. For a time the consumers would rejoice over the surplus supply of beef at amazingly low prices. They would eat T-bone steak three meals a day and fill their refrigerators and deep freezes, but there would be a limit to the amount that could be eaten and stored and soon appalling waste comparable to the destruction of the buffalo herds in earlier years would take place. After the cattle had been slaughtered and wasted, supplies of beef would dwindle, stores from the deep freezes would be exhausted, and then the price for the inadequate remaining supply of cattle would soar. The consumer would discover that his brief period of feasting on absurdly cheap meat would result in a long period of fasting on outrageously high and scarce supplies of meat.

If these assumed conditions existed it would be necessary both for the protection of the consumer and the producers of beef that some governmental authority prorate to each rancher his rightful share of the community supply and that the total quantity allocated daily or monthly to the various ranchers be only that quantity which the public would consume. It is, of course, readily acknowledged that the demand for beef is not an absolute quantity, but that it does vary to some extent with price. It would be the task of the regulatory authority to allocate the quantity of beef to be slaughtered so as to assure the consuming public of a constant dependable supply with adequate reserves for the future and at the cheapest possible price, but the cheapest average price would not be obtained by temporary, wasteful surpluses which would depress prices followed by soaring prices from consequent scarcities.

Thus it is with oil. Without proration by a state regulatory authority, each producer is legally entitled to all the oil he can capture and sell from a common oil reservoir. There are no fences underground. It is always open range and the law of capture applies as far as the oil man is concerned. Without proration a wasteful flood of oil would recur as in the early life of the East Texas Field.[7]

The upshot of this is that from the 1930s to at least 1970—but definitely not since April 1973—the U.S. crude oil producing market was not free. It was cartelized. A cartel exists when there are either restrictions on who can sell in a market or on how much anyone can sell. Oil production under market-demand prorationing was cartelized because producers' output was restricted by regulatory commissions. Entry into the industry as a seller. was and is unrestricted.

Most of us are familiar with a number of cartels or closed markets. Physicians, lawyers, public accountants, pharmacists, and taxicab operators are members of cartels because not just anyone can offer their services in these fields. Before setting up shop in any of these industries, one must acquire a license, usually issued by a state commission or board. Farmers are members of cartels not because entry into farming is restricted but because acreage controls limit production. Physicians justify their cartel by pointing out the higher standards of medicine brought about by licensing. Oil men justify their cartel by citing the greater conservation of oil. Both are unquestionably correct—the levels of medicine and conservation are higher. However, in addition, prices of both medical services and oil are higher because their supply is restricted. Thus, there was nothing unusual or devious about the domestic petroleum cartel. It was established by state laws, endorsed by federal law (the Connally Hot Oil Act), and even operated in Texas by officials elected in statewide voting. Like many cartels, it was the outcome of a highly democratic process.

How were prices and overall market supplies determined in this cartel? With regard to price, it appears that some large purchaser of crude (also a seller) would change his purchasing price. If a sufficiently large number of other purchasers followed suit, the new price would stick. If not, the price change would be cancelled. In this way, when large-volume crude purchasers wanted a different price, that price would be realized.

---

[7] "Market Demand Proration," in U.S. Congress, Senate, Committee on the Judiciary, *Governmental Intervention in the Market Mechanism: The Petroleum Industry,* Hearings before the Subcommittee on Antitrust and Monopoly, 91st Congress, 1st session (1969), Part 2, "Industry View," pp. 1070-1071.

In general, high-cost producers prefer prices higher than those preferred by low-cost producers. Thus, any actual price in the market would not reflect everyone's idea of what the optimal or profit-maximizing price is. Precisely how the opinions of different firms were weighted is unclear. All we know for certain is that the price prevailing in the crude oil market (before government price controls) was lower than some firms wanted and higher than other firms wanted.

But the price-setting process used by a cartel is not nearly so crucial to its survival as the system that controls production. Much of the success of the domestic crude oil cartel is owed to the procedure used for setting production levels. Again, no one has described it so well as William Murray:

> In regard to the Railroad Commission of Texas, the Attorney General reported that for seven of the eleven years under study Texas annual production was never as much as one percent above or below actual demand and that for the five year period from 1952 through 1956 the weighted average for Texas production missed the actual demand by only 11/100 of one percent.
>
> Following this revelation of amazing accuracy in balancing supply to demand, the skeptic finally inquires as to how the Texas Railroad Commission is able to do it. To better enable it to estimate future demand, the Commission is constantly making forecasts of all types, but it must be acknowledged that the Commissioners are not the economic wizards or the crystal ball gazers that they are sometimes credited with being. There is actually a relatively simple method for determining market demand. This method is sometimes compared with that used by the city of Austin to determine the demand for water. Water is pumped out of the city lake into a reservoir on top of a hill from whence it flows to the consumers. If too much water is pumped into this reservoir it will overflow and be wasted; if too little is pumped there will be inadequate pressure on the mains and some of the consumers will not have all of the supply they need. However, it is not necessary to accurately forecast the total demand for water on a hot summer day. Instead it is only necessary to observe the level of water stored in the reservoir. From experience those operating the pump at the lake know at what level the reservoir should be maintained. If water is below the proper level and is declining, then the consumers are using more than is being pumped and it is necessary to speed up the pumps. If the

water is above the proper level and is rising, then the pumps must be retarded else waste will occur.

This is essentially the method followed by the Railroad Commission. At periodic hearings the proper levels of crude oil stocks and products for the nation are determined. If crude oil and product stocks are above the proper levels and are increasing, then it requires no crystal ball to determine that production in excess of market demand is occurring and that if waste is to be avoided a reduction in allowables must be ordered.

On the other hand if stocks of crude oil and products are below the proper levels and are declining then an increase in allowables is desired in order to bring supply and demand in balance.

Once each month the Railroad Commission holds a hearing to determine the number of producing days to be set for the following month. Testimony is received from all interested parties, many factors are considered, but the primary determining factor is whether the above ground stocks of crude and four principal products are in excess or below the proper level.[8]

It is sometimes thought that the success of market-demand prorationing depended heavily upon monthly petroleum demand forecasts issued by the Bureau of Mines prior to the monthly TRC hearings.[9] Mr. Murray's statement belies the importance of this, as do TRC procedures. Furthermore, a 1971 White House directive, issued when allowables were still below 100 percent, delayed the release of the Bureau of Mines forecasts until after each monthly hearing with no perceptible effect on the TRC, the hearings, or the allowables set.

It must be stressed that the TRC and other state commissions did not set prices—they ratified prices set by refiner-purchasers by tailoring production to just meet demand at those prices.[10]

The surplus capacity generated by market-demand prorationing can be calculated from estimates of productive capacity and actual production data. The only source of productive capacity estimates on a state-by-state basis are those of the Independent Petroleum Asso-

---

[8] Ibid., pp. 1071-1072.

[9] For example, this is the view of M. Mann in his testimony before the Senate Special Subcommittee on Integrated Oil Operations, 28 November 1973, p. 444 of the transcript.

[10] Professor Adelman holds the view that on at least one occasion the TRC used its production allowables to force a price increase. See Adelman, *World Petroleum Market*, pp. 151-158.

ciation of America.[11] The association's estimates indicate that in 1965 Texas could have increased production from non-stripper wells by 84 percent, Louisiana, 62 percent, Kansas, 30 percent, California, 16 percent, and New Mexico, 10 percent.[12] The association estimated total U.S. productive capacity for all wells to be 3.7 billion barrels in the same year. Actual production was 2.7 billion barrels, indicating a surplus capacity of more than 25 percent. This is not to suggest that under a policy of compulsory unitization productive capacity would have been fully utilized. Some voluntarily held spare capacity would exist under compulsory unitization, but it certainly would be less than 25 percent.

How well did the domestic petroleum cartel do? The measure of cartel effectiveness is profits earned, which depend upon the proximity of cartel price to profit-maximizing price and actual costs to minimum costs. On the price side it is clear that the domestic cartel price was substantially above the price that would have existed in a competitive market with unitized fields (and substantially above the delivered foreign price when imports became a factor). How close the domestic cartel price was to the optimal price is hard to say.

What *is* obvious is that the costs of production under the government-operated cartel were enormously higher than they would have been under an efficient cartel or competition. The formula for allocating production shares among producers was extremely generous to small high-cost producers and extremely stingy to low-cost producers. Wells producing less than twenty barrels per day—so called "stripper wells"—were usually exempted from regulation entirely. Furthermore, there was no barrier erected to prevent new high-cost producers from entering the market, thereby forcing cutbacks in low-cost production and further raising costs. The result was a "system of organized waste" that would be difficult to parallel. Adelman's estimate of *added* costs over the competitive market in 1961 is eighty cents to one dollar per barrel or 40-50 percent of the delivered price of foreign crude.[13] By and large these excess costs were imposed on major oil companies and larger producers.

It is certain that numerous inefficient producers were enriched by the cartel. Tens of thousands of stripper wells owed their survival to

11 "Report of Productive Capacity Committee," mimeographed, May 1968.

12 See statement of Dr. Henry Steele in U.S. Congress, Senate, Committee on the Judiciary, *Governmental Intervention in the Market Mechanism: The Petroleum Industry*, Part 1, "Economists View," pp. 208-233.

13 M. A. Adelman, "Efficiency of Resource Use in Crude Petroleum," *Southern Economic Journal*, October 1964, pp. 101-122.

it. The profits of medium-sized and larger producers, however, appear to be substantially below the normal rate of return earned by U.S. industry during the past two decades. For these firms the added costs seem to have more than offset the higher prices.[14]

It should be stressed that this cartel was operated by the government and could *only* have been operated by the government. The structure of the crude oil producing industry was and is sufficiently competitive to make a private cartel impossible. Indeed, the major companies would never have designed a system so overwhelmingly hostile to their interests. The production control systems developed appear to be the work of small producers employing their relatively greater influence on state legislatures, another example of the tyranny of the small over the large familiar to students of political economy.

In April 1972, due primarily to changes in U.S. oil import policy which will be elaborated below, production allowables rose to 100 percent of the maximum efficient rate. Market-demand prorationing is no longer restricting crude oil production. But circumstances in the world market and shifts in import policy could easily change and again make market-demand prorationing an effective device for supporting artificially high petroleum prices, stimulating high-cost production, and raising the costs of more efficient producers. The institution of compulsory unitization and the abolition of market-demand prorationing would assure more efficient exploitation of petroleum resources in the future.

Oil Imports: A Brief History [15]

As late as 1946 the United States was shipping more oil overseas than it was receiving. But this positive balance was never realized again as exports fell from their modest wartime levels, while imports rose for more than a decade without interruption. By 1955 overseas imports had increased four times, and domestic producers were concerned that the substantial post-war price increases—in 1955 crude oil was selling at more than twice its wartime level—would be washed out by the foreign onslaught and that domestic production would have to be cut back to make room for the indefinite expansion of overseas imports.

The source of these rapidly growing imports was the burgeoning low-cost production of the Middle East and Venezuela. This pro-

---

[14] See my testimony before the Senate Interior Committee, Appendix B.

[15] This section draws freely upon my paper, "U.S. Oil Import Policy," *Business Economics*, January 1974.

duction potential seemed—and was—almost unlimited compared to the size of the market. From 1950 to 1957 the major Middle East producing nations—Iran, Iraq, Kuwait, and Saudi Arabia—more than doubled production, and there was far more oil just waiting for a drill bit. This potential is exemplified by the tenfold increase in Saudi Arabian production since 1950—and that country's production limit is nowhere in sight.

For U.S. producers there was no remedy for these bleak prospects in the private sector. The only recourse was political: join the trek to Washington and seek relief from an institution capable of applying coercion—the federal government. Initially, however, the federal response was not coercive. A voluntary import program was set up in the hope that importers would recognize their overall long-term interests—most importers were also domestic producers—and cooperate by limiting imports. At first an informal arrangement was set up. In 1957, as new firms continued to enter the import business, this informal approach was displaced by a more serious, but still voluntary, regulatory effort. The "newcomers" also undermined the second voluntary program, some small companies raising imports rapidly to take advantage of a fifty to sixty cent per barrel, or 20 percent, differential between delivered domestic and overseas crude. As a result, overseas imports rose almost 40 percent over the four-year life of the voluntary programs.

In March 1959 the Mandatory Oil Import Program went into effect. It continued until April 1973. The mechanism chosen to restrict imports was a quota fixed as a percentage of domestic production. Obviously there were many possible alternatives: a quota fixed in absolute amount, a fixed tariff, or a tariff varying with the level of imports. Given that a quota was chosen, there was still the choice of how to allocate import licenses. They could have been auctioned to the highest bidders. Instead they were mainly allocated to refiners on the basis of refinery inputs. Economic analysis suggests that, of the alternatives, this system assured the highest domestic crude oil prices given the proportion of imports to domestic consumption.[16]

The allocation of import licenses among refiners was not in proportion to refinery inputs. Small refiners were given a disproportionately large share. For example, in 1969 a 10,000-barrel-per-day refiner received licenses to import 1,950 barrels per day, or 19.5 percent, while a 500,000-barrel-per-day refiner received licenses to import 21,050 barrels per day, or 4.2 percent. With import licenses worth

---

16 E. Mitchell, R. Tollison, and E. Tower, "Tariffs versus Quotas to Control Oil Imports," mimeographed, November 1972.

$1.25 per barrel, this meant per-barrel subsidies of 24.4 cents to the small refiner and 5.3 cents to the large refiner. Uniform subsidies tend to be competed through to consumers while special subsidies do not. Much of the value of import licenses went to support inefficient operations or, in the short run, into the pockets of small refiners as excess profit.

If we are to judge the quota program by the extent to which it restricted imports, it would have to be judged a success, at least up until 1967. Overseas imports rose 27 percent in the first eight years of the program. Domestic production rose 29 percent, putting overseas imports in a slightly poorer relative position. Furthermore, almost two-thirds of the increment in imports was in the form of heavy fuel oil, which is highly competitive with domestic natural gas and coal, and on which domestic refineries had been cutting back yields for three decades.

Looking at the main target of the mandatory quotas, the domestic price of crude oil, the program must also be judged a success—again, up until the past few years. In spite of considerable excess capacity in the domestic producing industry, U.S. crude prices remained virtually constant through the 1960s, typically running $1.25 per barrel (or 60 percent) over the landed foreign cost.

The costs of the quota program have been assessed in several studies.[17] Estimates of added consumer costs of oil products run around $6 billion for 1969. Resources used unnecessarily in the domestic production of oil that could have been purchased at a lower cost abroad have been valued at $500 million to $1 billion per year. No estimates have been made of the costs of inefficient refinery capacity kept in existence by an import license allocation program that was, in effect, a subsidy to small refiners.

By the late 1960s it became clear that either the domestic price or the proportion of imports would have to be allowed to rise significantly. Additions to domestic reserves at the prevailing prices were insufficient to maintain the historical degree of U.S. self-sufficiency. Texas allowables were rising during the late 1960s. Production at 100 percent was just down the road. Left alone, under the protection of the import quota, prices would have risen substantially. Instead, operating under the constraints of a very different political environment—Johnson, Rayburn, and Kerr were gone—and an atmosphere of

---

[17] See J. Burrows and T. Domencich, *An Analysis of the United States Oil Import Quota* (Lexington, Mass.: Lexington Books, 1970), and Cabinet Task Force on Oil Import Control, *The Oil Import Question* (Washington, D. C.: Government Printing Office, 1970).

concern about inflation, the industry was able to gain only two twenty-five-cent-per-barrel increases, one in February 1969 and the other in November 1970. At the end of 1972 real U.S. crude prices (deflated by the wholesale price index) stood 5 percent *below* their 1967 level.

Quotas have been continuously expanded in recent years to keep the real domestic price down by meeting rising domestic demand through imports. Crude imports had been fixed as a percentage of domestic production in the 1960s. After 1970, they were allowed to fill the projected gap between domestic crude supply and total domestic demand at current prices. This meant sharply rising imports with domestic production peaking in 1970. In the two years following the decision to set quotas on a "gap" basis (1971-72), imports rose almost 40 percent.

Setting the quotas at the difference between domestic demand and domestic production at available capacity meant that control over price passed from the producing states and industry to the federal government. And federal policy aimed at keeping nominal or money prices relatively stable. Prices were neither as high as the industry would have liked, nor as low as they would have been with no quotas or larger quotas.

In the spring of 1973, due to a combination of higher f.o.b. foreign crude prices and higher tanker rates, the price of delivered foreign crude rose to levels comparable to domestic crude. In these circumstances the quotas served no function except to allocate the foreign crude among importers. The quotas were not keeping oil out, nor were they keeping domestic prices up. Even as allocators of the right to import they were no longer allocating anything of value because the spread between domestic and foreign prices had disappeared.

With the inevitability of shortages in gasoline and heating oil (if economy-wide price controls continued), the quota program became a curious anomaly, virtually without reasonable defense. In April 1973 the President announced the end of import quotas and their replacement by a system of license fees—a euphemism for tariffs—on crude and petroleum products. Thus the surplus policy that had dominated the U.S. oil market for almost three decades came to an end.

The New Oil Import Program

On 18 April 1973, the President signed the proclamation that removed mandatory quotas on crude oil and oil product imports and substituted a system of license fees to encourage domestic production and refining. The schedule of fees sets different rates for crude, gasoline, and the other covered products, and all the fees are to rise gradually, reaching their maximums in November 1975. The per-barrel fees are: 10.5 cents rising to twenty-one cents for crude, fifty-two cents rising to sixty-three cents for gasoline, and fifteen cents rising to sixty-three cents on the other covered products. No fees were imposed on ethane, propane, butane, and asphalt imports.

The higher fees on gasoline and other products as compared to crude are intended to encourage the construction of domestic refineries. The differential of forty-two cents per barrel (sixty-three cents minus twenty-one cents) between product and crude license fees after November 1975 is the measure of protection given to existing domestic refineries by the fee schedule. In addition, new refineries will receive 75 percent of their crude imports fee-exempt for the first five years. Thus, the total protection for new refineries is forty-two cents plus 15.75 cents (twenty-one cents times .75), or 57.25 cents for the first five years of operation. Protection and encouragement of domestic crude production is measured simply by the twenty-one-cent crude license fee.

Under the old quota program licenses were subject only to a 10.5-cent-per-barrel tariff imposed by Congress, but the quantities imported by each firm were restricted by the quota allocation. The new program drops this tariff and replaces it with new, higher license fees, but it also excludes from fees classes of importers that had held quotas under the old program. These fee-exempt licenses accounted for the overwhelming bulk of imports in 1973. In subsequent years the quantity of fee-exempt tickets will be reduced by formula, and by 1980 all imports will be fee-paying.

The major groups of importers and the quantity of fee-exempt tickets they received in 1973 were:

Refiners and petrochemical plants east of the Rockies: 1,992,000 barrels of crude and unfinished oils per day.

Refiners and petrochemical plants west of the Rockies: 670,000 barrels of crude and unfinished oils per day.

Importers of heavy fuel oil along the East Coast: 2,900,000 barrels per day.

Importers of heavy fuel oil west of the Rockies: 75,600 barrels per day.

Remaining importers of heavy fuel oil: 42,000 barrels per day.

Refiners of Canadian crude oil east of the Rockies: 960,000 barrels per day.

Refiners of Canadian crude oil west of the Rockies: 280,000 barrels per day.

Deepwater terminal operators on the East Coast: 50,000 barrels per day.

In addition, the Oil Import Appeals Board is empowered until 1980 to grant additional fee-exempt product tickets "in emergencies" or to firms experiencing "exceptional hardship."

A little more than two months after the announcement of the new program another presidential proclamation was signed. It modified the treatment of Canadian product imports refined from Canadian crude. Under the provisions of the proclamation, fees on these imports were postponed until May 1974, and will increase more slowly than those on other product imports, not reaching sixty-three cents per barrel until November 1980.

Two major economic issues are raised by the new program: (1) How do the levels of protection granted to domestic refiners and producers by the license-fee system relate to national security or reliability considerations, and (2) will windfall profits be realized under the program, and, if so, to whom will they accrue? The protection offered to a new domestic refinery is 57.75 cents per barrel for the first five years and forty-two cents per barrel for the remaining life of the refinery. The value added by a new foreign refinery would be about $1.20 per barrel. Thus, the protection offered runs close to 50 percent of the value produced for the first five years and 35 percent thereafter. These are high rates of protection by U.S. tariff standards. As a point of reference, consider the fact that in 1970 the Cabinet Task Force on Oil Import Control recommended a ten-cent-per-barrel, or less than 10 percent, level of protection.

The protection offered by the new license fee or tariff schedule would seem to be more than necessary to assure a high degree of domestic refining self-sufficiency. The cost advantages of the cheapest alternative—a Caribbean refinery—depend, of course, on many factors, including tax treatment by the foreign government concerned, the rate of return required on an inherently riskier investment, and the existence of U.S. East Coast superports. But even assuming no East Coast superports, zero taxes, and no risk premium on foreign Caribbean refineries, we arrive at a cost differential of only thirty-four cents per barrel.[18] A firm would most likely want to earn a higher rate of return to offset the risks of foreign operations, or to locate in

---

[18] These calculations are based on the National Petroleum Council's *Factors Affecting U.S. Petroleum Refining* (Washington, D. C., May 1973). They assume a "balanced" refinery as opposed to the type built recently in the U.S. which minimizes heavy products. The calculations also assume a discounted cash flow rate of return of 10 percent.

the U.S. Virgin Islands (which would involve higher taxes). Either of these alternatives would tend to lower the differential to between twenty and twenty-five cents, depending upon the particular tax arrangements or return premium. Thus, protection on the order of twenty-five to thirty cents per barrel would appear to be adequate to assure construction of refineries in the U.S., with a possible exception here and there due to some uniquely attractive foreign situation.

But how badly should we want a very high degree of domestic refining self-sufficiency? The concern about refineries in the past fifteen years has been that they were almost all being built outside the U.S. If that trend continued a question of national security might arise. It is doubtful, however, that national security requires that *all* new refineries built to supply the U.S. market be located in the U.S. Foreign refinery capacity is scattered over many nations. No one nation would supply an appreciable percentage of U.S. consumption, nor is it likely that any group of nations would conspire to cut off refined products to the U.S. The national security aspect of refining is very different from that of crude supply. A more modest degree of protection—twenty-five to thirty cents per barrel for all refineries [19]—would probably assure a high degree of security and at the same time enable some foreign refineries to compete in the U.S. market, providing independent marketers with wider sources of supply.

The protection offered to domestic producers will be twenty-one cents per barrel in 1975. This is about 3 percent of the current value of domestic or foreign crude. (The Cabinet Task Force recommended a $1.35 per barrel tariff. This was the normal differential between domestic and foreign crude prices under the old quota program of the 1960s.)

How much additional domestic production does this twenty-one-cent fee or tariff buy and how much imported crude oil will be displaced? The answer depends upon the long-term elasticity of supply of domestic crude with respect to price. A reasonable range of elasticities would be 0.5 to 1.0. This means a 1 percent differential in domestic price would result in a one-half to 1 percent increase in domestic supply. If we were producing 11 million barrels per day in 1980 without this twenty-one-cent tariff, production could jump to 11.3 to 11.6 million barrels per day with the tariff. If we were importing 10 million barrels per day in 1980, this would fall to 9.4 to 9.7 million barrels per day. Obviously, a tariff of twenty-one cents per barrel on

---

[19] The purpose of a subsidy to domestic refining is not only to get new refineries built, but also to keep old refineries in existence. Economic efficiency would suggest the same subsidy to old and new refineries.

crude oil makes little difference in the U.S. import picture or in its reliance on Middle East crude oil.

With recent sharp increases in world crude prices the United States can be expected to become far more self-sufficient—providing that domestic crude is permitted to sell at free-market prices. Still it takes considerable time for the industry to bring new crude sources on stream. The normal lag from initial exploration and discovery to the consumer is three to five years, and sparsely explored and distant areas, such as Alaska, will take longer than that. Furthermore, there will be the inevitable delays brought about by environmental suits and the normal sluggishness of government in setting up leasing programs on federal lands. Therefore, we must be prepared to import oil in large quantities for an interim period, particularly from the Middle East and North Africa.

Should a special government program, such as oil stockpiling, be created as a precaution against future cutoffs of imported oil? In a truly free domestic oil market such a program would be unnecessary. Businessmen face the problem of unreliable supplies every day and solve it by maintaining a diversity of sources, spare capacity, and additional inventories. They do this not because they are concerned about the hardships imposed on their customers in the event of a shortfall in supplies, but because it is expected to be profitable. When shortfalls occur, prices will rise and they will be able to profitably sell the additional inventories and produce from their spare capacity. It is the expectation of profit from exploiting these situations of unusual scarcity that makes the holding of added inventories and spare capacity worthwhile.

This approach to the reliability problem has two socially desirable consequences: first, it reduces the impact of any shortfall by providing additional supplies in times of scarcity and thereby reduces the price necessary to meet demand. Second, it reduces the likelihood of a deliberate cutoff of supplies since its impact on consumers is reduced.

For this approach to be optimal two conditions must be met: first, the suppliers in the private sector must have as much knowledge as possible about the likelihood of a cutoff. Second, the same firms must believe they will be able to profit in case future cutoffs occur—by selling at free-market prices in periods of scarcity. It is safe to assume that the first condition can be met. It is the second condition that has been and will be difficult to meet. Many do not support free-market prices during periods of unusual scarcity. The political process tends to choose shortage policies and price controls in such situations, at least for a time. Businessmen know this and therefore hold smaller inventories and less spare capacity than they would under optimal conditions.

To remedy this inadequate preparation for import cutoffs, the government could require importers to maintain extra inventories or spare capacity as a condition of importing. It is not desirable for the government to stockpile oil itself, or even to specify the manner in which importers stockpile oil. It may be cheaper for some firms to maintain spare capacity in some wells and in their transportation system than to store oil in tanks. Closing in some high-cost stripper wells and keeping them on tap for emergencies might prove economical in some cases. All the government needs to verify is that additional oil can be delivered when it is wanted. For the government to hold oil itself, or specify the method that private firms must use to hold oil, would result in unnecessary costs.

It should be noted that this suggested intervention of government is not the result of imperfections in the free market. As is commonly the case, the demand for this government action is the consequence of other government actions, actual or potential.

Product prices in the United States will be higher under the new import program as compared to prices under free trade. The price differentials will result from the following elements: higher resource costs to the nation in refining and producing, economic rents or windfalls to various segments of the industry, and revenues to the federal treasury. A detailed analysis of this breakdown is inappropriate here; however, one point is worth mentioning. Assuming that no significant amount of fee-exempt licenses will be issued by the Oil Import Appeals Board, there are likely to be windfalls to established importers of petroleum products, especially on imports of heavy fuel oil and home heating oil. Imports of these products are likely to exceed the amount of fee-exempt licenses issued in the coming years and fee-paying imports will still set the domestic price. For heavy fuel oil the value of fee-exempt licenses in 1975 will be $550 million per year if fee-paying imports are coming in that early. Without changes in the program this value will accrue to importers as a windfall.

The World Market

Until the past year events in the world oil market had only a minor influence on the U.S. market. The surplus policy adopted by federal and state governments effectively insulated the U.S. from developments abroad. The shifts after 1969 from a surplus policy to a free

46

market and then to a shortage policy have made the actions of Middle East producers, especially Saudi Arabia, a dominant influence on the U.S. market.

The broad facts regarding the world oil market over the last two decades are not in dispute.[20] After World War II, Middle East oil sold in the U.S. market at prices competitive with domestic crude. Three trends occurred over the next twenty years. First, the concentration of production among major producing countries and major producing companies declined sharply. In 1950 Iran, Saudi Arabia, Venezuela, and Kuwait accounted for 90 percent of the production of the major foreign, free world oil-producing countries, roughly 3.1 out of 3.3 million barrels per day. By 1969, they had 12.1 out of 21.3 million barrels per day, or 55 percent. In 1950 the four leading oil companies—Exxon, BP, Shell, and Gulf—had 83 percent of the output of the major foreign, free world oil-producing countries. By 1969 their share had declined to 56 percent.

Second, the price of crude in the Persian Gulf fell substantially. In 1950 the price of Arabian crude was $1.85 f.o.b., Persian Gulf. By 1969 this price had fallen to $1.27 (or ninety-eight cents when adjusted for changes in the U.S. wholesale price index). This was still well above the typical cost of production of Middle East crude (about ten cents per barrel), but the price trend was clearly down.

Finally, a turnaround in world prices began in 1970. By the fall of 1973 Persian Gulf prices had far surpassed controlled U.S. prices, reaching more than eight dollars per barrel by January 1974. An important device in raising the cartel price—and, thus, the world price—was the shift to per-barrel taxes. Key members of the Organization of Petroleum Exporting Countries (OPEC) had shifted to de facto per-barrel taxes by 1960 (although the taxes were still called income taxes). With adjustments for transportation and crude quality, these taxes gave the producing nations an improved mechanism for discouraging competitive production among countries by, in effect, selling licenses to produce at coordinated prices. It is generally agreed that the major oil companies were passive participants in this process.

What is in dispute is why the Persian Gulf price has turned around so sharply in the past few years. According to one view, this turnaround was inevitable because of increasing cohesiveness of the members of OPEC, the projected dominance of Saudi Arabia (and possibly Iran) in future markets, and the enormous revenues of OPEC members—particularly Saudi Arabia—relative to their domestic

---

[20] See Adelman, *World Petroleum Market*, passim.

needs.[21] According to this view, all that could be done was to make an attempt to stabilize the situation by international negotiation. Oil prices of five or ten dollars per barrel were a necessary outcome.

Another view has it that there was nothing inevitable about the turnaround in prices.[22] Rather, it was the result of incompetent U.S. State Department dealings with a highly fragile cartel. Had the U.S. not passively accepted Libyan production cutbacks in 1970, nor given what was tantamount to outright endorsement of higher prices in Teheran in 1971, the OPEC nations would have returned to the competitive pricing patterns of the past two decades and prices would have continued to fall.

Whichever view is correct, it is now obvious that the OPEC cartel has the upper hand and is fully exploiting its position.

Since September 1973, Persian Gulf export prices have risen from about $3.10 to $8.30 per barrel (as of January 1974). Perhaps the most critical aspect of future oil policy is the path of future prices. Some forecasters see still higher crude prices down the road. On the other hand, some economists, such as Professors Friedman and Houthakker, believe that current prices already exceed the level that would maximize long-run cartel profits. And one leading oil consultant, Walter Levy, sees serious problems for the cartel in maintaining current prices over the decade. Current prices, they argue, would so reduce demand and stimulate supply that cartel revenues would be smaller than if prices were cut back. The large expected response of demand and supply to changes in world crude prices is evidenced by a recent study done for the Organization for Economic Cooperation and Development which shows 1980 oil exports to North America, Western Europe, and Japan at half the level predicted before the recent sharp escalation in prices. Incidentally, most of the change in oil import demand is likely to occur in the United States since it has far better energy resource opportunities than most other OECD nations.[23]

The possibility of a decline in world crude prices is also taken very seriously by the U.S. Department of Commerce, and thus by implication, by some major U.S. energy companies since the department generally represents U.S. business interests and puts forward

[21] James Akins, "The Oil Crisis," *Foreign Affairs*, April 1973.
[22] M. A. Adelman, "Is the Oil Shortage Real?" *Foreign Policy*, no. 9 (Winter 1972-1973).
[23] This means that the dollar and the U.S. exchange rate will probably be favorably affected by continued high oil prices. See E. J. Mitchell and W. Eizenga, "The Oil Crisis and World Monetary Arrangements," Amsterdam-Rotterdam Bank N.V., *Economic Quarterly Review*, June 1974.

their views in the councils of government. The Commerce Department has recently offered a plan to provide a guarantee of high prices—in the same range as those prevailing now in world markets—for unconventional petroleum substitutes. There is hardly a need for a guaranteed price if one is confident prices will not fall.

Predicting the path of future oil prices requires a knowledge of world demand and supply responses to price. In addition, it requires a knowledge of precisely which nations comprise the world petroleum cartel. High cartel or monopoly prices can only be maintained if production is curtailed in the exporting nations. To the extent that an exporting nation does not curtail production, it is not a true member of a cartel in the economic sense, whatever its formal status in international organizations such as OPEC.

During the recent Arab embargo only Arab nations curtailed output. Most other exporting nations continued to expand production. Between September and November 1973 Arab producers reduced production by 23 percent, from 20.5 million barrels per day to 15.7 million barrels per day. This amounted to a reduction of 8 percent in world oil production. In January 1974 Arab production rose to 17.6 million barrels per day, and it is likely that, with the suspension of the embargo, production will return to the September 1973 levels in all Arab-nations, except Libya and Kuwait, which will apparently continue their production at the January levels.

The success of the Arab producers in achieving coordinated cutbacks in production for a brief period does not imply that curtailed production can easily be achieved in the long run. And yet that is what must happen if current (or still higher) prices are to be sustained. Oil demand and supply are very insensitive to price in the short run. Over a period of years demand and supply adjustments will necessitate far smaller exports than anticipated earlier, as the OECD study suggests. This is where the question of precisely who comprises the cartel comes in. If the cartel is composed only of Arab nations, then those nations must bear the full brunt of curtailment while "free-riders," such as Iran, Venezuela, Nigeria, and Indonesia, derive full benefits. But limiting the cartel to just the Arab nations may still be too broad. Iraq, the third largest Arab producer, did not curtail production during the Arab embargo. Actually, it increased production by 5 percent from September to January. Other smaller Arab producers will find that their curtailment has little positive effect on price and considerable negative effect on their income. While this is very speculative, it could turn out in the long run that the cartel will amount to just Saudi Arabia, Kuwait, and Abu Dhabi—and perhaps just Saudi Arabia. If so, the most profitable cartel price will be much lower than for an all-OPEC or all-Arab cartel.

The actions of Saudi Arabia at the Vienna OPEC meeting in March suggest that in the long run the cartel may be rather narrowly based and that the optimal cartel price may be lower than the March 1974 price. A majority of the members of OPEC wanted to raise prices but were dissuaded when Saudi Arabia threatened to resign from the organization.[24] While this disagreement may have been due partly to noneconomic considerations, it is certainly consistent with the view that the cartel is narrowly based and that the current price is higher than the price that would maximize cartel profits. The view that "political" as opposed to "economic" considerations may dominate future cartel decisions does not really change the analysis much. Political strength is largely a function of a nation's economic status. And, furthermore, it is not easy to imagine a nation sacrificing its own economic position to achieve political gains, especially if its actions simultaneously enrich other nations at its expense and therefore endow these other nations with greater future political influence relative to its own.

What can U.S. energy policy do to reduce the price charged by the oil cartel? At first glance, one might imagine that simply reducing imports would have that effect, but this is not necessarily true. What determines whether a cartel raises or lowers its price is the elasticity of demand it faces. It is not certain that reducing U.S. imports will make remaining U.S. oil import demand more elastic. U.S. energy policy vis-à-vis the cartel should focus directly on making import demand more sensitive to price, that is, more elastic. To put it simply, if higher prices mean a large drop in oil exports for the producing countries and lower prices mean a large increase, we are more likely to get lower prices than if imports are insensitive to price.

Unfortunately, some present and contemplated policies have the opposite effect. Price controls on domestic oil mean that any increase in the imported oil price is not passed on fully to the consumer. With domestic oil supplying 60 percent of U.S. consumption, an increase of one dollar per barrel in the cartel price means only a forty-cent increase in the U.S. consumer's price. Price controls, by partially insulating the U.S. consumer from the cartel, induce the cartel to charge him a higher price. (Fortunately, most major consuming nations have not adopted this policy.) Furthermore, the lower the

---

[24] Clyde H. Farnsworth, "Algerian Says Oil-Buying Nations Conspire on Price," *New York Times*, 21 March 1974, p. 37.

domestic price, the smaller will be domestic supplies—and the more high-priced foreign oil we must buy.

The recent proposal of the U.S. Department of Commerce to guarantee high prices on unconventional energy sources by means of government subsidies also would have this perverse effect. To the extent that U.S. domestic supplies are independent of the world price, there is little incentive for the cartel to lower that price.

U.S. oil policy should be founded on the premise that we will buy cheap, reliable foreign oil. This policy would make sense if we had no influence over the world price. With U.S. demand becoming a major determinant of the world price, it is doubly important to adopt this approach.

Recent Oil Policy Decisions

Throughout the 1950s and '60s, government, through the institutions of market-demand prorationing and import quotas, gave us a surplus policy toward the domestic producing industry. Excess capacity existed in domestic oil production because prices were higher than necessary to clear the market. While this policy gave consumers substantial protection against cutoffs of foreign supplies and insulated the U.S. market from the vagaries of the world market, it also placed heavy costs on U.S. consumers and wasted billions of dollars in unnecessary drilling activity. The beneficiaries of this policy were small stripper-well producers.

By 1969, uncertainty arose regarding the future of U.S. policy. At prevailing domestic crude and natural gas prices the petroleum industry could not be expected to maintain the historical relationship between domestic production and consumption. In 1969 the Cabinet Task Force on Oil Import Control was formed. It issued a report calling for a switch to a tariff system. The proposal was rejected by the President. Significantly, the President was given a choice of continued quotas or a tariff that would reduce the domestic price. The option of a tariff that would maintain the domestic price was not presented.

The federal Oil Policy Committee was then formed to deal with policy issues within the quota framework. (Formerly, the secretary of the interior had handled the oil import program. Under this arrangement, a number of dubious decisions had been made suggesting allocation of import rights on a highly political and partisan basis.[25]) Management of quotas by an interagency committee provided an image of stability and continuity. But the decisions of the committee had a different effect. In the first place, the quotas were expanded at an increasingly rapid rate. And second, special exemptions were given to petrochemical plants and independent fuel terminal operators after heavy political pressure from the petrochemical industry and New England congressmen. On top of this, crude oil prices were held down by informal pressures up until August 1971 and by compulsory price controls thereafter. In form the industry still had a quota program and market-demand prorationing, all the trappings of the earlier cartel. In practice it had control of neither price nor domestic production, for the policy in force required that imports be expanded sufficiently to keep domestic prices down.

Under these circumstances the domestic refining and producing industry could not be certain whether the future held unlimited imports at reduced prices or genuine import restrictions and higher domestic prices. This uncertainty led to the only prudent conduct that could be expected: complaints about the lack of clearly defined energy policy and avoidance of investments in U.S. crude production or refining until the policy became evident. The administration never really made an explicit policy decision on imports. The movement of domestic crude production to capacity and the rise of world oil prices to the domestic level made the quotas ineffective, and in the spring of 1973 they were scrapped.

When the world price passed the U.S. price, a policy decision had to be made. Do we have a free-market policy in oil or a shortage policy, with prices set below the market-clearing level? The shortage policy was chosen. New crude oil prices have been freed, but old crude oil prices remain controlled. With price controls on refining and marketing margins, petroleum product prices are below the market-clearing level.

Oil policy has turned 180 degrees since 1969. In that year consumers paid about $6 billion *more* for oil than they would have paid in a free market. Today, domestic crude producers receive roughly $11 billion *less* per year than they would receive in a free market.[26] If we are concerned not with what each special interest

---

[25] This is all covered in various issues of the *Oil and Gas Journal* in the mid- and late sixties. A useful summary is K. Dam's "Implementation of Quotas: The Case of Oil," *The Journal of Law and Economics*, vol. 14, no. 1 (April 1971).

[26] This is calculated by multiplying the difference between the delivered foreign crude price (roughly $9.50 per barrel) and the domestic crude price (roughly $6.50 per barrel) by the annual domestic production (currently running at roughly 3.6 billion barrels per year, including natural gas liquids).

group lost or gained but what was lost or gained by the nation as a whole then these are not the figures to concentrate on. Import quotas cost consumers $6 billion per year, but they benefitted producers significantly less, resulting in a national waste of $1 billion per year or more. Today's policy of low domestic crude prices is also wasting the nation's resources, as consumer benefits certainly fall short of producer losses, probably by more than a billion dollars per year. Perhaps the most consistent element in U.S. oil policy is economic inefficiency.

4

NATURAL GAS:
FROM FREE MARKET
TO SHORTAGE POLICY

Natural gas is largely a phenomenon of the last two decades. Prior to World War II there was no economical way of transporting gas more than moderate distances. Markets were confined to the immediate producing area. With the development of economical long-distance pipelines, the large natural gas reserves discovered in the search for oil became available nationwide as fast as pipelines and distribution systems could be constructed. In 1946, 4.9 trillion cubic feet (tcf) were produced in the United States. By 1970 this had risen more than fourfold to 22 tcf.

Natural gas has two basic markets: the residential and commercial market, where it is used for heating homes and offices, cooking, and hot water heating; and the industrial and electric utility market, where it is a boiler fuel used to produce direct heat or steam for industrial processes and electricity generation. In the residential and commercial market, which accounted for 33 percent of total gas consumption in 1968, gas competes mainly with home heating oil. In the industrial and electric utility market, 64 percent of consumption in 1968, it competes with coal and heavy fuel oil (as well as hydro and nuclear energy sources in the electric utility sector). The remaining 3 percent of natural gas production is used in the transportation sector.

Natural gas is produced in the same states by essentially the same companies that produce crude oil. Like crude oil, today natural gas in the field is sold in a competitive market. Entry into the industry is easy, concentration is low, and statistical studies of prices confirm the lack of influence over price by individual firms.[1]

---

[1] See P. MacAvoy, *Price Formation in Natural Gas Fields* (New Haven: Yale University Press, 1962); Clark Hawkins, *The Field Price Regulation of Natural Gas* (Tallahassee: Florida State University Press, 1969); E. Kitch, "Regulation and

Natural gas differs from crude oil dramatically in the degree of government price regulation. Oil prices (before the August 1971 price controls) were not regulated at the wellhead, at the refinery, or at the retail outlet. Common carrier pipeline oil transportation is regulated by the Interstate Commerce Commission, but most oil is moved by tanker, barge, or company-owned trucks. Prices for natural gas sold in interstate commerce are regulated at the wellhead by the Federal Power Commission. Interstate gas pipelines are also regulated by the FPC, and local gas distribution companies are regulated by state public utility commissions. Thus, from the wellhead to the basement furnace, prices of natural gas sold in interstate commerce are under government control.

The rationale for gas pipeline and distribution regulation is that there are positive returns to scale in both activities which would lead to a private monopoly in the absence of regulation. This is presumed to be worse from a public point of view than a regulated, government-imposed monopoly. Whatever the merits of this argument, the basis for regulating wellhead prices, as distinct from pipelines and distribution prices, has always been controversial and puzzling to say the least. As noted above, the crude oil and natural gas producing industries are very similar from the point of view of the firms involved and the degree of concentration of production.

Evolution of the Present Regulatory System

In 1938 Congress passed the Natural Gas Act for the purpose of placing pipelines selling natural gas in interstate commerce under the regulatory authority of the Federal Power Commission. The act was specifically made inapplicable "to the production or gathering of natural gas." Sales of gas at the wellhead by independent producers thus continued unregulated by the FPC until the 1954 Supreme Court decision in *Phillips Petroleum Co. v. Wisconsin*. In this decision, the Court concluded that Phillips, although engaged solely in production and gathering operations, was a "natural gas company" within the meaning of the Natural Gas Act and that its sales for resale in inter-

the Field Market for Natural Gas," *Journal of Law and Economics*, vol. 11 (October 1968); Norman Ture, "Testimony submitted on Behalf of the Gas Supply Committee to the Subcommittee on Antitrust and Monopoly," Committee on the Judiciary, U.S. Senate, 27 June 1973, mimeographed; Clark Hawkins, "Structure of the Natural Gas Producing Industry," in Keith Brown, ed., *Regulation of the Natural Gas Producing Industry* (Baltimore: The Johns Hopkins University Press, 1972); L. Cookenboo, "Competition in the Field Market for Natural Gas," *The Rice Institute Pamphlet*, vol. 44, no. 4 (January 1958); and E. Neuner, *The Natural Gas Industry* (Norman: University of Oklahoma Press, 1960).

state commerce were subject to FPC regulation. Natural gas produced and consumed within a state was not made subject to regulation.

Thereafter, attempts by the FPC to regulate the over 4,000 independent producers on a company-by-company basis resulted in a backlog so great that in 1960 the FPC was described by a former Harvard Law School dean as "the outstanding example in the Federal government of the breakdown of the Administrative process." [2] Recognizing the virtual impossibility of regulating each company individually, the commission initiated the area rate theory of regulation in 1960. Instead of determining the rates that each producer would be permitted to charge for selling its natural gas, the FPC stated that all gas sold in a particular producing area would be valued on a "commodity" basis.

In 1961 the FPC commenced the *Permian Basin Area Rate Proceeding*, which it completed in 1965. In 1968 the Supreme Court affirmed the commission's opinion and orders in this case as being within the FPC's administrative discretion. [3]

The *Permian* methodology used by the FPC to arrive at the rates which it would allow producers to receive was an adaptation of the utility rate-base, cost-of-service approach. This approach had been developed over the past half century for rate regulation of public utility monopolies, such as the gas pipelines and electric power companies. In developing the costs to be applied in determining the rate base and cost of service, the FPC attempted to use the average, composite costs of the entire producing industry. Since this data was not available, the FPC elicited the information from industry through the use of massive questionnaires. After compiling the responses, the commission then attempted the logically impossible task of allocating costs between the joint production of oil and gas. Confronted with a wide range of choices in making its cost calculations, the FPC made determinations to the nearest mill, invariably selecting figures which were at the lower end of the spectrum. The commission then applied a 12 percent rate of return and established "just and reasonable" ceiling rates for all gas produced from the Permian Basin area.

One economist specializing in gas regulation matters has written that

> it is quite beyond the FPC or anyone else to determine what
> is the cost of natural gas for an integrated producer. Let alone

[2] As quoted in U.S. Department of the Interior, "Natural Gas," an in-house background report cited in *Natural Gas Deregulation* (Washington, D. C.: American Enterprise Institute, 1973), p. 11.

[3] Permian Area Rate Cases, 390 U.S. 747 (1968).

for a segment of the industry [*sic*]. The way those presenting data and calculations of average cost of an MCF of gas in area hearings switch back and forth among sources, the way they make joint cost allocations, and the way they apply "factors" represent pseudo-science to a degree it would be difficult to equal by example. At the final determination the examiner's fumbling among the numbers and making a cafeteria style selection from those presented, plus the Commission adding a few delicate adjustments of its own makes the whole thing nothing short of ludicrous.[4]

The *Permian* decision also introduced a concept which became known as "vintaging." Gas dedicated to interstate commerce by contract prior to a certain date was known as "old," or "flowing," gas, while gas dedicated by contract at a later date was known as "new" gas. A higher ceiling was permitted for the new gas on the theory that this would provide incentive for future exploration. Vintaging has been criticized on the ground that the consumer has no interest in the date the gas was dedicated to interstate commerce: an old cubic foot burns as well as a new one. Additionally, it has operated to provide existing pipeline companies which have contracts to purchase large volumes of "old" gas with an advantage over newer pipeline companies which have to contract for the more expensive "new" gas. Similarly, customers of pipeline companies with a higher percentage of "new" gas volumes pay more for their purchases than customers of pipelines with contracts providing more "old" gas supplies.

In establishing "just and reasonable" rates, the FPC attempted to determine average costs within the industry, thus making it difficult for high-cost producers (generally those with a less fortuitous finding rate) to compete. However, while forcing down contracts that were priced above the "average cost," the commission did not counterbalance this by permitting lower-priced contracts to rise to the "just and reasonable" rate. Although it established minimum rates that were generally below almost every contract in the area, the FPC generally limited producers to their contract rates when these were lower than the area rate.

In 1968 the FPC, using the same methodology, established area rates for southern Louisiana. This time, however, the commission was even more restrictive than in the *Permian* proceeding. Area rates

---

[4] Clark Hawkins, "Structure of the Natural Gas Producing Industry," in *Regulation of the Natural Gas Producing Industry*, ed. K. Brown (Baltimore: The Johns Hopkins University Press, 1972), p. 165.

were established below what the commission had previously set as guidelines for producers, and the industry was ordered to refund hundreds of millions of dollars for collecting "excessive" rates in prior years.

Completions of new gas wells declined steadily after 1962, the year after the commencement of the *Permian Basin* proceedings. In each of the four years subsequent to the 1968 *Southern Louisiana* decision, the domestic consumption of natural gas exceeded the American Gas Association's estimates of new additions to reserves in the lower forty-eight states.

Since 1969 the FPC has taken some steps to mitigate the developing shortages. In 1971 the second area rate decision in *Southern Louisiana* raised the area rates by approximately 30 percent. Other area rate proceedings established rates consistent with that decision. Natural gas discoveries increased by 32 percent in 1972 and by 40 percent for the first nine months of 1973.[5] This, however, appears to be largely a response to rising unregulated intrastate shipment (except that coming from federal offshore leases).

The Natural Gas Shortage

Between 1946 and 1960 natural gas production rose from 4.9 to 13 tcf per year. At the same time the American Gas Association's estimate of proved reserves rose from 159.7 to 262.3 tcf. The reserve-production ratio thus fell from 32.5 to 20.1. These movements can be explained in elementary economic terms. Between 1946 and 1960 the real price of natural gas at the wellhead rose appreciably, and expectations during the period were for rising prices. These rising prices were due to the expanding gas markets spurred by the development of long-distance pipeline technology, and they spurred a continuing search for gas and additions to the stock of proved reserves.

The reserve-production ratio desired by producers depends upon the relationship between expected future prices and current prices. Producers will hold more reserves (inventories) if future prices are expected to be high relative to current prices. The fall in the actual reserve-production ratio indicates that it was above that desired by producers throughout the period, and that producers did not expand reserves as rapidly as production in order to lower the ratio to its target level.

---

[5] Statement of Stephen Wakefield, assistant secretary of the interior, before the Special Subcommittee on Integrated Oil Operations, Committee on Interior and Insular Affairs, United States Senate, 28 November 1973.

Figure 1

RATIO OF NATURAL GAS RESERVES TO PRODUCTION IN THE
UNITED STATES FROM 1950 TO 1971

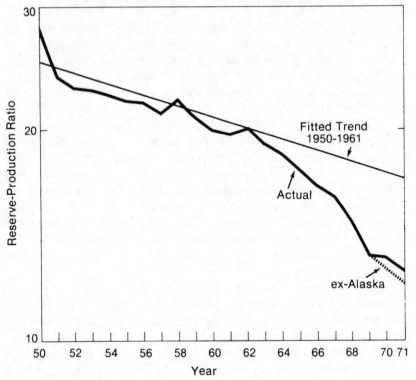

Source: American Gas Association, "Reserves of Crude Oil, Natural Gas Liquids, and Natural Gas in the United States and Canada and United States Productive Capacity as of December 31, 1971," vol. 26 (Arlington, Va., May 1972).

In 1961 the *Permian* hearings began. In the ensuing years it became evident that expectations of higher wellhead prices would have to be revised. The course of prices after 1961 completely reinforced that view, and real wellhead prices for "new" gas in 1969 were below the 1961 level. Whatever the target reserve-production ratio that was being approached prior to 1961, the target clearly must have been lowered with the advent of regulation. Prices were now expected to either rise at a lower rate or actually fall. With the target reserve-production ratio lowered, the rate of decline in the actual ratio accelerated. From 1950 to 1962 the ratio fell by 2.3 percent per year, and from 1963 to 1971 it fell at 4.3 percent per year, almost twice the earlier rate. These trends are shown in Figure 1.

60

Thus, for given reserves the price ceiling imposed by the FPC accelerated domestic production. Owners of reserves no longer expected future prices to yield an adequate return for holding reserves. The ceilings also reduced the incentive to explore for and develop new reserves. Despite the fact that future demand would obviously be much greater than current demand, reserve additions were below production every year the four years succeeding the 1968 *Southern Louisiana* decision. These trends in production and reserve additions could not continue indefinitely without creating a shortage in current supply. Dating the beginning of the shortage to consumers is not easy, but it probably occurred somewhere between 1968 and 1970. More important is the fact that the divergence between actual and free-market conditions occurred somewhere around 1963 when the *Permian* decisions were becoming clear, prices were beginning to level off, and the reserve-production ratio decline began to accelerate.

While this discussion gives us a feeling for when problems in the natural gas market began and what the causes of those problems were, it does not tell us how large the shortage is or what the market would have looked like in the absence of ceiling prices. The only serious attempts to simulate the natural gas market in the absence of regulation are those of Paul W. MacAvoy. In one paper he sets up an econometric model of the market and simulates the post-*Permian* period using market parameters estimated in the pre-*Permian* period.[6] In a more recent paper he develops a more complex model and simulates the late 1970s assuming, alternatively, continued regulation and a freeing of new contract prices as would occur under the President's deregulation bill.[7]

Although MacAvoy's 1971 model does not correspond exactly to the economic logic set out above, his qualitative results with regard to prices, reserve additions, and the reserve-production ratio confirm the interpretation in eastern and midwestern natural gas markets. MacAvoy concludes that under free-market conditions new-contract prices would have been more than double actual regulated prices from 1964 to 1967, new reserves added would have been 40 percent larger than reserves added at the ceiling prices, and the reserve-production ratio would have been substantially higher over the period.

The comparative levels of production under regulation and free markets is ambiguous in economic theory. MacAvoy's model suggests that production would have been slightly higher under free

[6] Paul W. MacAvoy, "The Regulation Induced Shortage of Natural Gas," *The Journal of Law and Economics*, vol. 14, no. 1 (April 1971), pp. 167-199.
[7] MacAvoy and Pindyck, "Alternative Regulatory Policies," pp. 454-498.

markets than under regulation, the results varying from year to year. Of course, in the long run, production under free markets would become continuously greater than under regulation because reserve levels would continuously diverge while the reserve-production ratios would tend to stabilize. MacAvoy's simulation extends only to 1967 and therefore does not reveal this trend.

It is not possible to adequately treat MacAvoy's complex econometric model in a monograph such as this. However, in the case of the shortage of reserve additions brought about by regulation, a ballpark figure can be arrived at by a much cruder analysis. Suppose we assume that the 2.3 percent annual decline in the reserve-production ratio of the 1950 to 1962 period had continued to 1967, and that annual production had been the same. Then by 1967 U.S. natural gas reserves would have been 319 trillion cubic feet instead of the actual 293 tcf. Reserve additions over the period would have been close to 130 tcf as compared with an actual 102 tcf—28 percent greater. If we extend this analysis to 1971, the reserve additions would have been 58 percent greater under the free market. These figures bracket Mac-Avoy's 40 percent shortage estimated for eastern and midwestern markets. Thus, by either sophisticated or very crude methods it can be concluded that new reserves added fell far short of what could be expected in a free market.

MacAvoy's more recent model simulates the gas market for the remainder of the 1970s. He considers three scenarios: (1) deregulation of new-contract prices with a national ceiling that would keep average wholesale prices from rising more than 50 percent over a five-year period, (2) strict "cost of service" regulation based on historical average costs, and (3) continuation of the current policy of allowing increases of two to four cents per thousand cubic feet each year. Under either "strict cost" regulation, or the status quo, the gas shortage continues through the 1970s. In the strict cost case the shortage grows from 4 tcf in 1972 to 8.9 tcf in 1980. In the status quo case the shortage grows from 4 to 5.3 tcf. In the deregulation case the shortage disappears in 1977.[8]

From the standpoint of economic efficiency these shortages—past, present, and future—represent social waste. Opportunities are eliminated for exchange between producers willing to develop and sell gas at prices higher than ceilings and consumers whose valuation of the gas exceeds the price ceilings. This production and consumption never takes place. Instead, these consumers must use less fuel or

---

[8] Ibid.

pay at least twice the free-market wellhead price for gasified coal or for liquified natural gas imports, or use more expensive alternative fuels.

Distributive Effects of Regulation

While the costs of regulation clearly exceed the benefits from an overall societal point of view, few policies are decided on this basis. It is common to advocate inefficient policies when they have "desirable" consequences for the distribution of income. Whatever the merits of these judgments about the relative moral worth of different individuals and groups, it is important to examine the distributional consequences of any policy. Many people believe they are important and, above all, the political process responds to such considerations.

The distributive consequences of FPC price regulation are dominated by one consideration: some people who would be paying more for natural gas in a free market are paying lower prices and getting gas. Others who would be willing to pay the ceiling price, or the free-market price, or even more, are not getting gas. They must either do without fuel or purchase more expensive or less desirable alternatives. The favored group consists of those who are rationed gas by interstate pipelines and those who buy gas in the intrastate market exempt from FPC regulation. Intrastate consumers are not now as favored as interstate consumers because intrastate prices have risen above the interstate level. But interstate consumers of gas are a dwindling group, since the low interstate prices attract little new gas from producers to replace dwindling supplies.

Only one-third of the natural gas sold is consumed by residential and commercial users. Nevertheless, in political terms this must be the group that the FPC is intending to benefit with low prices. Yet studies by MacAvoy and Stephen Breyer have indicated that it is not residential and commercial users but rather industrial users that have benefitted from low ceiling prices.[9] With the development of shortages, pipelines and distribution companies apparently devoted supplies to industrial users rather than connecting new residential and commercial users. The explanation for this diversion of supplies is that the FPC and many states do not regulate industrial sales of gas. Since industrial users are less "protected" by the regulatory authorities than homeowners, they get the gas and the new homeowner does

---

[9] P. MacAvoy and Stephen Breyer, "The Natural Gas Shortage and the Regulation of Natural Gas Producers," *Harvard Law Review*, April 1973.

without. This shifting of artificially cheap natural gas supplies to the industrial sector has apparently been very profitable for natural gas pipelines. The author has computed that a stockholder who bought the Standard and Poor's sixty utilities at the end of 1965 would have realized an 18.1 percent increase in the value of his holdings by the end of 1972, assuming he had reinvested his dividends. If he had instead invested in the Standard and Poor's natural gas pipeline stocks, he would have realized a 55.5 percent gain over the same period.[10]

A few statistics illustrate what has been happening. From 1950 to 1957, a period of rapid industrial expansion, gas consumption in the residential market grew at 10.9 percent compared with 9.4 percent in the industrial sector. From 1957 to 1962 both growth rates declined, but residential consumption growth widened its margin over industrial consumption, 7.5 percent to 4.8 percent. From 1962 to 1968, when price regulation began to take effect, the growth rate of residential consumption fell to 5.5 percent, but the rate of industrial consumption accelerated to 6.6 percent.

Another way of addressing the question is to compare how gas did in each of its markets relative to overall energy consumption in those markets. Between 1962 and 1968 total gas consumption grew faster than overall energy consumption. (As we have seen, this was because reserves were being depleted faster, not because they were becoming more abundant.)

Table 5 shows the market share of natural gas in five energy sectors in 1962 (at the start of the *Permian* hearings) and in 1968. In every energy market except the residential, gas increased its share. In the residential sector gas lost ground to electricity, a far more expensive source of heat. (This may be, at least in part, the result of a shift in the marketing tactics of electric utilities.) With the exception of the New England and Middle Atlantic states, 80 to 90 percent of the homes in all regions of the country were heating with gas in 1968. My estimates of the comparative economics of oil and gas heating in these areas suggest that gas was more economical in the Middle Atlantic states and roughly competitive in New England. In New York City in 1970 the cost of generating a btu for homes using oil appeared to be about one-third greater than the cost of using gas when incremental capital costs of oil heating are taken into account. Rougher estimates for seven other cities in the Middle Atlantic region suggest a 25 to 30 percent advantage for gas.[11] While gas heating

---

[10] Dividends were assumed to be reinvested at the succeeding year's closing price.
[11] A far more detailed research project would be required to ascertain with confidence the comparative costs of alternative heating systems to the homeowner.

Table 5

MARKET SHARE OF NATURAL GAS AS A PERCENTAGE OF TOTAL ENERGY CONSUMPTION IN EACH ENERGY MARKET

Market	1962	1968
Residential	50.7%	50.1%
Commercial	21.5	26.8
Industrial	40.4	43.3
Transportation	.35	.4
Electric utilities	25.9	26.1

Source: Stanford Research Institute, "Pattern of Energy Consumption in the United States," mimeographed, November 1971, various tables.

raised its share of households in the Middle Atlantic market from 12 percent in 1950 to 35 percent in 1960, its share had increased to only 47 percent by 1968.[12]

The shortages of natural gas to residential users mean that there is a greater demand for alternative fuels, namely, home heating oil and electricity, to heat homes. Since the supply of these alternatives is not perfectly elastic, this added demand must have increased prices beyond what they would have been if gas prices were unregulated. (The introduction of price controls in August 1971 has resulted in shortages in place of higher prices.) Thus, homeowners heating with oil or electricity must be worse off as compared to a free natural gas market. Table 5 shows that this group was approximately equal in size (when weighted by consumption) to the favored gas-consuming group in 1968, but growing faster. Thus we would expect more current statistics to show that more households (weighted by consumption) were made worse off by FPC price controls than were made better off.

One group clearly benefitted by FPC regulation of *interstate* prices is *intrastate* gas users. Because they are not "protected" by FPC controls, consumers in Texas, Louisiana, Oklahoma, and other large producing states can outbid New York and Chicago purchasers and obtain all the gas they want. And because the potential demand of interstate buyers is eliminated at prices above the ceilings, the effective national demand for natural gas is lower than it would be otherwise.

---

[12] In New England the market share of natural gas rose to 44 percent in 1968. Consideration of the poorer economics of gas versus oil heating in New England suggests a noneconomic allocation of supplies between New England and the Middle Atlantic.

The free-market intrastate price, therefore, is lower than it would be in a totally free national market. Thus intrastate gas users not only get all the gas they want, but get it at a price that is lower because of FPC attempts to protect *all other* gas consumers. This is one of those ironies so common to ill-conceived economic policies. But the ultimate irony is the bill before Congress to "solve the gas shortage" by extending FPC regulation to the intrastate market.[13] Having unintentionally bestowed benefits on some gas consumers, some senators and congressmen apparently feel they must correct that oversight and impose gas shortages on everyone—on grounds of fairness, of course.

The lower prices and lack of shortages in large gas producing states benefit not only gas users in those states, but also complementary factors of production. Armco Steel's decision to locate a plant in Texas because of an assured gas supply benefits Texas workers. Intrastate pipelines, such as Lone Star, have experienced dramatic growth that would not have occurred in a free national market. Conversely, complementary factors of production outside the major producing states have been injured—the 30,000 workers laid off for ten days in Cleveland in January 1970, to cite one early example.[14] The number of plants that were not built in gas-shortage areas will never be known.

The environmental consequences of regulation-induced gas shortages have not gone unnoticed. Natural gas is a far cleaner fuel than the cleanest heavy oil or coal, particularly with regard to sulfur content. Not only is the quality of air reduced overall by gas shortages, but the regional distribution of dirty air is distorted. Partly because New York and Chicago cannot compete against Dallas and Houston for gas supplies, 1975 clean air standards cannot be met. According to the Environmental Protection Agency, a four-fold increase in natural gas supplies to New York City would be required to meet the standards for atmospheric particulates. There is no possibility of this occurring under the present regulatory approach.

Arguments Against Deregulation

Two arguments have been made against deregulation. One is that the natural gas producing industry is monopolistic and cannot be

---

[13] See S. 2506, the Consumer Energy Act of 1974, 93d Congress, 1st and 2d sessions. The use of the word "consumer" in the title of this bill is clearly deceptive advertising if it is supposed to indicate the benefitted party.

[14] MacAvoy and Pindyck, "Alternative Regulatory Policies," p. 455.

permitted to exploit consumers by charging monopoly prices. This position has been advanced by some staff members of the Federal Power Commission.[15] The position and its supporting arguments have been dismissed by economists specializing in energy markets, such as Professors Adelman, Hawkins, MacAvoy, and Russell,[16] and, of course, contradicted by the studies cited earlier.[17] By every accepted measure—concentration, entry, market tactics, prices, profits—the industry is competitive, and, in some respects, it is among the more competitive of American industries. To argue monopoly in this case is to argue monopoly for most of the U.S. economy, an argument that falls of its own weight. Only in the realm of politics and journalism could the monopoly thesis survive.

The other argument against deregulation assumes the market is competitive but that natural gas supply is not sensitive to price. Higher prices would, therefore, mean greater earnings for producers but little additional supply for consumers. According to this line of reasoning, ceiling prices below the market-clearing level would result in shortages, but they would be small and manageable. While inefficiencies in the allocation of resources would result, they would be more than offset by the "positive" distributive effects on income. Note that advocacy of this shortage policy is based on the value judgment that consumers who are allocated gas are sufficiently more worthy than consumers who are not allocated gas (and, of course, gas producers) so that some small cost in economic efficiency is worth paying.

This argument, made by Professor Alfred Kahn during the *Permian* hearings,[18] is premised on one empirically testable proposition: the response of natural gas supply to price is small. Unfortunately, at the time the argument was made, little research had been done on the question. In the past several years a number of studies have been carried out. All show that the response of supply to price has been and is likely to be substantial. Thus, low ceiling prices

---

[15] Testimony of J. Wilson and D. Schwartz before the Subcommittee on Antitrust and Monopoly, Committee on the Judiciary, U.S. Senate, 27 June 1973.

[16] For the list of academic supporters of the competitive view, see Committee on Interior and Insular Affairs, United States Senate, *Natural Gas Policy Issues and Options: A Staff Analysis* (Washington, D.C.: Government Printing Office, 1973), p. 84.

[17] Footnote 1 of this chapter.

[18] Alfred Kahn, *In the Matter of Area Rate Proceeding*, Docket No. AR 61-1, Federal Power Commission, and "Economic Issues in Regulating the Field Price of Natural Gas," *American Economic Review*, May 1960. Professor Kahn seems to have revised his opinions in view of the shortages.

imply large shortages and injure many consumers as well as producers. Indeed, as suggested above, the number of consumers injured
(weighted by consumption) may well exceed the number benefited.

Natural Gas Supply Response to Price

Because many would not be prepared to deregulate gas prices unless
they had reasonable assurance of a substantial supply response, we
now turn to a more extensive discussion of what the various supply
models show. Five estimates were made of the response of gas supply
to price. These estimates are based on five independent studies or
models (not including the latest MacAvoy model, which has already
been discussed): (1) the National Petroleum Council (NPC) model,
constructed by a team of technicians from several major oil companies for use by the Department of the Interior, (2) the Khazzoom
model, developed under contract for the Federal Power Commission
by Professor J. Daniel Khazzoom,[19] (3) the Erickson-Spann model,
published by two university professors in *The Bell Journal of
Economics and Management Science*,[20] (4) the early MacAvoy model,
published in the *Journal of Law and Economics*,[21] and (5) the Garrett
study, a paper on the quantity of recoverable gas economical at
various wellhead prices, presented to the Potential Gas Committee by
Ralph Garrett of Exxon Corporation.[22]

Projections were made directly from the first two models, given
alternative assumptions about price. At the request of the author,
the NPC made the projection from its model and the FPC staff made
the projection from the Khazzoom model. Each of the other three
studies leads to an estimate of the price elasticity of gas supply.
These elasticities were utilized separately in a simple supply projection model constructed by the author. The projections made from
these latter elasticities, therefore, depend not only on the elasticities
themselves but also on the method of projection.

For each of these models two cases are considered:

Base Case:　　　　Wellhead price of natural gas constant at
　　　　　　　　　twenty-four cents per thousand cubic feet
　　　　　　　　　(mcf).

---

[19] J. D. Khazzoom, "The FPC Staff's Econometric Model of Natural Gas Supply in
the United States," *The Bell Journal of Economics and Management Science*, vol.
2, no. 1 (Spring 1971).
[20] E. Erickson and R. Spann, "Supply Price in a Regulated Industry: The Case of
Natural Gas," in ibid.
[21] MacAvoy, "Regulation Induced Shortage of Natural Gas."
[22] R. Garrett, "Effect of Prices on Future Natural Gas Supplies."

Deregulation Case: Wellhead price of natural gas rises to sixty-five cents per mcf (assumed free-market level) immediately and at 2.5 percent per year thereafter.

The assumption of a gas price of sixty-five cents per mcf after deregulation is consistent with recent uncontrolled intrastate prices, with MacAvoy's recent model, and with the Garrett study. Note that this is well below the costs of imported liquified natural gas and synthetic gas from coal or oil, which generally run $1.00 to $1.50 per mcf or more (wellhead equivalent).

While the assumption of a sixty-five cent wellhead price is useful for comparing the response of supply in different models, it has to be recognized that the response of gas supply will partially determine the price. In a free market price and quantity are determined simultaneously. This means that a model that forecasts a strong supply response to price is also forecasting that a smaller increase in price is required to clear the market. Furthermore, consumption of competing fuels, such as low-sulfur residual oil, home heating oil, and coal, will be depressed by the added gas supplies, and the prices of these fuels will be reduced.

Before laying out the supply schedules generated by these models, a brief description of how each model works is in order. The NPC model translates drilling footage into new reserves by means of a careful analysis of historical relationships between footage drilled and reserves discovered for fourteen different regions of the U.S. Each region has a separate engineering model with different parameters based on different historical experience and potential. For each region the model generates reserves, production, and capital and operating expenditures for any given drilling rate. For the industry to be in equilibrium, the flow of income from all production, old and new, must be such that, when compared to the total book value of capital, it yields a rate of return acceptable to the industry. The latter can be varied in the model. For the NPC forecast it was set at 15 percent return after taxes. Price is the variable that is adjusted so as to make the rate of return come out to 15 percent for a given drilling rate. Thus, there is a connection established between drilling rate (and hence production) and price. But it is drilling that "causes" price in the NPC model—not the other way around. Apparently one of the reasons for building the model "backwards" was to avoid the antitrust problem: the companies could not collectively agree on assumed prices.

To deal with the two cases the model had to be run backwards. Essentially what was done to find the pattern of drilling rate over time that yielded price patterns resembling the two cases. The model involves a choice of optimistic or pessimistic success rates in drilling, and the author averaged these two alternatives.

The Khazzoom, Erickson and Spann, and MacAvoy models are all econometric models. An equation, or set of equations, is postulated that represents the behavior of the industry as it responds to changes in price and other variables. Then the parameters of these equations are estimated by "fitting" the equations to the numerical data from some historical period: Khazzoom uses the period 1961-68, Erickson and Spann, 1946-59, and MacAvoy, 1954-60. All arrive at the conclusion that gas supply responds significantly to price. Erickson and Spann's elasticity of supply estimate is .69, meaning that a 10 percent increase in price yields a 6.9 percent increase in new reserves found. MacAvoy's estimate is .45. Neither the Khazzoom model nor the industry model yields a constant elasticity of supply.

To the elasticities of Erickson-Spann and MacAvoy can be added another estimate derived from the work of Garrett of Exxon Corporation. He estimated the quantities of potentially discoverable reserves that would be economical at various prices. The elasticity of his curve between current prices and seventy cents per mcf is roughly .6. If it is assumed that the industry tends to find in any year a constant fraction of the total reserves worth producing at contemporary prices, then a given percentage increase in price has the same proportional effect on reserve additions each year as it has on ultimately recoverable reserves. On this assumption Garrett's elasticity can be used in the same way as the others. It should be stressed, however, that this assumption is made by the author and is not implicit in the Garrett study.

To develop projections from these three estimates of elasticity of supply, it was assumed that the reserves added in 1969, 1970, and 1971 were in response to the 1966-70 FPC authorized price of eighteen cents per mcf. Any given percentage change in price was then translated into reserve additions by applying the particular elasticity to the 1969-71 reserve-addition data. For example, a 100 percent increase in price in 1973 would result in a 60 percent greater quantity of reserves added if the elasticity were .6. The reserve-production ratio was assumed to be ten to one in 1975 and thereafter. This type of projection has been labelled a constant elasticity of supply (CES) projection.

Table 6 gives the figures for the five projections of natural gas supply for the two cases. Only one projection is shown in the base

Table 6

NATURAL GAS PRODUCTION
(trillions of cubic feet)

Study	1970	1975	1980	1985
Base Case				
NPC	22.0	18.8	13.5	8.6
CES	22.0	19.9	16.4	14.4
Khazzoom	22.0	18.0	17.0	16.6
Deregulation Case				
NPC	22.0	24.1	26.9	30.5
CES:				
e = .5 (MacAvoy)	22.0	24.0	24.4	25.7
e = .6 (Garrett)	22.0	24.7	26.1	28.2
e = .7 (Erickson)	22.0	25.4	27.8	30.7
Khazzoom	22.0	20.5	27.3	31.5

case for the three CES projections because they are very similar in that case.

In the base case every model shows production falling. Khazzoom is the most optimistic with a drop from 22 tcf in 1970 to 16.6 tcf in 1985. CES shows a drop to 14.4 tcf by 1985, and NPC is most pessimistic with a predicted drop to 8.6 tcf.

In the deregulation case production increases in each model. The smallest gains came from MacAvoy's early model, just 3.7 tcf per year more in 1985 than in 1970. The largest gains came from the Khazzoom model, an increase of 9.5 tcf in 1985 over 1970.

But the question relevant to this discussion is: How much more natural gas is supplied in the deregulation case than in the base case? Taking each model separately, the smallest difference in 1985 between the two options is 11.3 tcf (early MacAvoy) and the largest is 21.9 tcf (NPC). These are enormous magnitudes. Converting these figures to oil equivalents, the smallest difference is 5.5 million barrels per day and the largest is 10.7 million barrels per day. For perspective, consider that in 1972 total U.S. oil imports were 4.7 million barrels per day and total U.S. crude oil production was 9.5 million barrels per day. While any modeling of this sort must be taken with some skepticism, the fact that five independent studies (some using totally different analytical frameworks) conclude that supplies will be much larger under deregulation is hard to ignore.

The shortage of energy now facing the nation is not a problem for public policy—it is a public policy. Shortages can be eliminated very simply: remove price controls on energy. The task for policy makers is to make energy less scarce and less costly. This means removing artificial scarcities created by price controls and reversing the policy of hoarding the nation's resources by government.

Are energy resources growing more scarce? There is no evidence that energy will be as scarce in the long run as current market conditions seem to suggest. Any forecast of future energy consumption and costs is extremely speculative. What knowledge we do have of future supplies suggests that they may cost more than we are accustomed to but not so much more as to result in dramatic changes in styles of living.

Why is there an energy crisis? One thesis is a spontaneous acceleration in demand. While the fact is that consumption growth accelerated in the late 1960s the data suggest that this acceleration was not so much a result of economic growth or exogenous forces as of consumption induced by rapidly falling prices. The acceleration in price decline was in large part the consequence of shifts in public policy over the past decade rather than a growing abundance of energy resources.

These public policies tended to stimulate current consumption while discouraging the discovery of energy reserves that would provide for future demand. The inevitable consequence of these policies was an artificial scarcity of energy that became obvious to the consumer only in 1973.

One of the major reasons for continuing error in energy policy making is a false perception of the problem. The view that public policy must address itself to gaps between supply and demand is resulting in support for policies that have little social value and great social cost. Much of energy research and development activity, such as the aggressive coal gasification programs, falls into this category. The large-scale importation of liquified natural gas from overseas is an example of another activity artificially stimulated by government but indefensible on public interest grounds.

The history of U.S. oil policy is one of surplus policies in the 1950s and '60s evolving into a shortage policy in the 1970s. This shift appears to be due mainly to movements in political sentiment and influence and not to changes in energy resource conditions. Neither shortage nor surplus policies are in the public interest, and particularly not in the consumer's interest.

The principal devices by which surplus policies were effected were market-demand prorationing and the import quota system. These permitted higher crude oil prices to prevail in the domestic market than abroad by restricting both domestic production and imports. The surplus policy hurt consumers. It also injured more efficient producers by raising the cost of production from efficient wells. The principal beneficiaries appear to have been small inefficient stripper-well producers.

In 1970 this surplus policy began to change. Import quotas were expanded rapidly. Domestic crude prices were held down, at first by informal pressures and then, in 1971, by strict price controls. By April 1972 all U.S. productive capacity was in use, and all incremental demands had to be met by imports. In early 1973 world prices reached the domestic level as the cartel of producing nations achieved remarkable successes in raising prices. At this point the quota program no longer served a useful purpose, and it was scrapped.

Later in 1973 the world price passed the domestic price and a crucial decision had to be made: adopt a free-market or a shortage policy. The U.S. government chose shortages. Facing the same choice, many European governments chose essentially free markets, avoiding shortages.

To deal with the world cartel and artificially high world oil prices, the United States should adopt policies that make U.S. imports highly sensitive to the cartel price, thereby creating incentives for lower prices. The domestic price controls have the opposite effect in that they subsidize high import prices with artificially cheap domestic oil.

One of the major causes of the artificial scarcity of energy in the United States is the extraordinarily low regulated price of natural gas.

74

Natural gas is the largest single domestic source of energy and accounted for a large part of the growth in energy consumption since 1950. But much of the gas produced in recent decades was discovered before 1950 in the search for oil. Since the imposition of strict Federal Power Commission price regulation in 1960, discoveries have fallen off substantially.

The natural gas shortage policy is one of the least defensible economic policies in American history. Attempts to justify the shortage on grounds of keeping consumer prices low fail because most consumers have to pay higher prices for alternative fuels, and because the benefitted group will steadily dwindle in numbers. The principal beneficiaries appear to be consumers and complementary factors of production in producing states, such as Texas, Louisiana, and Oklahoma, and foreign oil suppliers.

The argument that higher natural gas prices will not result in significantly greater supplies is contradicted by a number of serious studies by academicians and by oil companies. On the contrary, supplies can be expected to be far greater without cost-of-service price regulation, thus substantially reducing U.S. dependence on foreign oil supplies.

An artificial scarcity policy affecting both oil and gas resources is the system used to lease federal lands. It is estimated that most future petroleum resources will be found on these federal properties. The government has been extremely reluctant to permit Americans to make use of their own resources. In the future this policy will have to be drastically changed if domestic supplies are to approach their potential.

The only economical way out of the present energy dilemma is to allow energy markets to clear. If a free-market policy is not adopted, the shortages will tend to grow larger and supplies will dwindle. Or worse, the taxpayer will be called upon to contribute many tens of billions to subsidize federal energy corporations or the development of very high-cost unconventional sources.

APPENDIX A:
MEASURING ENERGY
CONSUMPTION AND PRICES

Aggregating an Energy Market: The Heat Approach

We have dealt with the primary fuel markets and with the degree of market overlap and inter-fuel competition. But many interesting and important questions make it necessary to aggregate these separate markets into an overall energy market. How fast is energy consumption growing? What is happening to energy prices? To answer these questions, we need a definition of energy and a unit of measurement. Those in the energy business measure oil in barrels, coal in tons, and natural gas in cubic feet. Since these are not comparable units, some common yardstick must be found.

The measure invariably used by energy researchers is the quantity of heat potentially derivable from a given quantity of a given fuel. The most common unit is the British thermal unit (btu), the quantity of heat necessary to raise the temperature of one pound of water one degree Fahrenheit. In these units a barrel of crude oil typically measures 5.8 million btus; a ton of coal, 24-28 million btus; and a cubic foot of gas, 1.03 thousand btus. Oil, coal, and gas can thus be added, subtracted, and otherwise statistically compared to ascertain energy consumption, production, and price patterns. The Bureau of Mines, Resources for the Future, the National Petroleum Council, and other energy research bodies have adopted this measure.[1]

In the past, in some parts of the energy market, this approach has served well. Consider what might be called the furnace or boiler-fuel market: industry, commercial establishments, electric utilities, and large residential units purchased fuels simply to burn them in furnaces

---

[1] See, for example, H. Landsberg and S. Schurr, *Energy in the United States: Sources, Uses, and Policy Issues* (New York: Random House, 1968).

to provide heat for offices and factories, to provide steam for industrial processes and electricity generation, or simply to heat water or space for apartment buildings. Although the handling, storage, and capital costs of oil, gas, and coal differed somewhat, as did the proportion of potential btus actually provided by the furnace, consumers of furnace fuels were in many cases interested primarily in purchasing btus, regardless of their form. They made their choice of which fuel to consume simply on the basis of the price per btu. In short, oil, coal, and gas were highly substitutable and highly competitive on a btu basis. Attesting to this fact is the close correlation between choice of fuel and average price per btu to electric power plants in different parts of the United States. Because of the locations of mines and wells and different transportation costs, delivered costs per btu of oil, coal, and gas will be different in various regions of the country. Invariably, electric plants chose to use the fuel that was cheapest per btu.[2]

The significance of this high degree of competitiveness and substitutability is that when we record someone using a btu of coal or a btu of oil, we are recording units of energy of a similar value to the user. The same can be said on the production or supply side, to the extent that markets are competitive. If marginal costs of delivering a btu of oil or coal or gas to the same point are equal, as they would be under competition, the economy gives up capital and labor resources of the same value whether a btu of oil or coal is delivered. Thus, under these conditions, btus of energy, whether in the form of oil or coal or gas, always mean the same thing in terms of marginal value to the consumer and marginal cost to the supplier.

While this situation may have prevailed to some extent in the furnace-fuel market for several decades, it never existed in some energy markets, does not exist in the boiler-fuel market today, and will not in the future. Take the gasoline market as an example. Historically a btu of gasoline has cost about twice as much as a btu of home heating oil. This is due not only to greater refining costs but in large part to greater distribution costs and taxes (which mostly go to pay for the use of public roads). Thus the value of a marginal btu of gasoline will be twice the value of a marginal btu of home heating oil. Adding together gasoline and heating oil btus is adding as equals things that are quite different from the point of the consumer.

---

[2] See Tables 1-14, p. 44, and 1-15, p. 45, in John Schanz and Helmut Frank, "Natural Gas in the Future Energy Pattern," in Brown, ed., *Regulation of the Natural Gas Producing Industry.*

The same is true from the point of view of the producer or supplier. It costs the economy more in labor and capital resources to supply a btu of gasoline than to supply a btu of heating oil. What sense does it make then to add them as if they were equal?

In short, gasoline is one kind of bundle of potential heat that is not the same to the consumer or the producer as other bundles of potential heat, much as an orange is not the same kind of bundle of citric acid as a grapefruit. We do not add oranges and grapefruits by their citric content to understand what is happening in the citric fruit market. That is because people buy citric fruits on the basis of properties other than their citric acid content. If we are to understand the energy market, we cannot add fuels as if their only physical property was the potential units of heat they can be converted to.

Where the heat approach gets into serious trouble is when it has to deal with electricity. An oil-fired electric generating plant uses roughly 11,400 btus of oil to deliver one kilowatt hour (kwh) of electricity to the consumer. But the kwh supplies only 3,400 btus to the consumer due to the waste of heat in generation and transmission. How many btus of energy do we record when one kwh is generated, 11,400 or 3,400? Viewed from the supply side, clearly 11,400 btus have been used up. But from the demand or consumer side only 3,400 are received. The answer has generally been to count the btus used up by primary suppliers rather than those delivered to consumers. The argument here would have to be that we are concerned only with heat used up and not with what the final consumer actually receives.

What happens then when we come to hydroelectric power, which is generated by the kinetic energy of falling water with no btus used? The approach has been to set down the number of btus that *would* have been used up had the electricity been generated by a coal-fired plant. Clearly this is inconsistent with the decision to measure btus used up rather than btus received by the final consumer.

This method of aggregating primary energy supplies—oil, gas, and coal—with secondary energy supplies—electricity and manufactured gas—using "heat" weights, either total btus used up, or btus consumed by the final consumer, is logically unsound and can lead to absurd statistical conclusions. R. Turvey and A. Nobay of the British Electricity Council found that the use of weights based on final consumption leads to the conclusion that nonindustrial energy consumption in the United Kingdom *"fell* by 3.6 percent from 1954 to 1964. Yet no one would seriously assert that fewer resources were used to provide domestic fuel and light in the latter year or that domestic consumers then had a lower standard of heating and lighting."[3] Apparently this quirk was due to the rapid growth of electricity, which provides more usable heat relative to btu potential than coal, which was declining as a heat source.

Suppose we concede that the electric power, motor vehicle transportation, and petrochemical sectors are ill suited to the use of heat weights. Can we not fall back to the position that within the boiler-fuel market the heat measure is appropriate and should at least be used there? Unfortunately, we can no longer answer affirmatively to this question. While one btu may have been as good as another in the past, this is not true today. The impact on air quality of burning fossil fuels has been introduced as a factor influencing the decision as to what fuel should be used. Sulfur oxides are a serious source of air pollution, and coal usually contains many times as much sulfur as low-sulfur heavy oil. Thus, in many places where coal could be supplied at a much lower cost than oil per btu, oil is used. Coal is not highly substitutable with oil today even in much of the boiler-fuel market.

The upshot of this discussion is that we cannot use heat units, or any other physical units, to measure a phenomenon that is essentially economic. Heat is supplied in every use of energy. But calories are supplied in every use of grain, and vitamin C in every use of citrus fruits. Yet we do not measure grain production in calories, or citrus fruit production in milligrams of vitamin C. We measure them by price-weighted indexes. In a free, competitive market relative prices will be proportional to relative consumer valuations at the margin and relative producer costs at the margin. Not all energy is traded in competitive markets. Electricity in all states must be sold by a regulated monopoly. Not all energy is traded in free markets. Natural gas prices are set well below the free-market level by the Federal Power Commission. Yet these deviations from the ideal are not fatal.

The deviation from free markets is serious, but it may be possible to statistically adjust for it. Despite problems in constructing price-weighted indexes, there is a strong presumption that they will give more sensible results. When Turvey and Nobay used price-weighted indexes in the U.K. several improvements over physical or heat indexes were observed. For example, we would expect an energy consumption index and the index of industrial production to be highly correlated. Taking first differences of all series, they found that the correlation between a heat index, such as that used in the U.S., and

---

[3] R. Turvey and A. Nobay, "On Measuring Energy Consumption," *The Economic Journal*, December 1965, p. 789.

industrial production was .67. The correlation between their price-weighted index and industrial production was .82.[4]

This suggests the possibility that some of the peculiar and unexplained phenomena in U.S. energy consumption may be less peculiar or more explainable if price weights are used. For example, would the sharp upturn in the ratio of U.S. energy consumption to gross national product occur in a price-weighted index? If so, would changes in relative prices of energy explain this shift?

Value-Weighted Indexes of U.S. Energy Consumption and Prices

The objective here is to measure the consumption and price of energy to the final consumer. For example, oil consumption in the form of gasoline must be distinguished from other forms and weighted according to consumer prices of gasoline. Heavy fuel oil consumption receives a much lower weight, since its price per gallon to the final user is lower. Heavy fuel oil prices are deflated by the wholesale price index (WPI), while gasoline prices are deflated by the consumer price index (CPI), because these commodities are sold in different markets. Heavy fuel oil consumed by electric utilities is not counted as final consumption. We measure electric power consumed weighted by its value and exclude all the oil, gas, and coal consumed in electric plants.

The classes of energy consumption and their weights based on 1960 values are:

Oil		63.0%
Gasoline	46.3%	
Distillates	13.7	
Heavy fuel oil (less utility use)	3.0	
Natural Gas		11.8
Residential	6.5	
Commercial	1.6	
Industrial (less utility use)	3.7	
Coal (less utility use)		2.9
Electricity		22.3
Residential	9.8	
Commercial	5.7	
Industrial	6.8	

[4] Ibid., p. 789.

Table A-1

INDEXES OF U.S. ENERGY CONSUMPTION, 1950–1970
(1960 = 100)

Year	Heat Index	Value-Weighted Index
1950	79	59
1955	89	81
1960	100	100
1965	120	125
1970	151	163

Source: U.S. Bureau of Mines and author.

Table A-2

AVERAGE ANNUAL ENERGY CONSUMPTION AND GROSS NATIONAL PRODUCT, RATES OF GROWTH, 1950–1970

	1950–55	1955–60	1960–65	1965–70
Heat index	3.4%	2.5%	3.9%	5.3%
Value-weighted index	7.7	4.6	4.9	6.2
Gross national product	4.7	2.3	5.3	3.4

Source: *Annual Report of the Council of Economic Advisers, 1973*, p. 194, and Table A-1.

The weights implicit in the heat index of consumption for 1960 are:

Oil	45.0%
Natural gas	28.5
Coal	22.8
Hydroelectric power	3.7

Nuclear power accounted for less than one-tenth of a percent.

It must be stressed that the value-weighted indexes are merely a first step toward better measurement of energy consumption and prices. A more detailed explanation of these statistics and their sources is given in the "Sources of Data" section of this appendix.

Table A-1 shows the heat index and the value-weighted index every five years from 1950 to 1970. The principal difference between the two series is that the value-weighted index grows faster in every period. This is shown even more clearly in Table A-2, where average annual rates of growth are given for each five-year period. Notice that this difference in rate of growth is much less pronounced after 1960.

The much heavier weight given to electricity and gasoline consumption in the value-weighted index accounts for most of the difference. Electricity consumption, in particular, grew much faster than nonelectric energy consumption over the whole period.

In general, the rates of growth in the two energy consumption indexes parallel the rates of growth of the real gross national product. The growth of both energy indexes slowed down in the 1955-1960 period when the growth rate of GNP slowed down, and then accelerated again when GNP grew faster from 1960 to 1965.

Only two cases diverged significantly from the parallel patterns of the economy and energy consumption. First, the value-weighted index grew exceptionally fast in the 1950-1955 period. Since the heat index did not, the answer must lie in the difference in weighting. The value-weighted index is much more sensitive to increased consumption of gasoline by automobiles and electricity by home appliances. Because of war-time shortage policies, there was enormous unmet demand for durable consumer goods, particularly automobiles and electrical appliances, in the immediate post-World War II years. From 1945 to 1950 consumer expenditures on durable goods rose at an average annual rate of 45 percent, while the real GNP was constant. It seems likely then that it is because electricity and gasoline consumption are more closely related to the stock of consumer durable goods than other forms of energy consumption that the value-weighted index showed a much higher growth rate than the heat index during the following five-year period.

Second, both energy consumption indexes accelerated during the 1965-1970 period, while the rate of growth of GNP slowed down, as compared to the previous five-year and ten-year periods. This is significant since it occurs in both energy indexes, indicating a general explanation and not a peculiarity of one index, and because it is in sharp contrast to the patterns of the previous fifteen years.

Much of the answer is to be found by looking at the value-weighted price index. Table A-3 shows the values of the index from 1950 to June 1973. Table A-4 shows the rates of change in the index. Energy prices have fallen dramatically since 1950 at a continuously accelerating rate of decline. The acceleration is particularly marked after 1960. Between 1960 and 1970 energy prices fell at more than twice the rate of decline from 1950 to 1960. If we consider that the consumer response to price takes time, probably several years because of the durability of energy-using equipment, the timing of the

Table A-3

VALUE-WEIGHTED INDEX OF ENERGY PRICES, 1950–JUNE 1973

(1960 = 100)

Year	Index
1950	107.2
1955	103.9
1960	100.0
1965	93.5
1970	85.4
June 1973	80.7

Source: Author.

Table A-4

AVERAGE ANNUAL RATE OF CHANGE OF ENERGY PRICES, 1950–JUNE 1973

Period	Rate of Change
1950–55	− .62
1955–60	− .75
1960–65	− 1.31
1965–70	− 1.73
1970–June 1973	− 1.87

Source: Author.

acceleration in consumption is readily interpreted. An accelerating rate of decline in energy prices induced an accelerating rate of growth in energy consumption.

This interpretation is reinforced by attempts to find factors that might have brought about exogenous shifts in the demand for energy after 1965. Even under very generous assumptions about what is an exogenous factor, it does not seem possible to ascribe the post-1965 acceleration to exogenous shifts in demand. The most ambitious attempt was made by Bruce Netschert who was able to account for only one-third of the acceleration in the heat index by factors such as the growth of air conditioning and the recent decline in electric plant efficiency, neither of which can be regarded as a truly exogenous development.[5]

From what we know of price elasticities of energy consumption, it is clear that the accelerating decline in energy prices can only be a partial explanation for the acceleration in consumption. The rate of price decline in the 1960-1965 period was only six-tenths of a percent per year greater than that of the 1950s, and the rate of decline from 1965 to 1970 was only seven-tenths of a percent per year greater than in the preceding ten years. Accounting completely for the 1.4 percent increase in the consumption growth rate (the 1965-1970 rate of 6.2 percent less the 1955-65 average of 4.8 percent) requires a price elasticity of demand of about -2.0. This is well above recent estimates of long-run elasticities of gasoline and electricity [6] and, of course, the overall price elasticity of energy must be smaller than the average elasticity of individual energy components. A careful econometric exercise would be required to say much more about this.

Sources of Data [7]

Total oil was divided into three groups—gasoline, which included motor and aviation fuel, kerosene, and jet fuel. Consumption data were taken from the United States Bureau of Mines *Minerals Yearbook* (various editions). Gasoline prices used were taken from *Platt's Oilgram Price Service* and were deflated by the CPI.

The subdivision distillates include distillate oil, still gas, liquified gases, and the "miscellaneous" category of the *Minerals Yearbook*. Price data are those for Number 2 fuel oil as given by the U.S. Bureau of Labor Statistics, *Retail Prices and Indexes of Fuel and Utilities*. Prices for 1950 and 1955 were obtained by extrapolating 1960 figures backward at a rate of 3 percent lower in 1955 and 3 percent lower again for 1950. All were deflated by the CPI.

The subdivision heavy fuel oil includes residual fuel oil, lubricating oil, wax, coke, asphalt, and road oil. Quantities were obtained from the *Minerals Yearbook*. Prices from 1960 on were obtained from the National Coal Association's *Steam Electric Plant Factors*. Price

---

[5] National Economic Research Associates, "Energy Consumption and Gross National Product in the United States: An Examination of Recent Changes in the Relationship," privately circulated, March 1971.

[6] Houthakker and Verleger, "Dynamic Demand Analyses of Selected Energy Resources."

[7] Constance Boris assembled and computed all the data discussed in Appendix A. She has my gratitude for a job well done.

data for 1950 and 1955 were obtained from the New York Bunker "C" oil price series in early editions of the American Petroleum Institute's *Petroleum Facts and Figures* by a linking adjustment of .89 times the Bunker "C" prices. This adjustment factor was based on the normal relationship between the series where they overlapped historically. All heavy oil prices were deflated by the WPI.

Data on natural gas quantities and prices were obtained from various issues of the Bureau of Mines *Minerals Yearbook*. Residential and commercial prices were deflated by the CPI, while industrial prices were deflated by the WPI.

Coal consumption data were obtained from the *Minerals Yearbook*. Coal price data were obtained from *Steam Electric Plant Factors*. Prices for 1950 and 1955 were not available from this source. Prices for 1955 were therefore assumed to be the same as for 1956. Prices for 1950 were determined by taking the *Minerals Yearbook* f.o.b. mine values and calculating the average freight charge as the average difference between the f.o.b. mine value and the price at the electric power plant *(Steam Electric Plant Factors)* for 1956-60. All coal prices were deflated by the WPI.

Electric power consumption and price data were obtained from the Edison Electric Institute's *Statistical Yearbook* (various issues). Residential and commercial prices were deflated by the CPI, while industrial prices were deflated by the WPI.

Unpublished price data for 1971, 1972, and June 1973 were obtained from sources by telephone. Only natural gas and coal prices could not be obtained up to June 1973. Since these receive only a small weight in the overall price index they were extrapolated in the following way: Natural gas prices were extrapolated to June 1973 by assuming the same rate of increase as for 1971 and 1972. (The latter were obtained by telephone from the Bureau of Mines.) Coal prices for 1972 and June 1973 were obtained by extrapolating the rate of increase of 1970 to 1971.

The main objective of petroleum policy is to provide the consumer with petroleum products at the lowest cost consistent with meeting demand. Obviously this objective is not being met. Supply is falling short of demand, and there is widespread suspicion that if past policies had been different, petroleum would be much more abundant today.

This suspicion is warranted. Public policy in the energy field has been deficient and has caused substantial injury to producers and consumers. Price controls on natural gas and oil, together with restrictive federal leasing policies, have created an energy crisis.

The subject of these hearings is the competitive market structure of the oil industry and possible reforms in that structure. The importance of this subject cannot be underestimated. The working of an efficient competitive market is fundamental to meeting our objectives of abundant supplies at lower costs. But we should be under no illusions regarding the role of competition in the present crisis. Imperfections in competitive structure have little to do with our current ills. Reforms in that structure will contribute little to resolving the problems consumers face today. Indeed, as is often the case with economic reforms, they may be disruptive in the short run even if beneficial in the long run. For these reasons we can indulge in a measure of deliberateness in these hearings that we could not afford in some other aspects of energy policy.

The focus of petroleum policy is the consumer. The optimal structure of the industry is the one that provides what he wants at the lowest possible price. The consumer could not care less whether

This statement is reprinted here substantially as presented by the author to the Special Subcommittee on Integrated Oil Operations, Committee on Interior and Insular Affairs, United States Senate, 21 February 1974.

the firms that supply him are large or small, integrated or noninte-grated, publicly run or privately owned. Whatever combination of in-dustry characteristics results in the lowest costs in producing what he wants, and competes these low costs through to him, is the best system.

In assessing the present structure, these two questions are central: (1) are there features of the present structure that result in un-necessarily high costs, and (2) are all existing efficiencies passed on to the consumer, or are they retained as excess profits by suppliers? In my current study of the competitive structure, I have reached two preliminary conclusions: (1) some inefficiencies, traceable to govern-ment policies, have raised the cost of supplying petroleum, and (2) existing efficiencies are passed on to the consumer in the form of low prices. There are no excess profits.

Inefficiencies in the Petroleum Market

So long as the most efficient firm is allowed to do the job, the lowest costs will be realized. This will tend to occur in a free and open market. The search for inefficiencies is, therefore, largely a search for restrictions on the activities of firms.

The following inefficiencies exist in the petroleum market:

1. Because of price controls and the federal allocation system, supplies of crude oil and gasoline do not necessarily go to the firms and consumers that can offer the most for them and can make the best use of them. Refineries that would yield the most valuable products from a barrel of crude oil are not allocated the crude oil. Marketers that could more efficiently market gasoline are not allocated the gasoline. And finally consumers who might value a gallon of gasoline more than others do not receive it.

I have not attempted to quantify the distortions generated by price controls and governmental allocation, but it could be done fairly quickly, and the distortions might prove sizable. Americans returning from Europe remark at how much easier it is to buy gasoline in Europe than at home in spite of the fact that Europe is far more dependent on oil imported from boycotting producers. The few European countries that tried price controls and rationing quickly abandoned them, and the remainder ignored them from the start.

2. Current price controls on crude oil favor the small inefficient producer. The Trans-Alaska Pipeline Authorization Act of 1973 exempts from price ceilings wells producing less than ten barrels per day. In recent months this has meant a price for costly or "less

efficient" crude oil about double that for more economical crude. This may have an air of "fairness" about it, and I have no doubt that many regard this as reasonable. After all, if you have higher costs, should you not get a higher price?

The trouble with this policy is that it means higher costs, higher prices, and smaller supplies to the consumer. It means that $6.00 per barrel crude—the ceiling price is $5.25—cannot be produced, while $10.00 crude can. Furthermore, a stripper-well producer contemplating production of ten or fifteen barrels per day will find it more profitable to produce ten barrels at $10.00 than fifteen barrels at $5.25. (As one might expect, the price control rules do not allow the $10.00 price if one is producing less than the maximum feasible rate. But as a practical matter, there is no way of applying these restrictions to the more than 300,000 stripper wells throughout the United States.[1])

The upshot is that we are discouraging production of more economical crude in favor of more costly crude and getting less oil in the end. It has been argued that we are favoring small business and *thereby* promoting competition. We are certainly favoring small business. But we are obviously *curtailing* competition and making oil more scarce.

3. The Federal Power Commission regulation of natural gas prices has for more than a decade created enormous distortions in the energy market. Natural gas is selling for an average of about eighteen cents per million btus, while crude oil from abroad sells for almost ten times that much. The economic waste from this policy is readily calculable, given assumptions about supply and demand elasticities of natural gas and other fuels. By the most conservative assumptions the nation is wasting billions of dollars per year in scarce capital and labor resources, and, by creating an unnecessary reliance on foreign oil, reducing the international exchange value of the dollar. Millions of consumers of home heating oil would be either heating with cheaper natural gas or cheaper home heating oil were it not for this policy.

Just as with crude oil, natural gas prices are not regulated in the case of smaller producers. The Federal Power Commission exempts firms producing less than 10 billion cubic feet per year from price regulation, resulting in the same kind of distortion as with crude oil production.

4. The Department of the Interior in disposing of royalty oil from OCS leases does not sell it to the highest bidder but allocates

---

[1] The rules are contained in the Code of Federal Regulations, Title 10, Part 210.31-32.

almost all of it to small refiners. Royalty oil from inland federal leases is also allocated disproportionately to small refiners. Again, this may help small business, but it reduces competition and creates inefficiency.

5. In the past enormous inefficiencies were created in some major producing states by the system of market-demand prorationing. Under this system small inefficient wells were allowed to produce without output limitations while efficient wells were required to cut back production substantially. In 1965, a costly stripper well capable of producing ten barrels per day in Texas was allowed to produce ten barrels per day while an efficient flush well might have been allowed as little as 28 percent of its potential production. To cover the high cost of production from the inefficient wells, prices had to be higher, and to sustain these higher prices, production had to be cut back on efficient wells, thereby artificially raising their production costs.

6. The mandatory oil import quotas established in 1959 discriminated against large refiners in favor of small refiners. Licenses to import oil from overseas were distributed to refiners on the basis of refinery throughput and a so-called "sliding scale." In 1969, for example, refiners with throughput of 10,000 barrels per day received licenses to import 1,950 barrels per day—or 19.5 percent—while refiners with throughput of 500,000 barrels per day received licenses for imports of 21,050 barrels per day—or 4.2 percent. Since these licenses were valued in the market at about $1.25 per barrel, the small refiner received a subsidy of 24.4 cents per barrel of throughput while the larger refiner received a subsidy of only 5.3 cents.

Elementary economics tells us that a uniform subsidy will tend to be passed through to consumers, while any special subsidies to particular firms will go either to offset inefficient operations or into the pockets of the small refiner as excess profit. Thus, the consumer would be better off if licenses had been distributed on a proportional basis.

Neither the oil import quotas nor market-demand limitations on crude oil production exist today. Production allowables in Texas reached 100 percent in April 1972, and a year later oil import quotas were scrapped.

7. Under the new oil import program launched by the President in April 1973 quotas have been dropped, but a small license fee—a euphemism for tariff—has been placed on crude oil and more substantial license fees have been placed on products. Some crude, however, may be imported without payment of a fee. These fee-exempt

licenses will be allocated to refiners on the same kind of sliding-scale basis used under the old oil import program. Thus the differential subsidy to small refiners continues, and with it inefficiencies and/or windfalls. Under the plan announced by the President these fee-exempt licenses will be phased out by 1980.

In citing these inefficiencies, I am not suggesting that all of the programs and policies that created them were unwise. In some cases, such as the oil import program, the inefficiency cited was a minor aspect of the program and a judgment about the overall value of the program would require analysis of many other aspects. In other cases, such as regulation of natural gas prices, the inefficiency mentioned was a major consequence of the policy. Also, there is no presumption that these inefficiencies are of the same order of magnitude. For example, the inefficiencies caused by the biased allocation of royalty oil are probably much smaller than the others.

In spite of all the qualifications that have to be made, there is still a definite public policy theme underlying all but two of these inefficiencies: the policy was motivated by concern for small business. To the extent that these policies are justified by the rationale that the assistance of small business is socially desirable for its own sake, one can only urge that the full costs of achieving this objective be weighed against its value. Consumers are suffering, and we had better be sure that their suffering is not too high a price to pay for this objective. Also, there are much simpler ways of subsidizing small business without creating significant market distortions. Finally, I would point out that many of these "small" businesses are firms worth tens of millions of dollars.

To the extent these policies are justified by the rationale that by promoting small business we are promoting competition and thus lowering consumer prices, the policies are seriously mistaken. In each of the cases cited, the small business subsidy curtails competition and results in higher costs and prices.

Competition, Entry and Profits

Three decades of congressional hearings on the petroleum markets have attempted to identify small business and competition. To a great extent they have established this connection in the public mind. We are told that there are twenty giant oil companies in the petroleum industry and a large number of small companies that provide them with some competition. These twenty giant companies "control" production, refining, transportation, and marketing sectors of the industry. This "handful" of twenty giant companies form an "oligopoly," a notion that makes my dictionary pitifully obsolete.

There is no systematic evidence that the petroleum industry is not highly competitive as it stands. There is no evidence that it would be substantially less competitive if the numerous small firms disappeared. (It would certainly be less efficient, since many small firms are very efficient. On the other hand, some small firms exist only by virtue of the aforementioned subsidies.)

The belief that small firms and less concentration are needed is based on the theory that the larger firms systematically exclude smaller firms from the industry, and therefore prices are not driven down to costs (including normal return on capital). This theory has one clear implication: if prices are not driven down to costs, then monopoly or excess profits will be made by the large companies.[2] Indeed many economists have regarded profitability as the premier test of monopoly.[3] Nevertheless, the connection between monopoly and profits is a highly qualified one. Perhaps the strongest statement that can be made is that the persistence of abnormally high profits over long periods of time in a particular industry make it more likely that the industry is monopolistic than competitive.[4]

Note the three qualifications in the statement: First, the statement is probabilistic. High profits are not a sure indicator of monopoly. Competitive industries earn high profits when favorable unanticipated shifts in demand and supply occur, and monopolies can earn normal or below-normal profits when unfavorable, unanticipated shifts occur. Second, the statement refers to the persistence of high profits over a long period of time. The larger the time span, the more likely that high profits are due to monopoly as opposed to favorable market conditions: the probability of perpetual good fortune is infinitesimal. Third, the statement refers to industry profits, not company profits.[5]

---

[2] Note that the special features of the petroleum industry—market-demand prorationing, import quotas, price regulation of natural gas, the depletion allowance—do not have long-run effects on the rate of profit in the industry because they do not affect entry into the industry. Those that make prices higher or costs lower merely attract more firms into the industry until prices fall or costs rise, or both, and profits fall to normal. Those that make prices lower, such as natural gas price regulation, drive firms out of the industry until profits rise to normal levels.

[3] Fritz Machlup, *The Political Economy of Monopoly* (Baltimore: The Johns Hopkins University Press, 1952).

[4] J. S. Bain, "The Profit Rate as a Measure of Monopoly Power," *The Quarterly Journal of Economics*, vol. 42, no. 2 (February 1941), p. 274.

[5] Yale Brozen, "Significance of Profit Data for Antitrust Policy," in J. Fred Weston and Sam Peltzman, eds., *Public Policy Toward Mergers* (Pacific Palisades, Calif.: Goodyear, 1969), p. 113.

Monopoly profits are due to higher prices which in turn are brought about by curtailed output. All firms in an industry benefit from higher prices, not just those that curtail output. (The requirement that excess profits be long-lived to indicate monopoly suggests the absurdity of recent claims that high oil company accounting profits recorded in the last quarter of 1973 demonstrate a conspiracy or monopoly power. Profits of one quarter or one year or even a few years provide no evidence regarding monopoly. Furthermore, there was a clearly unanticipated supply shift favorable to industry profits: the Arab oil boycott brought on by the October Arab-Israeli war.)

When we turn to measuring long-term profitability, we are faced with two alternatives: accounting measures derived from balance sheets and profit and loss statements, and realized profits to the stockholder as measured by stock price appreciation and dividends paid. Accounting measures of profits suffer a number of serious defects because accounting conventions are only vaguely related to economic theory. Expenditures that should be capitalized, such as advertising and research and development, frequently are not. Depreciation charges usually reflect simple arithmetic rules rather than actual changes in the value of assets. Future income not yet confirmed by sales contracts is ignored. Even without these problems, the procedure of estimating the rate of return on capital by the ratio of income to stockholders' equity or invested capital can give widely disparate answers for a given true rate of return depending upon the particular time pattern of cash flows.[6] Finally, we must hope that the accountants have not imputed capital values to any future monopoly profits acquired by the firm at times of organization, merger, or acquisition.

The alternative approach is more closely related to the economist's conception of profit. If a firm that is worth $100 million at the beginning of the year is worth $120 million at the end of the year, there has been a profit of $20 million, and the firm has earned 20 percent on its capital investment. Instead of attempting to estimate the true value of the firm from accounting records, we observe the value the market places on the firm. After all, buyers and sellers of shares of the firm have access not only to accounting statements, but to all kinds of other facts that affect valuation. The importance of this other information is indicated by the fact that the market value of a share of stock of a company is usually very different from the ac-

---

[6] E. Solomon, "Alternative Rate of Return Concepts and Their Implication for Utility Regulation," *Bell Journal of Economics and Management Science*, vol. 1, no. 1 (Spring 1970).

countant's book value of a share of stock. This is particularly important in the producing sector of the petroleum industry where there are enormous discrepancies between the value of oil discovered and the dollar value of capital assets used in the search for that oil.

If we engage in the following procedure, we will not miss any profits .the firm has realized, and we will measure the actual rate of return to a stockholder. Take the price of a company's stock at a beginning point in time; invest all dividends back into the firm by buying shares at the market price after the dividends have been paid; then calculate the wealth of the stockholder at the ending time point, a wealth increased by virtue of price appreciation and the greater number of shares due to reinvestment of dividends. We will not have missed any profits to the company because profits must be either paid out in dividends or used by the firm to purchase new assets, and these assets will enhance the market value of the firm and be reflected in stock prices. (We ignore any additional executive compensation paid out of profits as being too small to be concerned about for the large firms we will be dealing with.) Therefore, there can be no fear that some kind of financial sleight-of-hand has removed from the figures profits that are really there.

The rate of return calculated is simply the annual rate of return, which, if realized every year, would result in the same increase in wealth as experienced by the stockholder. The stockholder does not, of course, experience the same increase in wealth each year. The calculated rate of return must therefore be interpreted as an average.

One criticism of this approach is that initial period stock prices may already capitalize expected future monopoly profits. Therefore, rates of return calculated on initial stock prices would only reflect normal rates of return, even though monopoly profits were being earned. (Note that a similar criticism applies to accounting profits since book values may include some capitalized monopoly profits.)

As a practical matter this probably has little effect on our calculated rates of return. Any monopoly profits earned in the petroleum industry would—even industry critics would agree—require lax antitrust and regulatory policy and a passive Congress and executive. The uncertainty of future public policy would mean that these monopoly profits would be discounted at a very high rate and that monopoly profits that might accrue four or five years in the future would be accorded a very small value in present stock prices. If we are dealing with a period of twenty years, the influence of capitalized profits of a few years should be very small. Monopoly profits earned continuously for a couple of decades should definitely show up in our figures.

When my study is completed, it will deal with both accounting and market-related measures of profitability. At the present time only the market data have been adequately analyzed. The Standard and Poor's COMPUSTAT tapes available at the University of Michigan contain accounting and market data on oil corporations listed on the New York Stock Exchange and American Stock Exchange from 1953 to 1972. Only twenty-three petroleum companies were listed on these exchanges for the entire period. By also considering the period 1960 to 1972, it was possible to expand the number of petroleum companies to forty-nine.

As a standard of reference or norm, the rate of return of the Standard and Poor's (S&P) 500 stock composite index was calculated. The results for forty-nine petroleum companies and for the S&P composite are shown in Table B-1. (The classification of petroleum companies and the exclusion of some companies from the list would require considerable discussion. The basic principle of exclusion was that a company must have a majority of its assets in petroleum or a majority of its earnings from petroleum to be considered a petroleum company. Companies such as Tenneco, Penzoil, and Signal, which are primarily in nonpetroleum businesses, were excluded. Natural gas pipeline transportation and contract drilling were not considered part of the "petroleum industry" as defined here.)

Some of the significant conclusions to emerge from these figures are:

1. American petroleum companies were significantly less profitable than the S&P 500 over the 1953 to 1972 period. Indeed, not one of the twenty-one American petroleum companies equalled the S&P 500's rate of return!

2. The eight companies charged by the Federal Trade Commission with monopolizing the industry earned an average rate of return of 12.1 percent, more than 20 percent below the S&P norm for the 1953 to 1972 period.

3. Canadian and overseas producers were far more profitable than domestic producers, domestic refiners, or internationals, and significantly more profitable than the S&P 500. Canadian refiners were much closer to the norm.

4. Domestic refining was far more profitable than domestic production over the 1960-1972 period, and based on just two domestic producers, was more profitable over the whole 1953-72 period.

Table B-1

OIL INDUSTRY STOCKHOLDERS' AVERAGE ANNUAL RATE OF RETURN[a] AND STANDARD & POOR'S 500 STOCK COMPOSITE INDEX, 1953–72 AND 1960–72

Refiners	1953–72	1960–72	Producers	1953–72	1960–72
Domestic			**Domestic**		
American Petrofina	—	18.5%	Aztec	—	8.9%
Ashland	13.8%	13.6	Baruch-Foster	—	0.9
Atlantic Richfield	12.8	14.6	Consolidated	—	4.9
Cities Service	10.5	9.7	Crestmont	—	−4.8
Clark	—	19.0	Crystal	—	4.8
Commonwealth	—	11.8	Felmont	—	8.7
Continental	9.0	6.9	General American	8.9%	11.5
Crown	—	9.0	Louisiana Land	—	13.7
Getty	12.3	16.0	Superior	9.0	8.9
Husky	—	11.4	Westates	—	5.5
Kerr-McGee	14.6	18.3			
Marathon	9.7	10.2	Average	9.0%	6.3%
Murphy	—	10.5			
Phillips	9.4	7.8	**Canadian**		
Reserve	—	−5.2	Canadian Export	—	6.4%
Shell	9.9	6.8	Canadian Homestead	—	24.9
Skelly	10.2	12.5	Canadian Superior	—	14.3
Standard (Indiana)	11.7	15.3	Dome	21.4%	32.0
Standard (Ohio)	15.4	16.1	Home	—	15.8
Sun	7.1	9.4	United Canso	—	20.3
Union	11.1	12.8			
			Average	21.4%	19.0%
Average	11.3%	11.7%			
			Overseas		
International			Asamera	—	37.5%
Exxon	11.6%	10.7%	Belco	—	4.7
Gulf	12.3	8.9	Creole	—	5.2
Mobil	13.3	15.3	Occidental	—	23.8
Standard (Cal.)	11.4	10.2			
Texaco	13.7	9.7	Average	—	17.8%
Average	12.5%	11.0%			
Canadian					
Gulf Oil of Canada	—	11.1%			
Imperial Oil	12.4%	17.2			
Pacific Petroleum	—	12.3			
Average	12.4%	13.5%			

Standard & Poor's 500 Stock Composite Index

1953–72	15.6
1960–72	12.8

[a] Annual rate of return that would yield same increase in value over the period as realized price appreciation with dividends reinvested. Figures shown are averages of three rates of return based on three alternative price assumptions: (1) Stock purchased at initial year's high, sold at final year's high, with all dividends reinvested at succeeding year's high, (2) stock purchased at initial year's low, sold at final year's low, with dividends reinvested at succeeding year's low, and (3) stock purchased at initial year's closing price, sold at final year's closing price, with dividends reinvested at succeeding year's closing price.

From 1960 to 1972 domestic producers realized less than half the rate of return of the S&P 500.

These figures provide strong evidence that no excess profits were earned by domestic petroleum companies and thus contradict the theses that firms have been deterred from entering the petroleum industry and that prices are above costs.[7] The immediate task for economists is to explain why the industry has been so unprofitable and why capital continued to flow in. That explanation will not be attempted here.

If the exclusionary thesis is wrong, then there must be something wrong with the logic of that thesis or with certain key factual assumptions. To examine the thesis, I will set out an oversimplified version. Any version must be oversimplified because the charges against the larger petroleum companies are so numerous, so varied, and often so contradictory, that it would take a dissertation just to sort them out.

First, it is usually asserted that the industry is dominated by a small number of firms. In the economist's jargon, it is concentrated. This, it is alleged, permits monopoly power.

Second, it is alleged that the high degree of vertical integration further enhances this monopoly power. One of the most popular theses asserts that refining margins are artificially low and crude prices artificially high because of the favored tax treatment of production. This makes it impossible for firms to enter refining without integrating into production and thus raises further barriers to entry. (This argument seems to have been developed by Melvin de Chazeau and Alfred Kahn and has been used by the Federal Trade Commission and Professors Fred Allvine and G. Patterson—the latter, in these hearings—and in numerous popular pieces.) Small marketers are injured because there are fewer small refiners to purchase gasoline from and because the larger companies will not sell to them.

Third, refiners and small marketers are further excluded or handicapped by the fact that crude and product pipelines are overwhelmingly owned by large companies either singly or in joint ventures.

While I would like to deal with all of these theses, my research on the marketing and pipeline sectors is too preliminary to be used

---

[7] I have examined the question of whether it is possible that capitalized monopoly profits formed so large a part of the initial year's price that they masked a monopoly rate of return on the competitive value of assets. For the FTC Eight it turns out that for monopoly profits to have been earned, capitalized monopoly profits must have accounted for an overwhelming portion of 1953 market value, an implication that cannot be reconciled with the 1953 accounting data on assets.

here. However, there does appear to be an enormous amount of data to test theses regarding exclusion and cartelization. Considering the widespread charges, it is surprising that no systematic analyses have been carried out.

Consider the issue of concentration: In the first place, after an enormous amount of statistical research, there appears to be little, if any, correlation between concentration and monopoly profits across industries.[8] Thus concentration does not offer even a presumption of monopoly. Second, the petroleum industry is not highly concentrated: The average market share of the four largest firms for all U.S. manufacturing industries in 1966 was 39 percent.[9] In 1972 the four largest domestic refiners had less than 33 percent of the market, and the four largest domestic crude oil producers had 31 percent of the market.[10] In 1968 the four largest natural gas producers had 25 percent of the interstate market.[11] Most manufacturing industries are more concentrated than the petroleum industry.

Perhaps no other aspect of the petroleum industry has brought more confused discussion than vertical integration. The theory of vertical integration is simple: firms internalize operations when it is more economical than using the marketplace.[12] Indeed, the business firm itself is the first step in vertical integration. One would think therefore than an inquiry into vertical integration would focus on the economies that can be obtained by bringing certain market transactions within the firm. Surprisingly, the high degree of vertical integration in the petroleum industry has spurred a search for devious explanations.

The most popular thesis is that developed by de Chazeau and Kahn,[13] and can be summarized as follows: A firm that had crude production equal to its refinery output would be indifferent to the

---

[8] H. Demsetz, *The Market Concentration Doctrine* (Washington, D.C.: American Enterprise Institute, 1973).

[9] William G. Shepherd, *Market Power and Economic Welfare: An Introduction* (New York: Random House, 1970), p. 106.

[10] The *Oil and Gas Journal* staff, American Petroleum Institute, and U.S. Bureau of Mines.

[11] Federal Power Commission, *Sales by Producers of Natural Gas to Interstate Pipe Lines* (Washington, D. C.: Government Printing Office, 1969).

[12] R. Coase, "The Nature of the Firm," *Economica*, vol. 9 (1937), pp. 386-405.

[13] Melvin G. de Chazeau and Alfred Kahn, *Integration and Competition in the Petroleum Industry* (New Haven: Yale University Press, 1959), pp. 221-229. The opposite of this thesis was put forward by Eugene Rostow in *A National Policy for the Oil Industry* (New Haven: Yale University Press, 1948), and is now being examined by a committee of the California legislature. This is but one illustration of the contradictory nature of the charges against the industry.

price of crude oil for a given product price. Its total revenues would be the same regardless of the crude price and, given its costs, its profits would be the same. However, crude production is favored by the tax system. Higher crude prices mean a greater value to the depletion allowance and, thus, lower taxes. Thus, for any product price and profit before taxes, a greater profit after taxes can be realized by taking minimum earnings on refinery operations and maximum earnings in crude production.

Few refiners have complete self-sufficiency in crude production. But even if they have a fairly high degree of self-sufficiency, it can be shown arithmetically that they will benefit from a rise in crude prices even if product prices remain unchanged. When the depletion allowance was 27.5 percent, a refiner with 77 percent self-sufficiency or higher would benefit from higher crude prices even if product prices remained unchanged. If only a part of the crude price increase were passed on in the product price, a correspondingly lower degree of self-sufficiency would suffice to make the crude price increase profitable. (The FTC's report on the petroleum industry succeeds in proving the impossible: that the reduction in the depletion allowance increases the incentive to higher crude prices!) [14]

Thus, an artificially high crude price and artificially low refining margin will exist. This makes it difficult for refiners that are not integrated to survive and discourages entry into refining since the refiner must also be a crude producer.

This artificial price structure obviously implies that crude production will be more profitable than refining, and therefore both crude producers and highly self-sufficient refiners will be more profitable than less integrated refiners. In fact, de Chazeau and Kahn show that from 1947 to 1957 security prices of producers and highly self-sufficient refiners substantially outperformed less integrated refiners. Also, from 1946 to 1955 accounting profits on total invested capital were higher for producers than for refiners. [15]

This argument is not sustainable in logic or in fact. It is true that artificially small refining margins would drive nonintegrated refiners out of the business. However, they would also drive integrated refiners out of the refining business. If the refining business is unprofitable, it is unprofitable to everyone. The argument requires integrated

---

[14] This is due to an arithmetic error. See *Preliminary Federal Trade Commission Staff Report on its Investigation of the Petroleum Industry* (Washington, 1973), Appendix B. I am grateful to my colleague, Richard Mancke, for pointing this out and the fact that when the arithmetic is corrected, the argument collapses.

[15] Ibid., pp. 321-332.

refiners to continue investing in activities that yield subnormal earnings and thus not to maximize the total profits of the firm. The rational integrated firm would cease investing in refineries and invest in super-profitable crude production. Indeed, anyone, whether refiner, producer, or outside the oil business, would want to invest in production and avoid refining. Thus, capital would continue to flow into production and avoid refining until each sector's rate of return became normal and equal.

But, it will be counter-argued, this is a conspiracy, and even though it is not rational for the individual firm to build refineries, the group must build them and so they will be built. Adding the assumption of conspiracy does make the argument more logical, but it makes it even less realistic. If a cartel is requiring its members to invest in unprofitable activities, then it must divide this burden among the firms in some equitable manner. But, in fact, refining and production activities—that is, unprofitable and profitable activities—are shared very unequally among large firms. Getty's ratio of crude oil production to refinery runs in 1972 was 149 percent. Standard of Ohio's ratio was 7 percent. How does Getty induce Standard of Ohio to keep sinking money into refineries? For this cartel to work, literally billions of dollars of bribes would have to be paid among the top twenty or so companies. No evidence has been presented that this happens. To my knowledge, no one has suggested that it happens.

What about refining and producing profits? Everyone knows that producing is more profitable than refining. As with so many things everyone knows, this is untrue. During the period examined by de Chazeau and Kahn (1947-1957) crude prices rose 64 percent. During the same period spare capacity in refining rose from 4.9 percent to 10.1 percent. It would certainly be surprising if stock prices of producers had not performed better than those of refiners.

Economic theory suggests that production and refining should be equally profitable in the long run, although they may certainly differ in the short run. Therefore, over the long run producers should earn rates of return similar to refiners, and refiners with relatively large crude production should earn rates of return similar to less integrated refiners.

Looking back at Table B-1 we find only two producers for the period 1953 to 1972, and they earned 9 percent. Fourteen refiners averaged 11.3. It would be hard to say profitability was significantly different given only two observations on producers. In any case it certainly contradicts the de Chazeau-Kahn thesis which requires that the producers do better than the refiners. When we turn to the 1960-

1972 data, we find ten producers averaging 6.3 percent, much lower than the twenty-one-refiner average of 11.7 percent.

To compare profitability of more integrated and less integrated refiners, I have plotted the rates of return against the so-called "self-sufficiency ratio," the volume of crude production divided by refinery runs. Figure B-1 shows the 1953 to 1972 period, and Figure B-2 shows the 1960 to 1972 period. In both cases there is an absence of correlation. The most profitable firms include crude-poor and crude-rich refiners.

The notion that vertical integration is a device by which large firms monopolize the industry is also inconsistent with some other facts. For one thing large companies are not especially integrated as compared to small companies. The most recent analysis of the degree of integration of large and small firms was done for 1960. In that year the twenty largest domestic refiners had an average ratio of crude production to refinery runs of 49.7 percent. Of the next twenty-five largest refiners, only eighteen offered data adequate to calculate this ratio, and the average ratio for these eighteen refiners was 44 percent.[16] And a comprehensive survey of refiners in 1950 showed that refiners that were totally nonintegrated accounted for less than 2 percent of U.S. refinery capacity.[17] The notion that there is a group of "independent" refiners significantly less integrated than "major" refiners is apparently a myth.

Have small firms been deterred from entering the refining business? The FTC has explicitly stated that barriers to entry into refining are "overwhelming" and that "there has been virtually no new entry into the industry."[18]

It is difficult to find a good yardstick for ease of entry, but perhaps the simplest approach is just to count how many firms have entered and relate the number to the size of the industry. The Bureau of Mines survey of refineries for 1972 indicates that thirty-one refiners had capacities of 50,000 barrels per day or greater. In 1951 the number was twenty. Nine of these thirty-one companies were not in the refining business in 1950 and ten of the fourteen newcomers (three 1950 companies merged with others in the top twenty) entered by

16 Statement of Morris Livingston before the U.S. District Court for the Northern District of California, Southern Division, in the case of United States of America v. Standard Oil Co. (Indiana), Civil No. 40212.

17 John McLean and Robert Haigh, *The Growth of Integrated Oil Companies* (Washington, D. C.: Howard University Press, 1954).

18 Testimony of James T. Halverson of the Federal Trade Commission before the Subcommittee on Antitrust and Monopoly of the Senate Judiciary Committee, 27 June 1973, pp. 21-25.

Figure B-1

PROFITABILITY AND "SELF-SUFFICIENCY" OF FOURTEEN REFINERS, 1953-1972

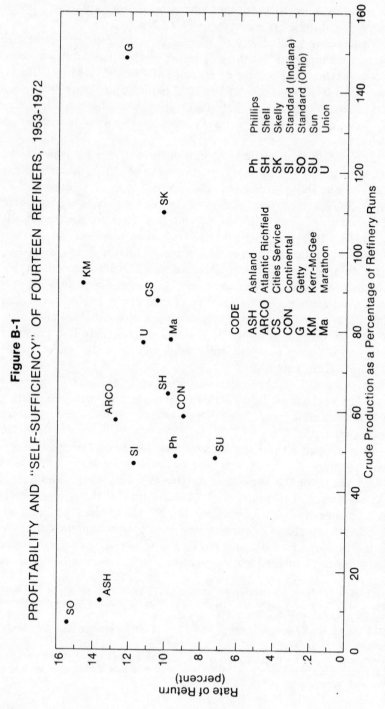

Source: Profit data is from Table B-1; self-sufficiency data is from *Rice/Kerr Chemical Service* (Laguna Beach, California, November 1972).

102

Figure B-2

PROFITABILITY AND "SELF-SUFFICIENCY" OF NINETEEN REFINERS, 1960–1972

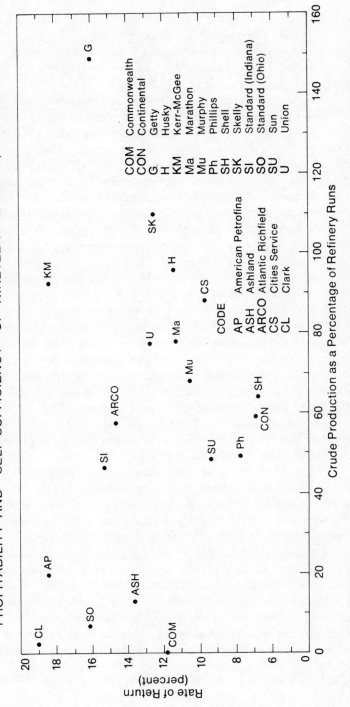

CODE

AP	American Petrofina	COM	Commonwealth
ASH	Ashland	CON	Continental
ARCO	Atlantic Richfield	G	Getty
CS	Cities Service	H	Husky
CL	Clark	KM	Kerr-McGee
		Ma	Marathon
		Mu	Murphy
		Ph	Phillips
		SH	Shell
		SK	Skelly
		SI	Standard (Indiana)
		SO	Standard (Ohio)
		SU	Sun
		U	Union

Crude Production as a Percentage of Refinery Runs

Rate of Return (percent)

Source: Profit data is from Table B-1; self-sufficiency data is from *Rice/Kerr Chemical Service* (Laguna Beach, California, November 1972).

building totally new capacity—not by purchasing existing refineries.[19] While it is hard to construct an absolute standard for ease of entry, the fact that 30 percent of the larger refiners in 1972 were not in the refining business in 1950 does not suggest "overwhelming" barriers to entry.

Why then are petroleum companies so integrated? There seem to be three major reasons. First, there are economies of management. Each stage of the industry—production, refining, transportation, and marketing—is highly dependent upon the others. The success of a refinery is more a function of success in the raw materials and product markets than of success in refinery operations. It is apparently more efficient in many circumstances to plan jointly corollary and supporting investments than to rely on other firms at other stages to make the right investments at the right time in the right place. This is not to say that other firms could not make these investments, but rather that they will make them less efficiently.

A second motive for integration is the reduction in variability of profits. When a petroleum company finds itself with additional funds for investment, beyond what can profitably be used in its own sector, it seeks out investments whose returns are not highly correlated with the company's main business so as to stabilize earnings. Remarkably, it happens that the profitability of the production, refining, and marketing sectors of the petroleum industry are not highly correlated with one another. Over the period 1920 to 1952 John McLean and Robert Haigh found that a nonintegrated mid-continent refiner would have average monthly fluctuations in gross margins four times the size of a fully integrated refiner. Substantial stabilization of earnings were also shown for producers and marketers who integrated.

A third reason for integration is to assure "availability" of supplies. In a few cases a refinery may be geared to process a very special type of crude for which the market is thin. Integration will assure supplies at relatively constant costs. But most refineries are equipped to process a range of crudes that are sold in active markets. This permits them to outbid rivals for limited supplies. What probably motivates a concern for availability here is the fear of price controls. Petroleum prices were controlled in World War II, in the Korean War, and since 1971 under the President's New Economic Program. At other times informal government pressure has been placed on petroleum companies to hold prices down. Judging by the spurts in crude prices when these controls have been relaxed, we must conclude that

---

[19] National Petroleum Refiners Association, *Washington Bulletin*, 29 June 1973, p. 2.

the shortages created were large and that the value of crude oil substantially exceeded the ceiling price. Since the probability of price control, formal or informal, has remained high in recent decades, it is not surprising to find businessmen providing for the eventuality. Since the FPC regulation of natural gas prices in the 1960s, pipeline companies have been integrating backward into production. The recent controls on crude oil prices have motivated firms as diverse as Bethelehem Steel, Ryder Systems, and Dow Chemical to move into crude oil and natural gas production. The list also includes General Motors, Ford, International Paper, St. Regis Paper and W. R. Grace. By internalizing the sale of crude oil within the firm, these companies can avoid the problem of price controls. Given price controls, this is a socially useful response, but it is of course far less efficient than simply removing the price controls.

Conclusions

The consumer is best served when (1) the petroleum industry is efficiently organized and the lowest costs of supply are realized, and (2) the benefits of these low costs are passed through to the consumer by competition. The consumer wants an efficient and a competitive industry.

Some inefficiencies in the petroleum market exist and are traceable to government policies. An important theme running through many of these policies is an attempt to favor or assist small business.

Prices paid by consumers for petroleum products reflect the actual costs of suppliers and are not "padded" by excess profits. The competitive process has held industry profits down. The petroleum industry over the past two decades has, in fact, earned subnormal profits.

**PRICE CONTROLS
AND THE NATURAL
GAS SHORTAGE**
Paul W. MacAvoy
Robert S. Pindyck

This appraisal of the natural gas shortage and of ways to reduce the shortage is based on the authors' technical work in modeling the industry in the last few years. Under a grant from the National Science Foundation to the M.I.T. Energy Laboratory (RANN Grant #GI-34936), we developed a large-scale econometric policy model of natural gas. The model is described in the Appendix; for greater detail on theoretical structure and estimation see *The Economics of the Natural Gas Shortage (1960–1980)* by P. W. MacAvoy and R. S. Pindyck (Amsterdam: North-Holland Publishing Co., 1975).

This work departs from the model at a number of points, however. Although the North-Holland book contains extensive forecasts of the size and location of the shortage, policy changes have rendered them somewhat dated. Recent Federal Power Commission reviews of ceiling prices on field sales of gas have resulted in revisions of the ceilings. Statements by the Canadian government in the last few months have placed new limits on gas exports to the United States. New forecasts have been made on the basis of these changes, and they are reported here. Also, new forecasts of a critical variable "outside" the model—the size of undiscovered gas reserves—have been incorporated here by inserting the new estimates into the equation sets and forecasting policy effects therefrom. All these changes show that the gas shortage will be more extensive than forecast in the North-Holland book, and solving the shortage will require more new policy than previously expected.

The model and forecasts could not have been done without considerable assistance from our friends and our "enemies." Our experience with Federal Power Commission officials, members and staff of the relevant Senate and House Committees and members of various executive departments contributed significantly to our judgments on the causes and consequences of the shortage. Scholars in economics and statistics taught us theory; at the same time employees of oil and gas companies tried to teach us the practical art of supplying a stock resource under regulation. The staff and faculty in the M.I.T. Energy Laboratory provided daily criticism. This legion of educators made our work towards this monograph possible. We hope that they find it worthwhile.

Current Conditions

Parts of the United States have experienced substantial natural gas shortages in the past few years. Rather than hour-long queues, as at gasoline stations in early 1974, the shortages have resulted in partial or total elimination of service for groups of consumers, both residential and industrial. Service has been terminated for interruptible buyers—those buyers taking gas only seasonally or at off-peak times—and new potential full-time consumers have not been allowed to connect to delivery systems. In some areas, industrial and commercial consumers have been told to replace gas with oil. Overall, there has been extensive unfilled demand: the Federal Power Commission found that interstate gas distributors fell 3.7 percent short of meeting consumption demands for communities and industries in 1971. The distributors are expected to fall 10 percent short of meeting consumption demands in 1974.[1]

Consumers in some regions of the country have fared worse than those in other regions. So far, buyers in the North Central, the Northeast, and the West—in that order—have suffered most of the shortages. Both new residential and oil industrial buyers in those regions continue to be kept off distribution systems and it will get worse. By the late 1970s, shortages in the North Central region could exceed one-half of total demands. Industrial and commercial establishments will then face 100 percent elimination of supply in order that there will be enough gas to meet the "old household" demands on local utilities. In other regions, industry may not be cut off entirely from natural gas supplies, but large industrial buyers seeking to expand

[1] FPC Bureau of Natural Gas, *National Gas Supply and Demand, 1971-1990* (Washington D. C.: Federal Power Commission, February 1972).

their use of gas would generally face curtailment. Some of these buyers might be able to obtain larger supplies by moving their operations to southern states currently unaffected by the shortage.[2] If they were to relocate in significant numbers, however, this would lead to important changes in patterns of regional development. Growth in the energy-related industries of the upper Midwest would be reduced relative to growth in the South-Central part of the country.

The Federal Power Commission regulates this industry. There is little prospect that Federal Power Commission policy could reduce these shortages in the near future. Unless there are large discoveries not now expected, or unless FPC regulation changes radically, excess demand should grow to more than one-quarter of total demand.[3] Indeed, natural gas experts on the FPC staff forecast that (assuming continuation of present regulatory conditions) the shortage will grow to be at least 30 percent of demand by 1980.[4] Consumers now being told to curtail consumption or to switch to other fuels are not likely to be told anything different in the future unless public policies change.

As service is curtailed, these consumers might well ask where the shortages came from and how they developed. In particular, they might want to know how long they will last and whether they will grow under present policies, and whether they can be reduced or shortened by policy changes of any kind. To answer these questions, it is important to know how shortages develop, in order that appropriate policies can be formulated for eliminating conditions that create these shortages. The next three sections of this chapter describe the processes of production and distribution in gas field and wholesale markets, and show how shortages evolved in these two sets of markets.

Production and Distribution: Field Markets

The field markets for natural gas center on contracts in which petroleum companies dedicate reserves of natural gas for production into

---

[2] These statements are predictions from the econometric policy model developed by the authors and described in detail in the Appendix. The forecasts for 1975-1980 shortage conditions are developed at length.

[3] For this forecast, the econometric policy model has been used to simulate continuation of present geological and regulatory constraints over the period 1975-1980.

[4] FPC Bureau of Natural Gas, *National Gas Supply and Demand.* This forecast called for almost as much shortage as the econometric forecast; presumably it is based on the continuation of present price regulation although this is not explicit. It has been revised and the shortage made larger by FPC Bureau of Natural Gas, *A Realistic View of Natural Gas Supply* (December 1974).

pipelines. The petroleum companies have established property rights by drilling wells into gas reserves. They bring gas to the surface through these wells, remove saleable liquid by-products, and deliver the "dry" gas into the buyer's gathering lines. The pipeline companies then take the gas from the field to wholesale industrial users or to retail distributing companies, who in turn deliver it to individual households, commercial establishments, or retail industrial users. Ultimately, more than 45 percent of the natural gas production goes to residential and commercial consumers, while the rest is used as energy or process material in industry.[5] Reserves, production, and the pattern of consumption depend on a combination of engineering and economic conditions. Although these conditions cannot be dealt with in detail here, the most important of them are sketched in the flow diagram in Figure 1. (Each of the boxes is presented in more detail in the Appendix.)

The natural gas reserves of the producing companies are accumulated through a complex and time-consuming process. To begin with, the companies discover that there are in-ground deposits of "associated" gas in newly discovered oil reservoirs and "nonassociated" gas found in reservoirs not containing oil. The companies claim these reserves in drilling wells for new discoveries or for extensions or revisions of previous discoveries. (Extensions come from exploration beyond the limits of known field boundaries. Revisions are changes in estimates of reserves in place within known field boundaries.)

The process of adding to reserves has begun long before commitments are made to pipelines. Years earlier, the producer has undertaken geophysical exploratory work to show the existence of potential in-ground hydrocarbon reservoirs. After this he has sunk wells into the reservoir to determine if it holds oil, gas, or water. The decision to conduct preliminary geophysical research and drill wells is essentially an investment decision under uncertainty. As the expected profitability of such an investment increases, the number of wells drilled (as also ultimately the total discoveries) increases. Profitability depends upon future prices and costs, and these are

---

[5] The percentage of total consumption by residential and commercial buyers was 45 percent in 1962 and 43 percent in 1968. As the natural gas shortage appeared on the horizon, the amount of residential consumption declined. See Federal Power Commission, *Statistics of Natural Gas Pipelines* (annual) and S. Breyer and P. W. MacAvoy, "The Natural Gas Shortage and Regulation of Natural Gas Producers," *Harvard Law Review*, vol. 86, no. 6 (April 1973), p. 977 and following.

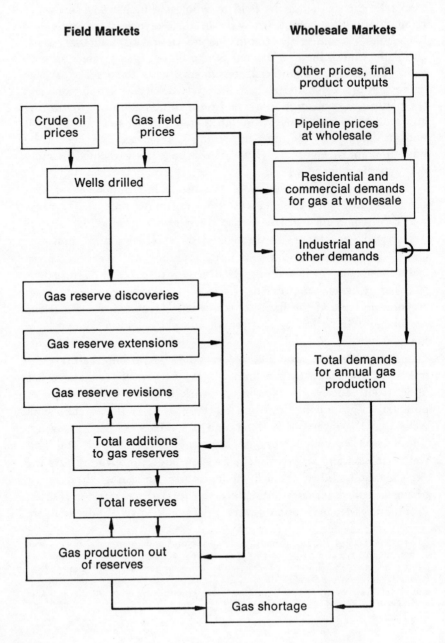

Figure 1

SIMPLIFIED ECONOMIC MODEL FOR THE
NATURAL GAS INDUSTRY

Field Markets

Wholesale Markets

Crude oil prices

Gas field prices

Wells drilled

Other prices, final product outputs

Pipeline prices at wholesale

Residential and commercial demands for gas at wholesale

Industrial and other demands

Gas reserve discoveries

Gas reserve extensions

Gas reserve revisions

Total additions to gas reserves

Total reserves

Gas production out of reserves

Total demands for annual gas production

Gas shortage

related in a complicated but positive way to present prices and costs—which means that if present prices increase, there should be an increase in exploratory work. New exploratory work should lead, in a year or two, to additional drilling activity and, subsequently, to the offer of additional reserves for sale to pipeline buyers.[6]

Prices are by no means the only determinant of reserves. There is only a fixed stock of gas to be discovered in any producing region, and it is likely that the larger deposits in the region are discovered first. Technical progress may compensate for the limits to discovery in any area by pushing down costs of finding the smaller deposits and of course some unexplored areas have not yet experienced the initial stages of depletion.[7] But over time, at fixed prices and costs, we should find that the volume of discoveries declines per well drilled.[8]

After deposits are found, the producers "dedicate" them in contracts calling for production over a five-to-twenty-year period. The producers estimate the size of newly found in-ground deposits and provide sufficient documentation to support the commitments they make to pipelines for production over the period of the contracts. Reserves, of course, are never known for sure (as is indicated by the revisions made each year), so that the contracts are, in effect, "futures"

---

[6] An important part of the econometric model is the exploration and discovery process. Our view of this process is described in more detail in the Appendix.

[7] This again is dealt with explicitly in our econometric model described in the Appendix. The summary here does not take into account the relative importance of the variables (1) prices, (2) technical progress, and (3) earlier discoveries in explaining additions to reserves. The econometric model includes these important details.

[8] At the present time, the limits on total reserves do not appear to be constraining. We are not out of discoverable reserves in the United States. The sum total of past production and of present discovered reserves, as of 1970, totaled 648 trillion cubic feet (Tcf), less than 40 percent of the amount of ultimate discoverable reserves expected in most forecasts. The amount remaining to be discovered has been estimated to be 851 Tcf by the National Petroleum Council and by the Colorado School of Mines' Potential Gas Committee, and to be 2,100 Tcf by the U.S. Geological Survey. See U.S. Department of the Interior, National Petroleum Council, *U.S. Energy Outlook: Oil and Gas Availability;* and Colorado Schools of Mines, Potential Gas Agency, Minerals Resources Institute, *Potential Supply of Natural Gas in the United States,* October 1971 (the latest report, issued in November 1973, gives 1,146 Tcf and the U.S. Geological Survey, Circular 650, "U.S. Mineral Resources," states that the range of estimates is between 1,178 and 6,600 Tcf). Of course, the amount actually found will depend on the level of exploratory activity, and thus on costs and prices offered by the pipeline buyers. These are the most important technical and economic limiting factors; the reserve estimates show enough additional reserve inventory to support at last two decades of production at forecast rates exceeding 30 Tcf per annum.

agreements—promises to deliver an uncertain volume of a commodity at a future time.[9]

Field markets for natural gas are thus similar to minerals futures markets in which present inventories are dedicated for future refining and delivery. The important characteristics of these markets generally are that more of the commodity—in this case gas—will be dedicated as the buyers offer higher prices, and that the lag between price increases and the development of additional reserves is likely to be considerable. With natural gas, moreover, production lags behind dedicated reserves. In the end, of course, the larger the volume of reserves available and the higher the contract prices, the greater production is likely to be.

Production and Distribution: Wholesale Markets

Buyers of reserves at the wellhead are for the most part natural gas pipelines seeking gas to deliver under long-term contract to industrial consumers and retail gas public utility companies. Their scheduled annual deliveries to utilities and industry determine their demand for reserves to be dedicated at the wellhead. These annual deliveries in turn depend upon the prices they charge for gas at wholesale (that is, the prices paid by industrial consumers and retail public utilities to the pipelines), the prices for alternative fuels consumed by final buyers, and such factors as population, incomes, and industrial production that determine the overall size of energy markets.

Gas wholesale prices depend upon field prices and delivery charges for the transportation of the gas from wellhead to final consumer. The pipelines offer instantaneous deliveries of gas as it is burned by the final buyer, and for this they charge a markup over their field purchase prices. Markups (at least for the interstate pipelines) are determined by the historical average costs of transmission and by the transportation profit margins allowed under Federal Power Commission regulation.

The regulation of wholesale prices creates significant lags between changes in field prices and changes in final consumers' prices. The policy of the Federal Power Commission has been to allow wholesale prices to equal the historical average field price paid for gas at the wellhead plus the markup. This average wellhead price—called

---

[9] In the econometric model, the equations are such that the level of production will be greater the greater the volume of reserves in place and the higher the prices in the contract commitment.

116

a "rolled in" price—changes slowly as prices rise on new field contracts. It changes slowly because new contracts in any year provide only 5 to 15 percent of all gas under contract: on the average (assuming that percentage of deliveries in each year come from new contract dedications) the full impact of a change in new contract prices is realized only after the change has been in effect for almost a decade.

This lag between changes in wholesale prices and changes in wellhead prices softens the impact of large increases in new contract prices in field markets. In addition, since pipeline construction costs or allowed returns on capital investment change slowly (at least as allowed by the Federal Power Commission), average transmission costs also change slowly over time.[10]

Flows of gas across the country also change slowly over time. From 35 to 40 percent of natural gas remains in the South Central region of the country where it is produced; approximately 19 percent moves to the Northeast, 20 percent to the North Central, and 7 percent to the western parts of the country. These figures held over much of the 1960s, with only the flow to the North Central region showing increases of 3 percentage points over the period from 1962 to 1968, while the flow to the Northeast region was reduced by the same percentage.

The flow in the ideal works out to satisfy demands of households and industry across the country. At a given level of field prices, the additions to reserves meet the needs of the pipelines (as evidenced by their new contract demands). If they do not meet the needs, and there is excess demand, then the prices these pipelines offer in new contracts rise above previous prices. These higher prices bring forth additional production from old contract reserves, as well as some known reserves not under contract previously: they also reduce some of the marginal resales of the pipelines. After a time, the higher new prices also bring in additional new reserves from new discoveries. Eventually, at the higher level of new contract prices, the amount of new reserve commitments made by the producers will be the same as the amount sought and resold as production by the pipelines.

Effects of Shortages on Field and Wholesale Markets

Under normal conditions, the reserve and production markets operate so as to allow each pipeline buyer the reserve backing he desires— that is, the backing which will make secure continued production to

---

[10] The process of setting markups on field prices is described in detail in the Appendix using a truncated version (in equation form) of FPC regulatory practice.

meet his commitments to residential and industrial consumers over the lifetime of their gas-burning equipment. Price increases take care of this. When there are regulatory price controls, however, price increases may not be sufficient to clear markets. New discoveries fall short of the reserves demanded by the pipelines, and the amount of actual new field contract commitments is less than the desired increases of reserve backing. As a result the pipelines either limit their new delivery commitments to preserve reserve backing for old consumers or make new delivery commitments to draw down previously purchased reserves at a faster rate. If new delivery commitments are made, production demands by final consumers can be satisfied for some time if the pipelines use the reserve backing of old consumers. For this reason, reserve shortages in field markets may not be perceived by final buyers whose demands are being temporarily satisfied by present production (as was the case in the late 1960s).[11]

Production from previous reserve commitments cannot meet expanding demands indefinitely. Eventually, reserves from old commitments are so reduced that the amount remaining serves as an effective limit to production. As the reserve backing becomes smaller, production tends to fall, and a gap is opened between demand and available supply. Many years may pass, however, before the decline in additions to reserves is followed by production shortages.

Can the process be reversed? If prices in new contracts were to increase by a substantial amount, then more production could be derived from previously committed reserves (that is, the price increase would be compensating for additional costs from secondary recovery programs). This effect would be small, however, if reserves have already been greatly depleted. Higher prices would, however, add to incentives for exploratory drilling, and the drilling would increase new discoveries and extensions or revisions of reserves. After these additional reserves had been committed, the amount of production would again be increased.[12]

At the same time, over this extended period, demand for production would be curtailed by the higher price. Total demand would have increased because of increases in the size of energy markets and increases in the prices of alternative fuels. But higher gas prices should slow down the growth of new customers, so as to dampen this "normal" increase in gas demands.

---

[11] This is surmised from simulations with the econometric model as shown for the 1960s and 1970s in Chapter 4.

[12] As shown by simulations with the econometric model described below.

The combination of these two price effects should reduce excess demand. It may take several years, however, before the full effects are felt in field and wholesale markets. Under some conditions, however—large price increases and new government policies directly stimulating reserve discovery—most of the shortages expected to occur in each region of the country could be reduced or even eliminated by 1980.

2

THE FEDERAL GOVERNMENT'S POLICY TOWARD NATURAL GAS

The Phillips Case

That part of the history of regulation that bears on the natural gas shortage begins in 1954, the year of the Supreme Court's decision that required the Federal Power Commission to regulate the wellhead prices on gas sold to the interstate pipelines. The case was brought by the Attorney General of Wisconsin against Phillips Petroleum Company because a rise in the price Phillips was charging to the Wisconsin pipeline had caused increased charges to Wisconsin consumers. In lower court testimony and briefs, it was argued that the natural gas industry, although regulated at the pipeline level by the Federal Power Commission and at the retail level by the state regulatory commissions, was unregulated at the wellhead and, indeed, was controlled there by the large field producers. As a result, field price increases determined by a few large petroleum companies could be passed through as "costs" in pipeline wholesale prices and could thereby create high consumer prices. These "pass-throughs," it was argued, should be curtailed by FPC regulation at the wellhead. The Supreme Court, without explicitly finding that there was monopoly power in the hands of the producers, did find that the Federal Power Commission had a mandate to regulate wellhead prices.[1]

---

[1] Phillips Petroleum Company v. Wisconsin, 347 U.S. 622, 1954. See E. W. Kitch, "Regulation of the Field Market for Natural Gas by the Federal Power Commission," *Journal of Law and Economics*, vol. 11 (October 1968), pp. 243-281. Kitch notes on page 255 that "the court gave no reason for the regulation . . . considering the expertise of the Federal Power Commission . . . the court gave no indication of how the regulation was to be carried out."

For the next five years, the commission attempted to fulfill the mandate. The commission tried price control at the wellhead following the practices of state public utility commissions acting to set limits on electric power or gas retail prices. This procedure involves the estimation of (a) operating costs, (b) allowed rate of return applied to the undepreciated original investment per unit of gas produced under a contract and (c) depreciation of investment.[2] The permissible maximum revenues are set equal to the sum of these "costs."

There were difficult problems in the use of this procedure for controlling gas field prices. The attribution of previous dry hole costs to particular gas contracts and the allocation between oil and gas of joint costs for associated gas was essentially arbitrary and set arbitrary limits on prices. In addition, the usual standard for finding the proper rate of return—the usual standard being the average rate of return for public utilities—scarcely applied to petroleum exploration and development companies. As it was, higher returns were in fact allowed in partial compensation for exploratory risk, but risk premiums were arbitrarily chosen. The most important problem was that the commission, dealing in detail with a single case, was falling behind in its work. The Phillips case itself had produced more than 10,000 pages of briefs and records; moreover, by 1962, more than 2,900 applications for price reviews had been filed by other companies. The commission itself estimated that it would not finish its 1960 caseload until the year 2043.[3] This expected delay, together with the arbitrary nature of regulation required the FPC to try other ways of controlling field prices.[4]

---

[2] "Unit costs" are defined as $\{[(a)+(b)+(c)]/q\}$ for q annual production.

[3] See In re Phillips Petroleum Company, 24 FPC 537 (1960), p. 545.

[4] James M. Landis was particularly critical of the FPC's performance in natural gas regulation, charging it with delays as well as with disregard of the consumer interest. He wrote that

The FPC without question represents the outstanding example in the field of government of the breakdown of the administrative process. The complexity of its problems is no answer to its more than patent failures. These failures relate primarily to the natural gas field. . . .

Delay after delay in certifications and the prescription of rates has cost the public millions of dollars. . . . The Commission has literally done nothing to reduce the delays which have constantly increased. . . . The dissatisfaction with the work of the Commission has gone so far that there is a large measure of agreement on separating from the Commission its entire jurisdiction over natural gas and creating a new commission to handle these problems exclusively. . . .

See J. M. Landis, *Report on Regulatory Agencies to the President-Elect*, reprint of a report to the Senate Committee on the Judiciary (Washington, D. C.: U.S. Government Printing Office, December 1960).

Area Rate Regulation

The FPC, faced with an enormous backlog of individual cases and the difficulty of using orthodox procedures of price regulation, cut the Gordian knot by setting regional maximum prices on the basis of regional average accounting costs. At the outset, temporary ceilings were set at market levels established a year or two previously. This produced a freeze on prices at the 1958–1959 level; new gas committed to interstate pipelines after 1961 had to be priced at a level not higher than the level for 1958–1959. The freeze was to be temporary and was to be followed by "area rate" decisions to set permanent prices. The permanent prices were to be based on the average historical costs of gas within the area and in fact considerable attention in the area rate proceedings was given over to calculating regional production costs, investment outlays, and rate-of-return averages.

Unfortunately the new approach turned out to be as fraught with analytical difficulties as the old. When the commission set permanent ceilings, it used estimates of regional costs from a period when temporary ceilings were in effect. In that period producing companies took on only those drilling projects with prospective costs below the forecast prices, and the result was that the companies in fact showed average costs less than or equal to the level of temporary ceiling prices. The FPC, noting that average costs were close to the temporary ceiling prices, found the temporary ceilings to be appropriate as permanent ceilings. In other words, temporary ceilings on prices set temporary cost ceilings which then set permanent ceilings on prices.

These ceiling prices—though they may have been arbitrary—did serve the commission's interest: they did preserve the price level of the late 1950s. The commission gave no specific reason for preferring the early prices. Neither the case materials nor the commission decisions indicated a desire to prevent the dictation of higher prices by noncompetitive producers.[5] Instead, it seems that the commission did not want higher prices either because price increases were subject to litigation by the pipelines, or (given the Phillips decision) because they would have run into difficulties in court review.[6]

The courts added to the desirability of a "freeze" by arguing that price increases should be denied simply because they were in-

---

[5] The competitiveness of structural supply was never examined by the commission. See S. Breyer and P. W. MacAvoy, *Energy Regulation by the Federal Power Commission* (Washington, D. C.: The Brookings Institution, 1974), Chapter 3.

[6] Ibid., Chapter 3.

creases. This view was exemplified by the 1959 case in *Atlantic Refining Company* v. *Public Service Commission* where it was stated that a price increase was to be denied because the given "price is greatly in excess of that which Tennessee pays from any lease in Southern Louisiana."[7]

Throughout the 1960s the commission's determination to "hold the line against increases in natural gas prices" produced a constant price level on new contracts for gas going to the interstate pipelines.[8] The weighted average new contract price was 18.2¢/Mcf (that is, per thousand cubic feet) in 1961, and 19.8¢/Mcf in 1969.[9] The average wellhead prices on old and new contracts increased from 16.4¢/Mcf to 17.5¢/Mcf from 1961 to 1969, primarily as depleted old contracts at low prices were replaced by new contracts at the ceiling levels close to 19¢/Mcf.[10] The consumer (at wholesale) paid approximately 33¢ per million Btu for natural gas throughout the decade, with a range from 32.0¢ per million Btu in 1962 to 33.4¢ per million Btu in 1970. For comparison, it may be noted that prices for oil at wholesale increased from 34.5¢ to 39.8¢ per million Btu and prices for coal at wholesale from 25.6¢ to 31.2¢ per million Btu.[11] The commission

---

[7] The case number is 360 U.S. 378. See E. W. Kitch, "Regulation of the Field Market," p. 261. Kitch argues that "the court reasoned from the premise that prices higher than prevailing prices were questionable simply because they were higher." He shows that an examination of the increases that were occurring at the time does not support the argument that the increases came in response to demonstrated manipulation of the market by the producers.

[8] See Federal Power Commission, *Annual Report for 1964* (Washington, D. C.: Federal Power Commission, 1965), p. 15.

[9] These and the data series described in the next few sentences are from the data bank used in compiling the econometric gas policy model. Appropriate references are provided in the Appendix.

[10] At the same time, average drilling costs did not increase; otherwise, they alone would have been the justification for regional price increases given the process of regulation. But the combined effects of cumulative discoveries and faster rates of production must have increased marginal production costs. Simulations with the econometric model described below show declining reserve additions at constant prices.

[11] An example shows even greater disparities. As a result of frozen field prices, wholesale prices charged by Columbia Gas Transmission Company to the Baltimore retail gas company (Baltimore Gas and Electric) were 43.5¢/Mcf (or per million Btu) in 1970 while wholesale terminal prices for No. 2 fuel oil were 86.3¢ per million Btu at the same location that year. Although retail delivery charges could explain part of the difference, they could not explain all of it. The size of the difference increased by 30¢ per million Btu per annum in the succeeding three years.

The oil and coal price series are from Edison Electric Institute, *Statistical Annual of the Electric Utility Industry*, for these fuels consumed in electric power stations; this is as close to a wholesale price series as can be obtained for

succeeded in holding gas prices down, while prices of other fuels were going up from 10 to 25 percent.

Regulation Today

The commission's view apparently changed with the first indications of gas production shortages. In 1971 the regulatory freeze policy was reversed in a series of FPC rate decisions that substantially increased the level of field prices. "Recognizing the urgent need for increased gas exploration and much larger annual reserve additions to maintain adequate service," the Federal Power Commission "offered producers several price incentives." [12] For producing areas which contained more than 85 percent of already proved reserves, the commission increased prices 3–5.2¢/Mcf for new contracts signed that year. For all future contracts the FPC began a proceeding to set national ceiling prices. [13] The commission signalled its intention of providing substantial increases through the national ceiling by setting preliminary prices in one region that were 7¢/Mcf higher than those previously in effect. [14]

Further increases were also promised through the commission's new procedure for certifying sales above the prevailing area price ceilings. The procedure allowed higher prices when these higher prices were "shown to be in the public interest." [15] Although no explicit schedule of higher prices was set out at that time, the fact that an explicit path was designated for avoiding the ceilings pointed to further price increases.

As a result of these policy changes there has been a substantial increase in new contract prices in the last few years. The weighted average new contract price increased from 19.8¢/Mcf in 1969 to 33.6¢/Mcf in 1972. For 1973, preliminary estimates gave an average new contract price of 36¢/Mcf. In effect, the price freeze of the 1960s was abrogated in the early 1970s and new gas prices increased by 70 percent in four years. The question is whether the increase was too little and too late to clear excess demands for reserves and production over the rest of the decade.

comparability with gas sales by pipelines to retail gas utilities, electric utilities, or other industrial users.

[12] See Federal Power Commission, *Annual Report for 1971* (Washington, D. C.: Federal Power Commission, 1972), p. 36.

[13] Docket R-389A entitled "Initial Rates for Future Gas Sales from All Areas."

[14] This applied to the Rocky Mountain area. See Federal Power Commission, *Annual Report for 1971*, p. 42 and Docket R-389A.

[15] See Federal Power Commission, *Annual Report for 1972* (Washington, D. C.: Federal Power Commission, 1973), p. 99.

Table 1

ADDITIONS TO NATURAL GAS RESERVES UNDER ALTERNATIVE CEILING PRICES, 1968–1972

Year	(1) New Contract Field Prices (¢/Mcf)	(2) Total Additions to Reserves [a] (Tcf)	(3) Hypothetical "Unregulated" New Contract Field Prices (¢/Mcf)	(4) Hypothetical "Unregulated" Total Additions to Reserves [b] (Tcf)
1968	19.5	19.2	30.2	19.6
1969	19.8	17.8	36.6	18.7
1970	22.1	15.1	43.0	16.3
1971	25.6	14.4	49.7	15.9
1972	33.6	15.3	56.2	16.8

[a] Simulated using the econometric model with actual new contract field prices (see Chapter 4).
[b] Simulations with the econometric model using prices in column (3).

Behavior of Field and Wholesale Markets under Price Controls

Institutional and political conditions worked together to produce shortages.[16] Production conditions required long lags between new discoveries of gas and final production of that gas for the consumer. At the same time, regulation prevented price increases over most of the decade of the 1960s and was the critical precondition for emergence of excess demand.

As shown in Table 1, total additions to reserves declined over the period from 17 trillion cubic feet (Tcf) in 1967 to 15 Tcf in 1972 (with a low of 14 Tcf in 1971). This decline in reserves would not have taken place if new contract field prices had been higher—as can be shown by simulation of reserve accumulations at higher prices in the econometric model. Alternative sets of prices can be used in the model, where each set is a possible replication of what unregulated

---

[16] Much more detail could be provided on the operating practices and regulation of the pipelines before we go on to describe the actual development of the shortage. The pipelines are regulated by the FPC on the basis of the procedures described here as "orthodox" public utility price controls, except on charges to direct industrial consumers or interstate consumers. Suffice it to say at this point that in the econometric model equations stressing "cost averaging" capture the results from this regulation. The simulations from the model as a whole are stressed at this point.

Table 2

NATURAL GAS FIELD MARKETS, 1967–1972

Year	(1) Average New Contract Field Price (¢/Mcf)	(2) Average Wholesale Price (¢/Mcf)	(3) Simulated Production[a] (Tcf)	(4) Simulated Production Demand[a] (Tcf)	(5) Actual Production (Tcf)
1967	18.7	30.69	18.9	18.6	18.9
1968	19.5	31.30	20.1	19.6	19.9
1969	19.8	31.85	20.9	20.4	21.3
1970	22.1	33.23	21.8	21.2	22.6
1971	25.6	35.35	22.8	22.0	22.8
1972	33.6	38.43	23.6	22.7	23.3

[a] Simulated using the econometric model with actual new contract field prices (see Chapter 4).

prices would have been. There is no way of telling which set is more appropriate, but one likely hypothetical "unregulated" price set shown in Table 1 would probably have added more than 1 Tcf of additional reserves each year from 1969 through 1972 to prevent a drawing down of the total reserve stock.[17]

At the same time discoveries of new reserves were declining, gas pipelines were increasing their demands. The pipelines had the choice either of refusing buyers or of meeting new demands for production out of their inventories of committed reserves. The companies in fact continued to meet new demands for production out of old reserves. There was no production shortage in the late 1960s or early 1970s, as shown in Table 2; the econometric model shows simulated production and demands at frozen prices to be approximately equal in each of these years.

---

[17] This price level was inserted into the econometric model in order to simulate the behavior of additions to reserves over the period from 1967 through 1971. Reserves are estimated with the equation relationships for discoveries, extensions and revisions as a function of prices, costs, and potential reserve discoveries. The basis for choosing the "unregulated" prices shown in Table 1 was that they maintained a reserve to production ratio of fifteen to one—the lowest ratio actually experienced in the early and middle 1960s. Given that demand for reserve backing by final consumers was constant throughout the decade, this ratio is the lowest that is in keeping with equilibrium of demand and supply of reserves as well as of production throughout the period.

Table 3

NATURAL GAS PRODUCTION UNDER ALTERNATIVE MARKETING PRACTICES OF THE PIPELINES, 1967–1972

Year	(1) Actual Production (Tcf)	(2) Production at Typical Early 1960s R/P Ratio [a] (Tcf)	(3) Production at Hypothetical "Unregulated" Field Prices [b]
1967	18.9	16.8	18.6
1968	19.9	16.9	19.3
1969	21.3	17.0	19.5
1970	22.6	17.1	19.4
1971	22.8	16.9	19.0
1972	23.3	16.8	18.3

[a] Calculated by multiplying actual reserves each year by the inverse of a 17:1 reserve-production ratio.
[b] Simulated with the econometric model using the prices in Column (3) of Table 1.

Instead of drawing down old reserves, the pipelines could have refused to attach new customers to the system in the absence of new reserves for them. The interstate pipelines, acknowledging that there would be a reduction in the reserve backing committed to established customers, could have refused to take on new customers unless the new customers could be provided the reserve-production (R/P) ratio available to all customers in the early 1960s. The level of production from this policy would have been less than the level from drawing down old reserves in Table 2, as is indicated by the model simulations reported in Table 3. The estimates for production at the constant R/P for the early 1960s in column (1) are approximately 4 Tcf less than the actual production in column (5) of Table 2. This difference is the amount "diverted" from the inventory reserved for old customers in order to provide immediate increased production.[18]

---

[18] This reserve saving alternative would have required cutting back production to a lower level than what would have occurred without price controls. The amounts expected without controls are shown as column (3) of Table 2; they were generated by simulations with the econometric model at the hypothetical unregulated prices shown in column (3) of Table 1. Because actual production was extended to meet the additional consumption demands of new buyers induced into the gas market by low frozen prices, both "reserve saving" and "no regulation" alternatives would result in lower than actual production.

The price ceilings imposed by the Federal Power Commission, in conjunction with long lags from price increases to production, appear to have had a two-stage effect upon gas field and wholesale markets. First, the frozen prices reduced the amounts of reserves found over the last half of the 1960s. Second, the decline in additions to reserves was not matched by any decline in the growth of production. In fact, additional demands from both new and old consumers were met by taking additional production out of the existing reserve stock.[19] The established consumers with fifteen to seventeen years of reserve backing on annual production lost some of that backing up to 1972. After 1972, there was not enough reserve backing to allow production to meet all of the increased demands, and a "production shortage" set in.[20]

The Effects of Regulation on Consumers

Because of lags of changes in production and consumption behind reserve discovery, it is difficult—at least up until 1972—to say who benefitted and who lost from regulation. But consumers in the Northeast, the North Central region, and the West received a proportionately smaller share of the increased production out of old reserves than consumers in the Southeast and the South Central region. This is shown in Table 4, where demands at actual prices are compared with demands at hypothetical (higher) unregulated prices for each region and each year. The hypothetical prices are derived from the econometric model. The differences between actual and hypothetical "unregulated" behavior indicate that demands were increased by regulation more in the South Central and Southeast than in other regions; almost 45 percent of the increased national consumption occurred in the South Central region alone. Since the increased demands were satisfied in large part by production out of old reserves, the net result

---

[19] The demands in turn were increased by the relatively low prices at wholesale following from the frozen field prices. The additions to demands as a result of frozen prices can be seen by comparing "production demand" at actual average wholesale prices, shown in column (4) of Table 2, with the demands that would have been realized at the hypothetical "unregulated" prices, shown in column (3) of Table 3. Column (3) shows both production and demands at prices sufficiently higher to hold the 1965 reserve-production ratio through the rest of the decade. The additions to demand artificially induced by the lower frozen prices were on the order of 3 to 4 Tcf per annum by 1971-1972, and occurred mostly in the South Central and Southeast portions of the country as demands for boiler fuel.
[20] The 1973-1974 production shortages are shown in the Federal Power Commission staff study of the supply and demand of natural gas and in the econometric model simulations shown for those years in Chapter 4 below.

Table 4

REGIONAL PATTERNS OF DEMAND FOR NATURAL GAS, 1967–1972 [a]

Year	National Consumption Increase at Regulated Prices over That at Unregulated (Higher) Prices	Demands at Actual Prices	Demands at Unregulated Prices	Percent of National Increase in Consumption
----- NORTHEAST -----				
1967	0	3.3	3.3	—
1968	0.5	3.5	3.4	.20
1969	0.8	3.6	3.5	.13
1970	1.7	3.7	3.6	.06
1971	3.0	3.9	3.6	.10
1972	4.2	4.0	3.6	.10
----- NORTH CENTRAL -----				
1967	0	3.5	3.5	—
1968	0.5	3.8	3.7	.20
1969	0.8	4.0	3.8	.25
1970	1.7	4.2	3.8	.24
1971	3.0	4.4	3.8	.20
1972	4.2	4.6	3.7	.21
----- WEST -----				
1967	0	3.2	3.2	—
1968	0.5	3.4	3.3	.20
1969	0.8	3.4	3.4	0
1970	1.7	3.6	3.4	.12
1971	3.0	3.6	3.4	.07
1972	4.2	3.7	3.4	.07
----- SOUTHEAST -----				
1967	0	1.3	1.3	—
1968	0.5	1.4	1.3	.20
1969	0.8	1.5	1.3	.25
1970	1.7	1.6	1.3	.18
1971	3.0	1.7	1.1	.20
1972	4.2	1.7	1.0	.17
----- SOUTH CENTRAL -----				
1967	0	7.2	7.2	—
1968	0.5	7.6	7.5	.20
1969	0.8	7.9	7.6	.38
1970	1.7	8.1	7.4	.41
1971	3.0	8.4	7.1	.43
1972	4.2	8.6	6.7	.45

[a] All demand values are simulated using the econometric model.

was that the backing for old customers nationally was being used to cover additional regulation-induced demands in the South. Those losing the reserve backing were customers under the protection of regulation, while those gaining the additional gas for consumption were mostly intrastate or industrial consumers in the South not regulated by the FPC.

Northern consumers experiencing vanishing reserves were not the only losers, nor were these the sum total of losses. Those who lost included producers experiencing cutbacks in reserve discovery and overall profit reductions. The losses—which had they not been lost would have gone into dividends to stockholders of gas companies or into new investment in exploration and development—cannot be ignored entirely even if they were not taken into account by the regulatory commission. All that can be said is that the price freeze did short-term good for some buyers in holding down their monthly payments of gas bills but not for others losing reserve backing, and it did harm to producers in income and production losses.

The long-term losses are more extensive. These include the ultimate curtailments of demand caused by the smaller production from the smaller stock of reserves. They are dealt with in the next two chapters.

The development of production shortages in the last few years has had a strong effect on the conduct of regulation. Soon after these shortages showed themselves in the inability of pipelines to meet commitments to consumers, the Federal Power Commission brought about rapid increases in new contract field prices through the introduction of new regulatory procedures. This was done partly in response to widely expressed opinions that higher prices were needed to bring forth additional reserves and thereby additional production. The lags from price increases to additional production have been so extensive, however, that to date large price increases have been followed by relatively small changes in production. The continued shortage has led to new calls from producers for changes in the commission.

These calls have not been the only political reactions to the shortage. Congress and the Office of the President have become focal points for complaints that FPC policies have perpetrated gas shortages. Many of these complaints have come from buyers—that is, from the pipelines and retail gas utilities—in those northern and western parts of the country experiencing the shortages. With neither producers nor direct buyers supporting field regulation, there has been substantial pressure for change—pressure evident in calls for legislation that would reform the controls of the Federal Power Commission.

Reform has been sought in two contradictory directions. The first direction is toward more regulation, while the second direction is toward elimination of Federal Power Commission controls over field markets. The argument made for moving in either direction is the same—that the shortage would be reduced and consumption expanded for those users of natural gas needing it the most. The argument is unlikely to be correct in both cases. Either more or less regulation might be expected to reduce the shortage, but not both—unless of course we are just now enjoying the worst of all possible worlds.

This chapter will describe four proposals for eliminating the domestic natural gas shortage. These are (1) to strengthen the current regulation by instituting an overall price freeze, (2) to simplify the regulation by promulgating uniform rates among different geographical areas, (3) to maintain the regulation by allowing the FPC to increase the price of gas at the current rate, and (4) to deregulate the industry by phased elimination of controls. The first three alternatives depend more or less on some form of federal regulation, while the fourth would in time do away with regulation. In Chapter 4 the econometric model is used to simulate what would happen under each of these four proposals.

Strengthen Control: Price Freezes

Stronger controls over wellhead prices have been proposed in Congress and before the Federal Power Commission. The most pervasive argument for this proposal is that producers have been holding back reserves in anticipation of relaxed controls. Because of the lag from discovery to production, many years must pass before there is any effect from higher new contract prices. It is argued that this period can be further extended by producers if they think that prices are going to be higher after regulation has been relaxed. On this showing, the blame for the shortage lies with the FPC and its policies for price increases: "[The FPC], with the best motives, has so titilated the speculative expectations and ambitions of the producer industry with a promise of imminent deregulation and ever-higher prices, that it has become perfectly rational profit-maximizing behavior on their part to move slowly on development and production of reserves."[1] Strict ceilings should cause producers to see the futility of holding back supplies and, as a result, more gas should be forthcoming at frozen prices.[2]

The case for stronger regulation has sometimes been based on a second argument: that higher prices will have little effect on the size

---

[1] U.S. Senate, Commerce Committee, Gas Supply Committee, *Hearings on Gas and Oil Regulatory Bills*, 93rd Congress, 1st session, p. 737. The quotation is from the testimony of Peter Schuck, director, Consumers Union.

[2] Ibid., p. 457 and following. The quotation is from Mr. Lee White, chairman, Energy Policy Task Force, Consumer Federation of America. White's argument is an attempt to separate "increased demand" and "reduced supply" from "price" as factors contributing to the present natural gas shortage (see p. 478).

of the shortage. This is the view of Peter Schuck of Consumers Union, for example, who after reviewing past increases in the price of natural gas and the resulting quantity available, concluded that "deregulation would not significantly increase natural gas supplies." [3] The grounds for this view are that the response of production to price is limited by the lack of competition in field markets. In the words of David Schwartz of the Federal Power Commission's Office of Economics, "a review of the evidence indicates a lack of workable competition in the producer market, [and] due to structural imperfections, deregulation would result in extensive prices, windfall profits to the producers, consumer exploitation and little assurance of adequate supplies of natural gas." [4]

With no supply response, it is argued, there should be no need to weaken price controls. In Schwartz's terms, "if administered fairly and firmly, regulation can assure an equitable framework for producers and consumers. . . . There is strong evidence that the present unavailability of gas supply is related to the speculative anticipations of significantly higher prices." [5] Any new policy would be designed to affirm ceiling price regulation. Frozen prices would hold for so long a period of future time that to withhold gas for speculation would be futile.

Various proposals have been made as to how to determine the appropriate level of frozen prices and to decide which producers should be subject to the freeze. It has been suggested that regulation be extended to include intrastate sales, so that one speculative outlet (higher intrastate prices) would be foreclosed. It has been proposed that the freeze be limited to the large producers. The Consumer Energy Act introduced in the Senate in 1974 (S. 2506) called for abolition of the Federal Power Commission's alternative pricing procedures and establishment of a national ceiling on prices of gas and crude oil. The national ceiling would be calculated on the basis of historical costs plus a fair rate of return as determined by an orthodox

---

[3] Ibid., p. 737.

[4] Ibid., p. 220. Others, particularly Professor Alfred Kahn, have argued that supply is inelastic (thus assuming that markets are competitive enough for there to be a supply function); see Federal Power Commission, *The Permian Basin Area Rate Proceeding*, Docket ARG1-1 (1961). This assertion was not supported by evidence on supply elasticities. The econometric policy model used here deals directly with the extent of market imperfection by fitting equations for production out of reserves that contain terms for the degree of market imperfection. These terms then are used in equations for prediction of future production (as described in the Appendix).

[5] Ibid., pp. 221 and 223.

public utility rate review.[6] All these policies endorsing stricter controls are designed to slow down the rate of increase of prices while still making possible additions to reserves and production.

Simplify Control: Area Rate Regulation

The FPC could choose to combat the natural gas shortage with strictly enforced area rates similar to those in effect from 1960 to 1968. In those years, it will be recalled, the commission determined what ceiling prices were "just and reasonable" for particular producing areas. In all the "area rate" cases, a lower price was set for old gas than for new, because the lower price on old gas, which was "locked" into production contracts, would not affect the quantity of gas delivered to final consumers. With the "old" prices held down while demand increased, producers were denied the economic rents that come from additional revenues for the same production. In fact, as has been shown, all prices were held down. The FPC could return to that policy.

The commission recently moved in that direction in a decision that allowed gas from wells drilled from the beginning of 1974 to sell at 50¢/Mcf. This uniform "national" rate on new gas was established through the customary area rate proceeding that reviewed both the historical costs and the market conditions. The rate will be allowed to increase by small increments per year from the initial level. Old gas is to be held at previously set levels. This policy does not differ substantially from earlier price freezes: a uniform national rate —even with an annual rise—is simply a return to area rates based on historical costs and designed to hold for long periods of time.

Maintain Control: Price Increases

The FPC could simply continue its seven-year policy of increasing prices on new contracts an average of 5¢/Mcf each year. In this course of action the commission is not likely to be hindered by the Courts of Appeal; the Supreme Court has continually affirmed the

---

[6] But there would be more latitude within proposals to allow the commission to consider in finding the rate of return "factors which are relevant to assuring that the nation has adequate supplies of oil and gas at reasonable prices to the consumer." See "Congress Near Showdown on Proposal to Decontrol Gas Prices," *National Journal Reports*, May 25, 1974, p. 772. Although "supply and demand factors" could allow the commission to set any price ceilings it wished, without reference to a congressional mandate for stronger control, the desire for a price freeze still predominates in this type of legislation in 1975.

commission's right to proceed this way. In the most recent case, the Court once again quoted the words of *FPC* v. *Natural Gas Pipeline Company* according to which rate-making agencies "are permitted to make the pragmatic adjustments which may be called for by particular circumstances." [7] The courts "have consistently held that there is a presumption of validity that attaches to each exercise of the Commission's expertise. Those who would overturn the Commission's judgment undertake the heavy burden of making a convincing showing that it is invalid because it is unjust and unreasonable in its consequences. . . ." [8] In the 1960s these holdings were thought to imply the right to freeze prices. In the early 1970s the commission, without court objection, followed the practice of increasing prices on new contracts each year because "particular circumstances" of shortages require price increases. This judgmental practice, continued into the future, would constitute the lowest degree of continued regulation.

Eliminate Control: Phased Deregulation

One widespread reaction to increased shortages has been a call for the removal of wellhead price regulation. Since prices were frozen over most of the 1960s, and shortages first developed in reserves in the middle 1960s and developed in production in the early 1970s, it has been argued that controls were the cause of the shortages. Furthermore, given that it has been demonstrated that price freezes reduce production, total elimination of controls should increase prices and these increases should in turn hasten elimination of the shortage.

The deregulation of wellhead prices on new contracts would be a first step. Calling natural gas "America's premium fuel," the President in April 1973 proposed legislation to exempt gas newly dedicated to the interstate pipelines from ceilings so as to "stimulate new exploration and development." [9] This was echoed by the chairman of the Federal Power Commission when he noted that "gas supplies are short and the way to encourage more drilling and discoveries may be to let prices rise." [10]

---

[7] FTC v. Texas Inc. et al., 42 United States Law Week 4867, June 11, 1974.

[8] See Mobil Oil Corporation v. Federal Power Commission, 42 United States Law Week 4842, June 11, 1974. The words are quoted from the decision in Permian Basin Area Rates, 390 U.S. 747, 1968.

[9] See "Congress Nears Shutdown on Proposal to Decontrol Gas Prices," *National Journal Reports*, p. 764.

[10] See "Federal Power Commission Head Urges End to Gas Curbs," *New York Times*, April 11, 1973, p. 19.

The policy of deregulation is based on the belief that there would be substantial response in production and demand to increases in price. Although time lags are not assumed away, proponents of deregulation argue that it would eliminate shortages over the next five years. Decontrol would allow higher prices to clear markets of excess demand by increasing reserves and production, and decreasing demands at wholesale. Natural gas now being channeled away from controls into intrastate markets should go back to the interstate pipelines as the interstate prices either matched or exceeded those offered by local industry.

But there is less than perfect agreement among proponents of deregulation as to how and over what time period decontrol should take place. The administration has proposed gradual or phased deregulation of new contract prices. Price ceilings would still be in effect on old contracts. The prices of new contracts would be allowed to increase by steps over the next few years until presumably by 1980 any further increases would be determined by what the market would bear. The step ceilings would be administered by the Federal Energy Administration, and would be based on forecasts of future production and demand conditions rather than on backward-looking accounting costs.

Total deregulation of all contracts has been proposed as well (S. 371, sponsored by Senator John Tower in 1973). In addition, immediate deregulation of new contract prices was proposed, and came close to passage as an amendment to other energy-related legislation (the Buckley amendment to the Energy Emergency Act of 1973).

There have been many reasons advanced for choosing a particular form of deregulation besides the quickness of the market-clearing response. Almost all proponents of deregulation have agreed that the regulatory process itself produces systematic shortages: because price changes lag behind marginal exploration and development costs under historical-average-cost rate-setting procedures, there is no way of avoiding shortages under regulation. Regulated prices simply cannot catch up to rising resource costs.[11] Those who favor phased deregulation argue that without phasing there will be too large an immediate price increase while those who favor immediate deregulation argue there will be too long a production lag if deregulation is phased.

Without choosing exactly the best of these arguments, we should point out that the question here is whether decontrolled prices would

---

[11] This point leads to the question whether a process designed for public utility controls applies to a natural resource industry. See Stephen Breyer and P. W. MacAvoy, "The Natural Gas Shortage," p. 941.

"do better" in the late 1970s than controlled prices. Would higher prices of the sort proposed by deregulation significantly reduce the size of production shortages? This is an empirical question, and the answer must support either the general case for strengthened regulation or the general case for deregulation.

4

With long lags from price increases to increases in reserves and production, it might be expected that any price policy would be effective only after a number of years had passed. Moreover, there should be only gradual changes in demand as a result of new contract price policies, since "roll-in" regulatory procedures pass new field prices through to wholesale prices only after a number of years, and after that, the wholesale prices affect industrial or final consumer demands. Even so, there should be some change in the first few years, and a significant change by 1980. (No political policy taking a decade to show initial results is likely to be acceptable.) Thus, advocates of either stronger controls or of decontrol expect their policies to eliminate most of the gas shortage for consumers by the early 1980s.

To investigate these possibilities we introduce the four proposed policy changes—to strengthen, to simplify, to maintain, or to eliminate natural gas regulation—into the econometric model of gas field and wholesale markets. We must assume certain rates of growth of production costs, of economy-wide determinants of demand, and of oil prices; then the econometric framework leads to predictions of additions to reserves and production from each of twenty-nine production districts. By inserting the assumed new contract field price consistent with each of the alternative policies into the modules for reserves and production, and by marking up assumed field prices through roll-in pricing procedures in the modules for demand, we predict reserves, production, and demands for each policy. Thus, policies can be examined for the implications of their pricing schedules for levels of the production shortage.[1]

---

[1] The last half of the 1970s, assuming a more or less expansive economy, would have inflation rates of 6.5 percent, real growth of incomes and investment of 3.5 percent, and substantial oil prices (close to $7 per barrel in 1974 dollars).

Of the four policy alternatives considered in Chapter 3, the latter two—maintenance of current regulation and phased deregulation—were considered to be the most likely choices for the future. (Current regulation would follow from an accumulation of appeals to the FPC for more increases; phased deregulation would follow from the passage of bills proposed by the current administration.) Accordingly, these two alternatives are analyzed and presented here in much greater detail than are the other two. The variables being forecast—variables such as total reserves, supply, and excess demand—are identical for all four choices.

Before we present any results of the simulation, there should be a brief note on the technical background of these tests. All the simulated forecasts are based on a specific set of values for the exogenous variables: these values are expected to hold during the 1970s. The important exogenous determinants of demands for natural gas include state-by-state value added in manufacturing, population, income, capital equipment additions and fuel oil prices. It is assumed that value added, income, and capital additions will grow at 4.2 percent per annum in constant dollars.[2] We chose a conservative expected rate of growth of prices of 6.5 percent. The rate of inflation likely to prevail in the late 1970s is uncertain and is in fact under considerable debate: the 6.5 percent simply represents a rough average of several recent inflation forecasts. Thus, value added, income, and capacity grow at 10.7 percent per annum in current dollars. It is assumed that the rate of growth of population will be limited to 1.1 percent per annum for the rest of the decade (in keeping with the assumptions used in the economy-wide models from which were generated the rates of growth of value added and capacity). The domestic price of crude oil is assumed to be constant at $6.50 per barrel in 1973 dollars for the remainder of the decade, and wholesale prices for both distillate and residual oil are assumed to remain at comparable levels in real terms. Finally, average drilling costs are expected to increase at a rate of 3.3 percent per annum in real terms, in keeping with the trend of real cost increases over the late 1960s and early 1970s.

Simulation of Strengthened Regulation

The most restrictive of the policy alternatives—strengthened regulation—would require a price freeze at the 1974 level, with adjustments allowed thereafter only for changes in historical average drilling costs.

---

[2] This assumption is based on the *Data Resources Quarterly Economic Model* forecast for the period 1972 to 1980.

Given that average drilling costs in the last four years have increased by almost 3¢/Mcf per year, it can be expected that new contracts would be limited to the 1974 level of 39¢/Mcf, with 3¢ increases thereafter. Projections of supply and demand under these conditions are shown in Table 5.

The table shows that price restraints should keep additions to reserves and production close to pre-1970 levels. The model suggests that new discoveries should increase somewhat, from the 10 Tcf level in the early 1970s to 14 or 15 Tcf in 1980 primarily because of incentives for exploration from the assumed high level of oil prices (close to $7 per barrel in real terms). Total additions to reserves would be less than 25 Tcf each year, while production would rise to as much as 28 Tcf. As a result, the reserve base would decline from 230 to 211 Tcf by 1980.

The model shows demand to be much greater than production if ceiling prices are held at these levels. Total demand for new production is forecast to increase from 24 Tcf in 1973 to approximately 41 Tcf in 1980. This increase results from the increase in oil prices combined with the ceiling on gas prices (a ceiling so low that prices do not rise even as much as general price increases from inflation).

Excess demand is expected to increase for the remainder of the decade. The gap between production and demand should increase from approximately 4 Tcf in 1975 to 12 Tcf by 1980. Strengthened price controls appear to exacerbate excess demand, so that the shortage would be close to 30 percent of total demand for production by 1980.[3]

Simulation of National Rate Regulation

The Federal Power Commission itself has proposed a new form of regulation that may have about the same effect. As noted in Chapter 2, the FPC on June 26, 1974 allowed all gas produced from wells drilled after January 1973 to sell at a price of 50¢/Mcf. This uniform national rate would be 5¢ greater in 1975, and would increase by 2¢

---

[3] These results from strict controls can be expected whether we use values of exogenous variables assumed here, or reasonable "higher" or "lower" values. As is shown later in this chapter, when "high" values are used the size of the excess demand in 1980 is larger than for "medium" values, and when low values are used the excess demand is somewhat smaller than for "medium" values. The results are approximately as sensitive to changes in oil prices as they are to changes in the values of economy-wide variables. Simulations based on high values for exogenous variables differ from simulations based on low values by approximately 7 Tcf in forecast excess demand for 1980. But this amount of difference, while substantial, does not affect the conclusion that strict regulation cannot eliminate the present natural gas shortage, and is likely to make it worse.

Table 5

ECONOMETRIC SIMULATIONS OF STRENGTHENED REGULATION OF NATURAL GAS [a]

Year	New Discoveries (Tcf)	Total Additions to Reserves (Tcf)	Total Reserves (Tcf)	Supply of Production (Tcf)	Demands for Production (Tcf)	Excess Demand for Production (Tcf)	New Contract Field Price (¢/Mcf)	Average Wholesale Price (¢/Mcf)
1972	4.7	8.8	233.4	23.3	23.5	.2	31.6	39.9
1973	9.9	17.0	227.8	23.6	24.3	.6	34.6	41.7
1974	10.0	18.4	222.8	24.3	26.2	1.9	39.7	44.9
1975	12.4	20.9	219.9	24.9	28.7	3.8	42.7	48.6
1976	13.8	22.6	217.9	25.6	31.2	5.7	45.8	52.0
1977	15.1	24.3	217.2	26.1	33.7	7.5	48.9	55.6
1978	15.8	25.4	216.6	26.9	36.1	9.2	52.0	59.5
1979	15.3	25.2	215.0	27.8	38.6	10.8	55.1	63.4
1980	14.3	23.9	211.2	28.6	41.0	12.4	58.2	67.3

[a] All values are for the continental United States including offshore and Canadian imports.

144

per annum thereafter. The FPC did not expect these prices to be sufficient to clear excess demand immediately; indeed the commission said the demand for gas "is much higher than the supply and will remain so for the immediate future." [4] But the commission concluded that "these rates for natural gas sold in interstate commerce are adequate to bring forth the requisite supplies to fill reasonable demand" and "not so high that natural gas consumers are exploited during times of shortage." [5]

These proposed prices are not much different from strengthened regulation, even though they offer a somewhat higher national ceiling at the present time. In setting this national ceiling, the commission has, in effect, frozen prices on some contracts already at that level as "exceptions." These contracts are those with the most advantageous reserves and production (large in quantity and close to final delivery points). Because such contracts are frozen, the effect may be the same as a general price freeze, although the FPC did not intend it to be so. Moreover, the allowed annual increase of 2¢ per annum is less than enough to compensate for expected inflation. The effect over time as well as at certain locations may be that of a general price freeze.

The forecast results are shown in Table 6. New discoveries are expected to be 16 Tcf per annum by 1980 so that, given production close to 30 Tcf, the reserve stock in the United States is expected to fall below 220 Tcf by 1980. At the same time, demand is expected to be enhanced by the small annual increase in field prices and should grow to nearly 39 Tcf by 1980. Excess demand would then exceed 8 Tcf, or more than 20 percent of total demand. The forecasts suggest that the commission will be unable to reduce the shortage, but will not create greater excess demand than would otherwise occur by invoking the old "cost of service" procedures on a regular basis through the rest of the decade.

Simulation of Current Regulation

One alternative the FPC must consider is that of maintaining the status quo in regulation (that is, the status quo before the 50¢ ceiling). The commission, in the absence of new legislation, would continue its 1970–1973 policy of allowing sizable price increases each year on new contracts. Area rate reviews, along with individual case reviews, could result in the same 5¢ annual increases on new contracts as in

---

[4] J. L. Rowe, "Price Boost Approved for Natural Gas," *Washington Post*, June 26, 1974. The quotation is from the commission decision in Docket R-389, *National Area Rates*.

[5] Ibid.

Table 6

ECONOMETRIC SIMULATIONS OF FPC NATIONAL AREA RATE GAS REGULATION

Year	New Discoveries (Tcf)	Total Additions to Reserves (Tcf)	Total Reserves (Tcf)	Supply of Production (Tcf)	Demands for Production (Tcf)	Excess Demand for Production (Tcf)	New Contract Field Price (¢/Mcf)	Average Wholesale Price (¢/Mcf)
1972	4.7	8.8	233.5	23.3	23.5	.2	31.7	39.9
1973	9.9	17.0	227.8	23.6	24.3	.7	34.7	41.6
1974	9.8	18.2	222.4	24.6	26.3	1.6	49.9	45.2
1975	14.0	22.6	220.2	25.9	28.6	2.7	54.9	51.2
1976	16.3	25.3	219.8	26.7	30.7	4.0	56.9	55.9
1977	17.6	27.0	220.5	27.3	32.7	5.4	58.9	60.3
1978	18.4	28.3	221.4	28.3	34.6	6.3	60.9	64.7
1979	17.4	27.7	220.8	29.3	36.5	7.2	62.9	68.8
1980	16.1	26.0	217.5	30.3	38.5	8.3	64.9	72.7

earlier years. The basis would be the pragmatic judgment of the commission as to what was necessary to ease a growing shortage. By 1980 (as shown in Table 7) additions to reserves should increase to approximately 29 Tcf per annum as a result of substantial increases in discoveries, extensions, and revisions. Production would be expected to be comparable to the total additions to reserves each year. As a result, the total stock of reserves would be expected to decline somewhat by 1976, but to return to the level of 224 Tcf by 1980.

Unfortunately, neither the additions to reserves nor the level of production would appear to be sufficient to eliminate the shortage. Simulated demand increases at a slightly lower rate than under the strengthened regulatory policy discussed above, principally because the average wholesale prices would increase from 49¢ to 72¢ over the period from 1975 to 1980. Even so, the 1980 demand of 39.9 Tcf exceeds production by 10 Tcf. Worse still, because of smaller additions to production than to demand, the shortage would increase. Excess demand is a smaller percentage of total demand than under strengthened regulation, but still exceeds 20 percent of total demand. Thus this approach, like strengthened regulation, cannot by itself be expected to eliminate production shortages. Price ceilings appear to make the shortage worse.

Simulation of Phased Deregulation

Given the large number of alternative proposals under the general heading of "deregulation" of field prices, no single price schedule can be proposed as an exact picture of market conditions under decontrol. Most proposals, however, would allow new contract prices to seek their own levels after 1980, with rising ceilings on new contract prices in the intervening period.[6] The ceilings would not in fact eliminate

---

[6] It should be stressed that "phased deregulation" is in no way a synonym for complete deregulation within a few months' time. Although complete and instanteous deregulation is an alternative being considered, it has not been examined here. The chances of its acceptance by Congress seem so small that it does not merit space in this short chapter. Also, there is no ar.. lytically acceptable procedure for simulating complete deregulation, since the equation relationships in the model were constructed on the basis of data for two decades in which regulation was predominant. Extrapolation of relationships during regulation, to indicate other relationships in unregulated markets, seems unacceptable: the changes in patterns of price expectations alone would be so great as to eliminate any similarities of producer performance under the two regimes of control. Simulations of phased deregulation over the next five years seem to be legitimate, inasmuch as they involve the continued use of price controls of the nature of those in the 1960s and 1970s when the data for equation estimation were generated.

Table 7

ECONOMETRIC SIMULATIONS OF CURRENT NATURAL GAS REGULATION

Year	New Dis-coveries (Tcf)	Total Additions to Reserves (Tcf)	Total Reserves (Tcf)	Supply of Production (Tcf)	Demands for Production (Tcf)	Excess Demand for Production (Tcf)	New Contract Field Price (¢/Mcf)	Average Wholesale Price (¢/Mcf)
1972	4.7	8.8	233.4	23.3	23.5	.2	31.6	39.9
1973	9.9	17.0	227.8	23.6	24.3	.7	34.6	41.6
1974	10.0	18.4	222.9	24.3	26.3	1.9	39.7	44.7
1975	12.8	21.3	220.2	25.0	28.8	3.8	44.8	48.7
1976	14.9	23.8	219.1	25.8	31.2	5.4	49.8	52.7
1977	17.0	26.3	219.9	26.6	33.5	7.0	54.9	57.1
1978	18.6	28.5	221.7	27.6	35.8	8.2	60.0	62.0
1979	19.2	29.5	223.5	28.7	37.9	9.1	65.1	67.0
1980	18.7	29.0	223.6	29.9	39.9	10.0	70.2	72.3

excess demand in the middle 1970s because they would be set to prevent the short-term market-clearing price increases in the immediate future.

Many rules of thumb have been proposed for setting the interim prices. Among the most frequent suggestions is to keep average wholesale prices from increasing by more than 100 percent over the 1976–1980 period.[7] Using wellhead prices that would fit in with these interim ceilings, we could establish a sequence that would include a 25¢ increase in 1975, with a 7¢ per annum increase thereafter. Simulations with this price sequence have been completed as an indication of price and production behavior under phased deregulation.

The simulations indicate increased discoveries of up to 33 Tcf each year to 1980, with total reserves equaling 271 Tcf by that year (as shown in Table 8). The impact of the price increases on new discoveries would not occur immediately, but would begin to appear in the second and third year after the 25¢ price increase. Production out of reserves would increase somewhat faster than reserve accumulations themselves since production depends on price as well as on the reserve level. As a result, simulated production rises from 23 to 34 Tcf at the rate of more than 1 Tcf per annum.

At the same time, simulated increases in demand for gas are dampened as a result of the pass-through of higher new contract field prices to the wholesale level. The average wholesale price rises to 88¢/Mcf in 1980, while the new contract field price in 1980 is $1.00/Mcf. The increases are sufficient to hold demand down to the level of 34 Tcf per annum by 1980. Phased increases in gas prices curtail the growth in demand for production by almost 36 percent (when demand under this alternative is compared to demand under the current regulation alternative).

---

[7] These price equivalents were presented to members of the House of Representatives in individual briefings in the spring of 1974 by the Columbia Gas System of Wilmington, Delaware as part of a legislative proposal allowing higher gas prices. As a matter of fact, they would allow price increases that would still not place natural gas prices at the same level as oil prices forecast for New Jersey in 1980. The sequence of such "equitable" prices would be as follows. Gas wholesale prices start at approximately 44¢/Mcf in 1974 and increase to 88¢/Mcf in 1980. The final price is equivalent to crude oil prices close to $5 per barrel. But the addition of further delivery charges to places as far north along the eastern coast of the United States as New Jersey would add at least 30¢ to these average nationwide wholesale prices. The resulting East Coast oil and gas prices would be $7 per barrel in 1980 dollars—which is the level of oil prices in 1974 dollars used in the econometric forecasts.

Table 8

ECONOMETRIC SIMULATIONS OF PHASED DEREGULATION OF NATURAL GAS

Year	New Dis- coveries (Tcf)	Total Additions to Reserves (Tcf)	Total Reserves (Tcf)	Supply of Production (Tcf)	Demands for Production (Tcf)	Excess Demand for Production (Tcf)	New Contract Field Price (¢/Mcf)	Average Wholesale Price (¢/Mcf)
1972	4.7	8.8	233.4	23.3	23.5	.2	31.7	39.9
1973	9.9	17.0	227.8	23.6	24.3	.7	34.7	41.4
1974	10.0	18.4	222.9	24.3	26.3	2.0	39.7	44.3
1975	16.3	24.8	222.3	26.4	28.7	2.3	64.7	52.7
1976	21.4	30.5	226.1	27.6	30.4	2.8	71.7	59.6
1977	25.4	35.3	233.9	28.6	31.9	3.3	78.8	66.3
1978	30.0	41.1	245.8	30.2	32.9	2.7	85.9	73.7
1979	31.5	43.9	258.6	32.1	33.7	1.6	93.1	81.1
1980	33.0	45.6	271.2	34.1	34.2	0.1	100.3	88.3

Figure 2

EXCESS DEMAND UNDER ALTERNATIVE REGULATORY POLICIES
(trillions of cubic feet)

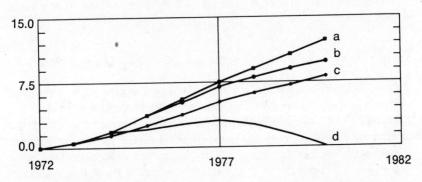

Notes:
a = National area rate (42¢ ceiling)   c = Current regulation
b = Strengthened regulation   d = Phased deregulation

The forecasts here seem to point toward a substantial reduction in the gas shortage within a reasonable time span. By 1980 the level of production and the level of demand are both expected to be approximately 34 Tcf. Of course, there is some chance that there would still be a shortage since these forecasts, based on probable values for economy-wide determinants of costs and demands, are not going to be perfectly accurate. But the most likely general result from phased deregulation should be amelioration of excess demand in production markets.[8]

Figure 2 above shows how excess demand behaves under the four policy alternatives. The graph shows that phased deregulation,

---

[8] Attempts have been made to assess the precision of the forecasts, by inserting different values of exogenous variables into the econometric model to determine how the size of forecast excess demand changes. The different values for exogenous variables are discussed later in this chapter. But, even with a wider range of values than is likely to occur, the size of the shortage would be as large as 2 Tcf if either high oil prices or high values for economic factors prevailed. If low oil prices and low values for economic variables were in effect, the shortage would become a surplus as large as 5 Tcf at prevailing phased deregulation prices. Under these latter circumstances, it would be expected that the price ceilings would not operate. Prices would be below ceiling levels, or reserves would be put back into the reserve inventory rather than produced, thereby raising the reserve-production ratio.

although extended over many years and requiring large price increases, should reduce the shortage to negligible levels by 1980. More regulation, on the other hand, would likely increase the shortage so that the excess demand would range from 8 to 12 Tcf out of 40 Tcf total demand per year. Thus, if policy changes should eliminate natural gas shortages, the proper direction to take would seem to be that of phased deregulation.

Further Analysis of Current Regulation and Phased Deregulation

As was pointed out earlier, the latter two policy alternatives are considered the most likely, and therefore deserve more attention than the first two. The values of the exogenous variables for each can be altered so that we can see how the forecasts depend on the particular assumptions that have been made. It is important to determine how they depend on the price of oil (the future of which is most uncertain), as well as how they depend on general economic conditions such as growth in output and the rate of inflation. In addition to the set of "medium" assumptions for exogenous variables that were used for the two policy analyses above, "high" and "low" assumptions for both oil prices and economic variables are used here.

In contrast to the medium assumption in oil prices, let us assume that the crude price on the low side declines by 25¢ per barrel each year from $6.50 per barrel in 1974 to $5.00 in 1980 or that on the high side the price increases from $6.50 per barrel in 1974 to $7.50 per barrel in 1980 (again in constant 1974 dollars). Wholesale oil prices (as well as prices for alternative fuels such as coal and electricity) are assumed to change at the same percentage rate as the crude oil price.

In contrast to the assumptions for medium economic growth, let us assume a low growth in which output variables (such as income, value added, and capital additions) grow at 2.5 percent in real terms with a rate of inflation of 4.0 percent, or let us assume high growth at 5.0 percent in real terms and a rate of inflation of 8.0 percent.

Alternative simulation results for the three oil prices are shown in Figures 3 and 4. In Figure 3 it is assumed that the current FPC regulation is in effect; alternative results for the phased deregulation price policy are shown in Figure 4.

Although this is not shown in the figures, new discoveries and additions to reserves are affected by oil prices. When gas prices are low, as under regulation, a high oil price serves as an incentive for additional exploratory drilling which results in moderate additional

152

Figure 3

EFFECTS OF CURRENT REGULATION UNDER ALTERNATIVE OIL PRICES
(trillions of cubic feet)

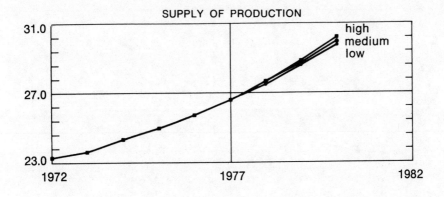

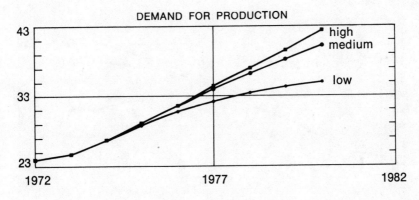

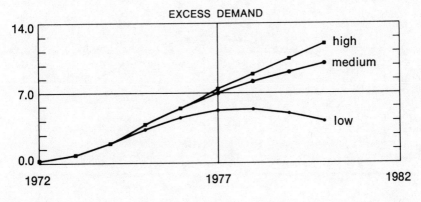

Figure 4

EFFECTS OF PHASED DEREGULATION UNDER ALTERNATIVE OIL PRICES
(trillions of cubic feet)

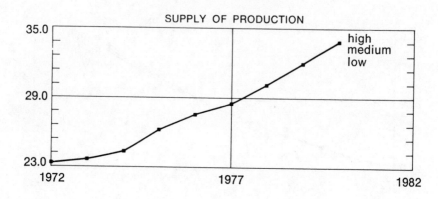

SUPPLY OF PRODUCTION

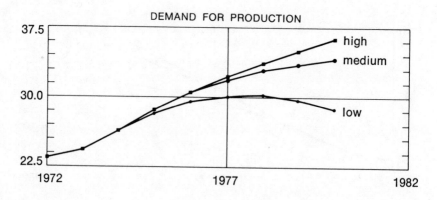

DEMAND FOR PRODUCTION

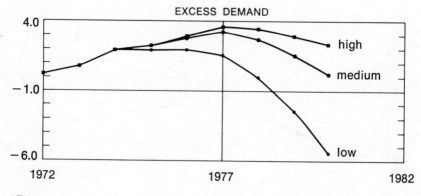

EXCESS DEMAND

gas discoveries. There is the opposite effect, however, under the phased deregulation policy. When the price of gas is allowed to rise, as under phased deregulation, there is already sufficient incentive for exploration on the extensive margin, and the additional incentive provided by the higher oil price largely functions to lead exploration toward oil drilling. In both policies the changes in oil prices lead to variations of somewhat more than 2 Tcf in total gas reserves. With small changes in reserves, the level of gas production remains almost the same under all three ceiling price simulations.

Demands for production, however, are more sensitive to changes in the price of oil. With low oil prices, there is a shift in demand from natural gas to oil, and in 1980 the excess demand for natural gas is only 4.1 Tcf under FPC regulation. Regulation does not create severe shortages, but deregulation eliminates shortages altogether. Under low oil prices with phased deregulation, the shortage of gas could be eased by fairly low price increases. Field price increases of only 10¢ or 15¢/Tcf in 1975 and 5¢ per year thereafter would be sufficient to clear markets by the end of the decade.

Alternative simulations for the three sets of general economic conditions are shown in Figures 5 and 6. Again there is relatively little variation in the level of production, but substantial variations in the demand for natural gas. Under conditions of relatively slow economic growth, for example, the excess demand for natural gas in 1980 under the current FPC regulation is predicted to be 5.5 Tcf. In comparison, excess demand is 10.0 Tcf under the "medium" assumptions and 12.4 under the high assumptions. These estimates are not unreasonable. Any decline in the long-term rate of growth of the American economy ought to reduce growth in the demand for natural gas. If the rate of economic growth actually turns out to be low, the field price increases necessary to clear the natural gas markets by the end of the decade will be smaller than they would otherwise be.

Other Ways to Alleviate the Shortage

There are, of course, other ways to alleviate or eliminate shortages. Let us briefly consider three other policies deliberately designed to eliminate the gas shortage.

The first is to tax consumption so as to reduce demand to the level of production forecast under current regulation (equal to "Supply of Production" in Table 7). According to the econometric model (Table 9), the taxes levied on pipeline buyers in new contracts would have to start at 15¢/Mcf in 1975 and increase to 90¢/Mcf in 1980.

Figure 5

EFFECTS OF CURRENT REGULATION UNDER ALTERNATIVE ECONOMIC CONDITIONS
(trillions of cubic feet)

SUPPLY OF PRODUCTION

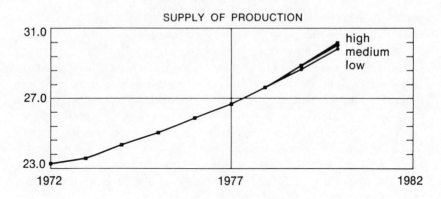

DEMAND FOR PRODUCTION

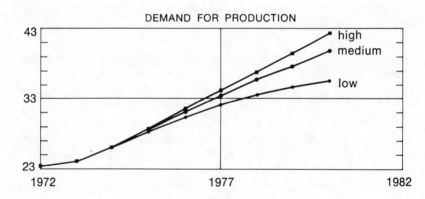

EXCESS DEMAND

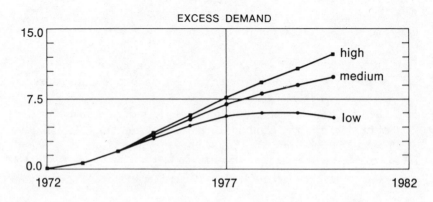

156

Figure 6

EFFECTS OF PHASED DEREGULATION UNDER ALTERNATIVE ECONOMIC CONDITIONS
(trillions of cubic feet)

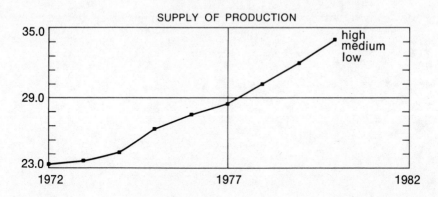

SUPPLY OF PRODUCTION

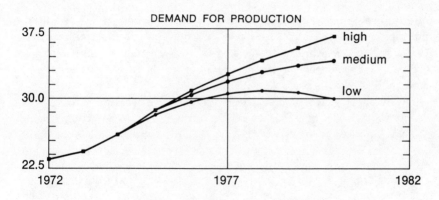

DEMAND FOR PRODUCTION

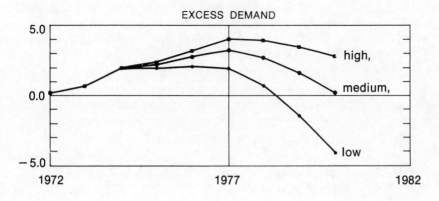

EXCESS DEMAND

Table 9

EFFECTS OF TAXES ON CONSUMPTION TO ELIMINATE THE GAS SHORTAGE

Year	Field Price on New Contracts (¢/Mcf)	Taxes on New Contracts (¢/Mcf)	Production Supply (Tcf)	Production Demand with Taxes (Tcf)
1974	39.7	0	24.3	26.2
1975	44.8	15.0	25.0	28.6
1976	49.8	30.0	25.8	30.5
1977	54.9	45.0	26.7	31.7
1978	60.0	60.0	27.6	32.0
1979	65.1	75.0	28.7	31.4
1980	70.2	90.0	29.9	29.8

These taxes would be added on to new contract field prices, so that the pipelines would pay $1.60/Mcf for new gas at the wellhead in 1980. When these prices are "rolled-in," they would be sufficient to cut back on wholesale and final demand so as to eliminate excess demand.

The shortage could also be eliminated by increasing gas supply an additional 10 Tcf. This could be done through the payment of subsidies on new contracts signed at regulated prices. The subsidies would provide income to the producer, but would not add to the field or wholesale prices paid by the buyers. Given current regulatory policy, Table 10 shows the subsidies required to produce the additional supply necessary to match demand of 39.9 Tcf at regulated prices. This simulation from the econometric model suggests that by 1980 market clearing could be achieved with subsidies of more than $1/Mcf on new contracts. Thus, the field producers would receive $2.02/Mcf that year on new commitments to interstate pipelines while buyers paid 70¢/Mcf on new contracts (and taxpayers paid $1.32/Mcf).

Both taxes and subsidies would seem to be more costly than phased deregulation, simply because each uses only one-half the market at any time. The tax policy uses the "demand dampening" mechanism of increasing prices to consumers, while the subsidy policy uses the "supply expansion" mechanism of increasing profits to producers. But phased deregulation uses both supply and demand incentives, so that the amount of price or profit increase required per unit

Table 10

EFFECTS OF SUBSIDIES TO ELIMINATE
THE GAS SHORTAGE

Year	Field Price on New Contracts (¢/Mcf)	Subsidy on New Contracts (¢/Mcf)	Production Supply with Subsidy (Tcf)	Production Demand (Tcf)
1974	39.7	0	24.3	26.3
1975	44.8	22.0	26.5	28.8
1976	49.8	44.0	28.8	31.2
1977	54.9	66.0	30.5	33.5
1978	60.0	88.0	32.9	35.8
1979	65.1	110.0	35.8	37.9
1980	70.2	132.0	39.3	39.9

of "excess demand reduction" is less than with either of the fiscal policies.

A third way to alleviate the natural gas shortage is through the leasing of offshore land for exploration, development, and production. Alternative offshore leasing policies can be simulated with the model since the number of offshore acres leased each year is an exogenous policy variable which (through reserve additions) affects offshore production. The simulated levels of excess demand shown in Figure 7 depend on how many acres of offshore land are leased to producers each year by the Department of the Interior's Bureau of Land Management.

Under current FPC regulation, excess demand for gas will increase steadily to 1980. Furthermore, variation in the number of acres leased has little effect on the ultimate level of the shortage. Under phased deregulation, however, excess demand peaks in 1977 and drops steadily, reaching a level between 0.5 and −0.2 Mcf depending on the number of acres leased. Again, phased deregulation proves to be more effective than any alternative in reducing the gas shortage.

Figure 7

EXCESS DEMAND UNDER ALTERNATIVE LEASING POLICIES
(trillions of cubic feet)

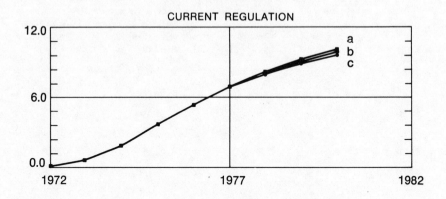

CURRENT REGULATION

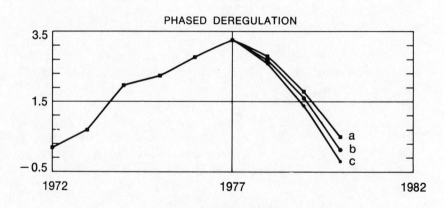

PHASED DEREGULATION

a = one million acres leased
b = two million acres leased
c = three million acres leased

160

The superiority of phased deregulation in reducing natural gas short-ages is so great that there would seem to be little economic basis for considering the alternatives. But there is concern over the income effects of substantial price increases from deregulation, since these would result in higher prices for consumers and higher profits for producers. What is involved is more than simple transfers of income from one group to the other; the shortage itself reduces total income. This last winter curtailments in commercial and industrial consumption of gas in the North left consumers with lower real incomes through higher prices for oil heat or reduced employment.[1]

Industry Gainers and Losers

Some of these effects can be seen if we study the patterns of shortages. If we assume maintenance of current regulation, excess demand would be greatest in the North Central and second greatest in the South-east region of the country (as in Table 11).[2] If all residential demands in the North Central and Southeast are met through FPC requirements that residential consumers be served first, the excess demand in these

---

[1] As can be seen by inserting the difference in gas supply into the energy sector of the Hudson-Jorgenson long-term growth model of the U.S. economy. See Edward A. Hudson and Dale W. Jorgenson, "U.S. Energy Policy and Economic Growth, 1975-2000," *Bell Journal of Economics and Management Science,* vol. 5, no. 2 (Autumn 1974), p. 461.

[2] There would be less excess demand in the Northeast and West because of access to pipelines going into the more likely productive new field areas, particularly offshore and in the Permian Basin. There should be no excess demand in the South Central region, because higher intrastate prices in that region allocate additions to reserves to buyers there first.

Table 11
NATURAL GAS SHORTAGES BY REGION, 1978–1980 [a]
(in Tcf)

Year	Excess Demand	Total Residential Demand	Total Industrial Demand
--------------------------------- NORTHEAST ---------------------------------			
1978	0.8	2.9	2.4
1979	0.8	3.0	2.5
1980	0.7	3.1	2.6
--------------------------------- NORTH CENTRAL ---------------------------------			
1978	4.4	3.9	4.6
1979	5.1	4.1	5.1
1980	5.7	4.3	5.6
--------------------------------- WEST ---------------------------------			
1978	1.2	1.9	3.1
1979	1.5	2.0	3.2
1980	1.8	2.0	3.3
--------------------------------- SOUTHEAST ---------------------------------			
1978	1.7	1.2	2.1
1979	1.8	1.3	2.2
1980	1.9	1.4	2.3

[a] The values are simulations with the econometric model, and derived from maintaining current regulatory conditions (see "Excess Demand for Production" in Table 7).

regions would be experienced by industrial buyers. Thus, from 90 to 100 percent of industrial demands in those regions would have to be cut off, with buyers going to alternative fuels or curtailing production of final products and services. Both would reduce employment, and consumers as job holders would lose. Whoever experiences the shortage, consumers and industrial employees in the North Central part of the country would experience increases in real income from phased deregulation.

Natural gas price decontrol also would have an impact on other energy industries. Without decontrol, a new industry providing liquified natural gas (LNG) could develop in the 1980s using gas from other parts of the world. This LNG could eliminate excess demands and sell at prices which should exceed $2/Mcf for demands greater than 2.5 Tcf per annum. But under phased deregulation, there would be negligible excess demands after 1980. In effect, the market for

LNG would be made by strong regulatory controls so that under phased deregulation LNG producers and transporters would be losers.[3]

Of course there are always potential gainers or losers from industry-wide changes in regulatory policies. Losers from phased deregulation—losers like the LNG companies—are not, however, to be mistaken for the general consumer. Under deregulation the substitution of domestic natural gas at 88¢/Mcf for LNG at $2/Mcf in fact should make the final consumers better off.[4]

Another group affected by changes in regulatory policies would be the producers and distributors of crude oil in the United States. If FPC price controls were discontinued, the demands for distillate and residual fuel oil would be substantially decreased. The econometric model has been used to simulate the changes likely to occur in fuel oil markets given that the alternatives are either phased deregulation prices or current FPC regulation prices.[5] Forecasts have been made for fuel oil demands in the Northeast under these two sets of natural gas controls. The forecasts suggest that residual demand will decrease by 1.0 million barrels per day and distillate demand by 0.3 million barrels per day as a result of gas decontrol. Sections of the country with even larger shortages of natural gas should have even more substantial decreases in fuel oil consumption as the result of deregulation.[6] The full effects of phased deregulation on these markets would

---

[3] No attempt is made here to describe the full market for LNG, nor to consider LNG as a solution to the gas shortage. To do this would require an analysis and forecasts of foreign reserves, production out of reserves, and demands in other countries than the United States. These forecasts would call for a world gas econometric model. The demand forecasts for LNG are described in detail in the Appendix.

[4] But it should be noted that there are economically substantial special interests for LNG. The licensing of LNG contracts by the Federal Power Commission would create large-scale new construction of storage facilities and of LNG tankers in domestic United States shipyards. These facilities would add considerably to the rate base for profit regulation of wholesale pipelines or retail gas utility companies, and the additions to the rate base would be welcomed in a period when the capital base from construction of pipelines in the 1950s has been in good part eliminated. Thus, important parts of the pipeline industry would benefit from the shortage or lose from phased deregulation.

[5] The procedure consists of finding that price P^*_2 that clears excess demands for gas (since the model does not recognize excess demands for one fuel as the determinants of demands for another fuel). Then oil demands at P^*_2 are compared with oil demands at P_2, the deregulated gas price.

[6] Forecasts cannot be made of decreased fuel oil demands in the North Central portion of the country because of our inability to construct a demand equation for fuel oil in which gas prices were significant. This vagary in the data for the 1960s prevents use of the approach given here for evaluating the impact of the shortage where it is greatest on fuel oil demands in that region.

163

be widespread and difficult to determine, but they should include reductions in imports of fuel and crude oil from abroad.

Consumer Gainers and Losers

There are important groups of consumers that would gain from phased deregulation, some of whom have been mentioned above. At this point, let us try to add up consumer debits and credits.

Some consumers are favored by regulation and they would lose if it were discontinued. To be able to get all the gas demanded for the rest of the decade at 1974 prices is a favorable position created for some consumers by strict regulation. Income transfers away from these consumers resulting from phased deregulation would exceed $1 billion per annum by 1975 and $4.8 billion by 1980 (where the alternative to phased deregulation would be a continuation of current FPC regulation). This income transfer would come from consumers now having uninterrupted gas service.[7]

Accompanying this loss from phased deregulation, however, would be gains to other consumers who would otherwise do without natural gas. The additional gas forthcoming at decontrolled prices would be available to meet excess demand in the northern parts of the country. The dollar gains from deregulation, measured by the prices these consumers would be willing to pay for this gas rather than do without in the period 1978–1980, should exceed $2.5 billion (in 1978) and $5.8 billion (in 1980).[8] Thus, this group should receive greater gains from deregulation than the losses inflicted on those who

---

[7] The amount of loss, estimated from the simulation results described below, is equivalent to Area A in the figure shown in footnote 8, below.

[8] This is equivalent to Area C in the figure below given that under FPC allocation rules certain consumers are doing without natural gas entirely:

GAINS TO CONSUMERS FROM DEREGULATION

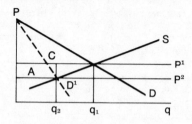

Thus, these losses are extended by the regulatory procedures which allocate the shortage entirely to new consumers and to industrial consumers in the regions experiencing excess demand.

164

would no longer be receiving the gas at lower prices. Since these are all consumers, there would seem at this time to be *general gains from deregulation* for consumers as a group through phased decontrol.

Regulation and the Reasons for the Shortage

Granted the results have been poor, it may be asked why regulation has operated in this way. There would seem to have been a classic failure of process in natural gas price controls. The regulatory mechanisms were mandated by court decisions, calling for price control without justifying that control according to special (monopoly) conditions of production or demand. These court decisions imposed a task on the Federal Power Commission that it was not able to perform, because of a failure of logic and perspective.

In part the FPC could not perform its task because of a failure of logic centered on reasoning by analogy. The process of regulation used by the commission followed time-honored procedures. The FPC had previously dealt in calculations of historical costs, and in finding a fair rate of return by comparing profit rates in the provision of pipeline services with those in other industries. These methods of control had been an accepted part of public utility regulation for decades. But these methods had not been applied systematically to the natural gas industry, where costs of new reserves could not be determined from historical accounting data on old reserves. New prices based on old costs guaranteed that increments to production would in the long run fall short of increments to demands. By asserting that controls developed in a public utility setting would work in natural gas field pricing, the regulatory agency made a logical mistake that undermined the efficiency of the results.

In part also the FPC could not perform its task because of a failure of perspective. To take a two- or three-year view of price ceilings, when industry reserve accumulation and production took place over much longer periods, was incorrect. Since this short-term view still predominates in legislative proposals for reform—quick results are expected from new policies—this part of the commission's mistake could well be repeated. The question that remains is how long it will take for policy makers to understand these mistakes and to learn from them in setting national gas policy.

APPENDIX: THE ECONOMETRIC
MODEL OF NATURAL GAS

Structure of the Model

The forecasts and policy conclusions presented in this book are based on an econometric model of the natural gas industry. The model consists of a set of equations that describe the behavior of natural gas reserves and production markets. By inserting into the model different wellhead prices as well as different numerical values for other economic variables and parameters, forecasts of natural gas reserves, production, demand, and prices can be made for alternative regulatory policies and alternative economic conditions.

An important aspect of the model is that production and demand are described in both the market for reserve additions (gas producers dedicating new reserves to pipeline at the wellhead price) and the market for wholesale deliveries (pipeline companies selling gas on long-term contracts to retail utilities and industrial consumers). In addition, the regional organization of these two markets is accounted for in the model. Reserve additions are contracted in regional field markets, and gas production is delivered by pipelines to regional wholesale markets. These regional markets are interconnected through the network of natural gas pipelines across the country. Individual wholesale markets receive gas from different combinations of producing markets, so that it would be possible for a shortage of natural gas production to exist in one wholesale market but not in another. The model will predict regional shortages because it describes the interconnection of regional field and wholesale markets.

[1] This model is described in considerable detail in P. W. MacAvoy and R. S. Pindyck, *The Economics of the Natural Gas Shortage (1960-1980)*. Information on how to access the model may be obtained from the authors at the Massachusetts Institute of Technology, Cambridge, Massachusetts.

The time-dynamics of the different stages of reserve accumulation, production and demand are another important aspect of the model. Policy questions are concerned not only with how much production or demand will be forthcoming at higher regulated prices, but also with how long it will take for the effects of the new pricing policy to occur. Appropriate time lags have thus been built into all of the relationships of the model. The overall structure of the model is shown diagrammatically in Figure A-1. (The diagram ignores—for simplicity—the spatial interconnections between production districts and regional wholesale markets.) We will survey each part of the model in connection with the diagram, and then later present the individual relationships as they have been statistically estimated.

The first block of equations in the model determines reserve additions for natural gas and oil. Reserve additions are made up of new discoveries, and extensions and revisions of previous discoveries. New discoveries are the largest component of reserve additions for natural gas, and include discoveries of both associated and nonassociated gas (associated gas includes both gas "dissolved" in produced oil and gas forming a cap in contact with crude oil). New discoveries also provide the major component of reserve additions for oil.

New discoveries begin with the drilling of wells, of which some will be successful in discovering gas, some will be successful in discovering oil (with or without associated gas), and some will be unsuccessful (that is, dry holes). Although wells are drilled in regions which offer some probability of gas or oil discovery, many are drilled without a priori knowledge of which hydrocarbon will be discovered. As a result, the exploration and discovery process for both gas and oil is here modeled simultaneously, and accounts for shifts in directionality between oil and gas in response to price changes.

Drilling takes place either extensively or intensively. On the extensive margin, few wells are drilled, but those that are drilled usually go out beyond the geographical frontiers of recent discoveries to open up new locations or previously neglected deeper strata at old locations. The probability of discovering gas in extensive drilling is relatively small, but the size of any discovery is likely to be large because it would be the first in the region. On the intensive margin wells are drilled in an area at or near a source of gas production. There the probability of discovering gas is larger, but the size of discovery is likely to be smaller than on the extensive margin.

Our model views the producer who is engaged in exploratory activity as having, at any point in time, a portfolio of drilling options available on both margins. In deciding where to drill, producers make a trade-off between expected risk and expected return, and thereby

Figure A-1

BLOCK DIAGRAM OF THE ECONOMETRIC MODEL

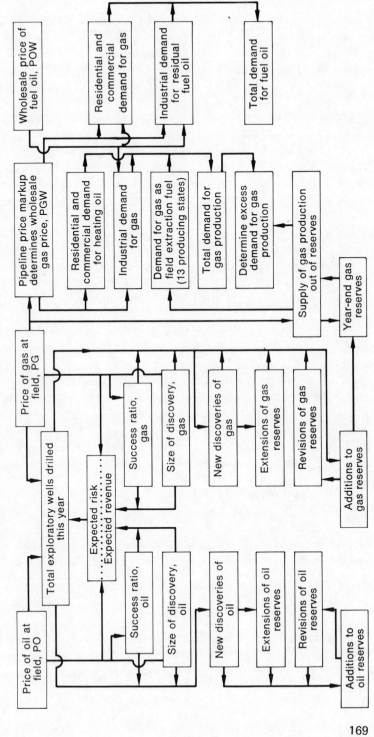

decide whether additional drilling will be extensive or intensive. This choice will be influenced by changes (or expected changes) in economic variables such as field prices of oil and gas and drilling costs. The model has an equation for the number of wells drilled: this equation assumes that producers have rational responses to economic incentives as they form portfolios of drilling ventures that may be extensive or intensive, or may favor gas or oil.

The number of wells drilled is the first step in determining new discoveries in the model. Equations are specified that predict the fraction of wells drilled that will be successful in finding gas, and the fraction that will be successful in finding oil. These "success ratios" depend on whether economic incentives (such as price increases) result in drilling on the extensive or intensive margin (something which must be determined empirically). For example, let us suppose that the choice is on the extensive margin. In that case the gas success ratio will depend negatively on changes in the gas price (that is, higher gas prices mean more extensive drilling for gas), and positively on the oil price (oil prices that are high relative to gas prices mean more intensive drilling for gas since oil becomes relatively more profitable than gas).

Two equations determine the size of discovery per successful well for gas and oil respectively. Discovery size is related to the number of successful wells drilled previously, to the volume of previous discoveries in that region (or to the "age" of fields there), as well as to gas and oil prices. The larger the number of previous successful wells the smaller will be the discovery sizes, since the large reservoirs are found early. The "age" of fields itself is a function of how much previous drilling has been done, so that size decreases with age. If economic incentives result in extensive drilling, then higher gas prices (or lower oil prices) result in a larger gas discovery size as the shift is made to the extensive margin.

The model generates forecasts of new discoveries separately for gas and oil as the product of number of wells, success ratio, and size of find per successful well. This level of detail gives explicit consideration to the process of long-term geological depletion as well as to the role of risk in determining the amount and nature of exploratory activity. It also accounts for the fact that oil and natural gas are in fact joint products that must be treated symmetrically. Finally, it allows for shifts in the relative proportions of intensive and extensive drilling in response to changes in economic incentives.

Extensions and revisions for both gas and oil also contribute to reserve additions. They depend theoretically on price incentives, past

170

discoveries of gas and oil, existing reserve levels for both gas and oil, and the cumulative effect of past drilling. In fact, extensions seem to be influenced most by past discoveries and total drilling activity. Revisions of established reserve levels, on the other hand, seem to be essentially proportional to prior discoveries and reserve levels.

As can be seen in the block diagram, additions to gas reserves are the sum of new discoveries, extensions, and revisions. Aside from changes in underground storage, subtraction from gas reserves occurs as a result of production. Additions to oil reserves are likewise the sum of new discoveries, extensions, and revisions. Since our model does not describe oil production and refining, we do not determine year-end oil reserves.

If the natural gas industry were not regulated, or if regulation of the wellhead price were ineffective (that is, if the ceiling price of gas were the equilibrium wellhead price), the model would also contain equations describing the demand for reserves. In particular, the demand for new reserves would be given by a wellhead price equation for pipeline offers to buy reserve commitments at specified new contract wellhead prices. Since 1962, however, there has been excess demand for new reserves, so that demand has not been observable and we therefore do not use a wellhead price equation. Instead the price is given by the exogenous wellhead ceiling price.[2]

Once the level of year-end natural gas reserves has been determined, we can determine the level of gas production. Production out of reserves depends not only on the size of the reserve base, but also on prices that buyers are willing to pay for increased deliveries. Production supply in the model is based on marginal cost pricing—that is, the marginal cost of developing existing reserves determines a particular level of annual flow (for example, by the drilling of development wells and then their operation). Marginal production costs are dependent on the relationship of reserve levels and production: as the reserve-to-production ratio becomes smaller, marginal costs rise sharply. It is assumed that the exogenous regulated price sets the upper bounds on marginal costs. Thus, as can be seen in the block diagram, the level of gas production out of reserves is a function of the field price of gas and the quantity of year-end reserves in any one production district.

The discovery and production of natural gas in offshore regions is a particularly important part of the econometric policy model.

---

[2] Note that it is possible to have at the same time excess demand for new reserves but clearing in production markets if the existing reserve-production ratio is run down. This was in fact the case in the late 1960s.

171

There are now, for geological and economic reasons, high probabilities that large discoveries will be found offshore. As both gas and oil prices increase and as more offshore acreage is leased by the federal government, offshore fields will probably provide an increasing share of gas production.

For both theoretical and empirical reasons, offshore reserves and production are described by a separate "submodel." This "submodel" describes relationships between reserves and production of gas off the coast of Louisiana and such policy variables as the new contract field price of gas and the amount of acreage leased annually. Important exogenous variables are interest rates, the price of oil, and the number of drilling rigs operating offshore. The "submodel" operates through three interacting blocks that determine, respectively, total acreage, producing acreage, and reserve additions and production.

The model's explanation of the offshore discovery process begins with the number of exploratory wells drilled, a number determined by an index of gas and oil field prices and total acreage leased. The average discovery size per well drilled (whether the well is successful or not) is determined by a second index of gas and oil prices and the cumulative number of wells drilled. This last variable serves to indicate a depletion effect in the model. New discoveries are determined as the product of wells drilled and size of discovery per well. Extensions and revisions are aggregated together, and are explained by a single equation.

As we have explained here and in the larger work upon which this book is based, regulation may give a level of production from reserves that is inadequate to meet the demands on that production after it has been transported to wholesale markets by pipelines. The wholesale demand for natural gas production is a function not of the wellhead price of gas but of the wholesale price. Average wholesale prices for gas are computed in the model for each consumption region in the country through a series of pipeline price markup equations. The price markups are based on operating costs, capital costs, and regulated rates of profit for the pipeline companies.

Of course wholesale gas prices are not the only determinants of wholesale gas demand. Residential and commercial demand, and industrial demand, also depend on the prices of alternative fuels, and "market size" variables such as population, income, and investment. Separate equations for residential/commercial and industrial use are formulated for each of five regions of the country. In addition, the demand for gas as field extraction fuel is formulated within the model. In the thirteen major producing states, a certain quantity of gas is used as fuel for operating pumps that extract gas from the ground and although this quantity is small it must be included for proper determination of total gas demand.

Natural gas is competitive with fuel oil both in residential/commercial and industrial markets. When we analyze the impact of alternative regulatory policies, it is desirable for us to determine not only changes in the demand for gas, but how changes in gas demand relate to changes in oil demand. The model therefore contains a set of wholesale demand equations for fuel oil.

Fuel oil demand is disaggregated into residential/commercial demand (for No. 2 and No. 4 oil) and industrial demand (for No. 6 residual oil). Separate equations are estimated for each of three consuming regions: the Northeast, the North Central, and a "South" region which includes the Southeast, South Central, and West regions of the country. The fuel oil demand equations have the same structural form as the natural gas demand equations, thus making it possible for us to compare changes in oil and gas demand in a consistent manner. As can be seen from the block diagram, the demands for oil depend on the wholesale price for oil and the wholesale price for natural gas, as well as on the same "market size" variables as gas demand.

The determination of natural gas production at the wellhead and, concurrently, of the volume delivered to buyers in wholesale markets, is accomplished in the model through an input-output table connecting production districts with consuming regions. A flow network is constructed according to the relative flows calculated from 1971 data. This flow network determines where each consuming region obtains its gas. It also helps determine the pipeline price markups for gas, inasmuch as those markups are functions of the volumetric capacities of the pipelines as well as of the mileages that gas must be transported across the country.

In its complete form, the model can be used to determine wholesale deliveries for each region of the country. Then, since we have the forecast demands from the wholesale demand equations, we can forecast excess demand on a regional basis.

The Model's Equations

The equations of the model were estimated through the use of pooled cross-section and time-series data. In most cases a number of alternative forms were estimated for each equation. In some cases these alternative forms were derived from different assumptions in the specification process and thus differed considerably from each other. In other cases the forms differed only in lag structure or choice of exogenous variables such as wholesale gas and oil demand. In all cases the final equation form was chosen according to considerations of overall statistical fit.

Estimation of the model involved the use of different regional groupings and time bounds for different equations. Obviously regional groupings are different for field market and wholesale demand equations, but even within field markets, exploration and discovery equations use different regional groupings from those used in production equations. In pooling data we designate regions according to their homogeneity in certain characteristics, and the relevant characteristics depend on what it is that is being modeled by the particular equation. Since the relevant characteristics change, the regional groupings change. An equation describing exploratory well drilling can be estimated to cover all production districts (with the exception of offshore Louisiana), since heterogeneities in the structure of final sales are not relevant. Those heterogeneities are, however, relevant to an equation that describes production of gas out of reserves, so that different production equations were estimated to cover four separate groups of production districts. The regional breakdown in wholesale demand is based on a similar criterion; separate equations were estimated for five separate "market" regions across the United States, each of which is roughly homogeneous.

The time bounds used in the regressions also differ for different equations. In part, this is because the time periods for which data are available differ for different parts of the model. In part it is because the time horizon should reflect a period of structural stability for the relationship described by the equation, and the period of structural stability may differ for different parts of the model. Moreover, we do not wish to include in the time horizon those years for which a particular equation is not identifiable. Thus, residential/commercial equations were estimated over the years from 1963 to 1971 while industrial demand equations for gas were estimated over the years from 1963 to 1969, because there was already excess demand for industrial gas by 1970, and the demand equations for industrial use would not be identifiable in 1970 and 1971.

The econometric estimation technique that was applied to the model is a variation of generalized least squares. This method, which is described elsewhere, is particularly applicable to estimation with pooled data.[3]

---

[3] See MacAvoy and Pindyck, *The Economics of the Natural Gas Shortage,* Chapter 4.

We will not attempt here to present the theoretical derivations of the structural equation forms used in the model, nor will we present the estimation results for alternative equation forms that were tested but rejected. That would involve a lengthy and technical discussion which would detract from the focus of the study. Besides, that material is presented elsewhere.[4] Instead we will simply list (and in some cases briefly explain) the final estimated equation forms that are used in the model. Each equation is presented with t-statistics for the coefficients in parentheses, as well as the R^2 (percent of explained variance) and standard error (standard deviation of the implicit error term on each equation).

New Discoveries. We begin with the equation for exploratory wells drilled (WXT). Economic incentives affect the number of exploratory wells drilled according to expected risk and expected return. This is done by calculating return as a function of current gas and oil prices, and also through average drilling costs and the interest rate (reflecting capital costs). Expected revenue per well is the sum of expected gas revenue and expected oil revenue, where each expected revenue is the product of current price, the estimated success ratio and the estimated size per successful well. Expected risk is an estimate of the variance of expected revenue. The estimated equation is:

$$
\begin{aligned}
WXT = {}& 796.16 - \underset{(-0.03)}{20.74 DD1} + \underset{(2.61)}{294.12 DD2} - \underset{(-0.02)}{1.49 DD3} \\
& {\scriptstyle(6.01)} \\
& + \underset{(0.53)}{234.29 DD4} + \underset{(7.074)}{0.00367} [S\hat{Z}G \cdot S\hat{R}G (PG_{-1} + PG_{-2} + PG_{-3})/3 \\
& + SZO \cdot SRO \cdot ((PO_{-1} + PO_{-2} + PO_{-3})/3] - \underset{(-2.49)}{(2.04 \times 10^{-8}} \\
& - \underset{(0.51)}{1.74 \times 10^{-8} DD1)} [S\hat{Z}G^2 \cdot S\hat{R}G^2 ((PG_{-1} + PG_{-2} + PG_{-3})/3)^2 \\
& + \frac{\sigma_0{}^2}{\sigma_G{}^2} \cdot S\hat{Z}O^2 \cdot S\hat{R}O^2 \cdot ((PO_{-1} + PO_{-2} + PO_{-3})/3)^2] \\
& - \underset{(-1.36)}{0.00204 ATCM} - \underset{(-5.85)}{64.15 INTA} \\
& R^2 = 0.81 \qquad S.E. = 1.781
\end{aligned}
\tag{1}
$$

where $S\hat{Z}G$, $S\hat{R}G$, $S\hat{Z}O$, and $S\hat{R}O$ are the estimated average size of gas find, the gas success ratio, the average size of oil find, and the oil success ratio respectively, PG and PO are new contract prices for gas

---

[4] Ibid., Chapters 3 and 4.

and oil, ATCM is a measure of drilling costs, INTA is an interest rate, and DD1, DD2, et cetera, are regional dummy variables. The fraction

$$\frac{\sigma_O^2}{\sigma_G^2} = \frac{(\text{S.E. of } SZO \text{ regression})^2 / (\text{Average number of successful gas wells})}{(\text{S.E. of } SZG \text{ regression})^2 / (\text{Average number of successful oil wells})}$$

$$= \frac{(5.46)^2}{(3.52)^2} \cdot \frac{1}{2.38} = 1.01$$

Following this, we estimate equations for the *size of gas discoveries (SZG)* and *size of oil discoveries (SZO)*:

Gas:

$$\frac{1}{WXG_{REG}} \log\left(\frac{SZG}{SZG_{REF}}\right)$$

$$= -0.0717 + 0.02687DD1 + 0.0638DD2 + 0.03825DD3$$
$$(-1.21) \quad (1.92) \quad\quad (1.53) \quad\quad\quad (0.0255)$$

$$+ 0.1146DEPG_{-1} + 0.00285\,((PG_{-1} + PG_{-2} + PG_{-3})/3)$$
$$(1.60) \quad\quad\quad\quad (1.21)$$

$$- 0.0241((PO_{-1} + PO_{-2} + PO_{-3})/3)$$
$$(-0.95)$$

$$R^2 = 0.95 \quad\quad S.E. = 3.519$$

(2)

where DEPG is an index of depletion of the natural gas resource base, and

SZG_{REF} = size of gas discoveries in the reference period immediately preceding the current period

$\quad\quad = (SZG_{-1} + SZG_{-2} + SZG_{-3})/3$

WXG_{REF} = index of number of successful gas wells completed in the reference period immediately preceding the current period

$\quad\quad = (WXG_{-1} + 2WXG_{-2} + WXG_{-3})/40$

Oil:

$$\frac{1}{WXO_{REF}} \log\left(\frac{SZO}{SZO_{REF}}\right)$$

$$= -0.08228 + 0.02074DD1 + 0.00464DD2 + 0.00233DD3$$
$$(-1.10) \quad (1.22) \quad\quad (0.66) \quad\quad\quad (0.37)$$

$$+ 0.02820DEPO_{-1} - 0.00195((PG_{-1} + PG_{-2} + PG_{-3})/3)$$
$$(0.35) \quad\quad\quad\quad (-2.08)$$

$$+ 0.02932((PO_{-1} + PO_{-2} + PO_{-3})/3)$$
$$(2.37)$$

$$R^2 = 0.84 \quad\quad S.E. = 5.46$$

(3)

where *DEPO* is an index of depletion of the oil resource base, and

SZO_{REF} = size of oil discoveries in the reference period immediately preceding the current period

   = $(SZO_{-1} + SZO_{-2} + SZO_{-3})/3$

WXO_{REF} = index of number of successful oil wells completed in the district in the reference period immediately preceding the current period.

The determination of new discoveries of gas and oil is completed with equations for the *fraction of successful gas wells (SRG)* and the *fraction of successful oil wells (SRO)*:

Gas:

$$\log\left(\frac{SRG}{1-SRG}\right) = \log\left(\frac{SRG_{REF}}{1-SRG_{REF}}\right)$$

$+\ WXG_{REF}[-0.04653 - 0.02706DD1 - 0.02502DD2$
$\qquad\qquad (-0.902)\quad (-2.60)\qquad\qquad (-1.88)$
$-\ 0.02891DD3 - 0.00312((PG_{-1} + PG_{-2} + PG_{-3})/3)$
$\quad (-2.382)\qquad\quad (-2.21)$
$\qquad +\ 0.04384((PO_{-1} + PO_{-2} + PO_{-3})/3)]$
$\qquad\qquad (2.14)$ (4)

$$R^2 = 0.76 \qquad S.E. = 4.32$$

where

$$SRG_{REF} = ((SRG_{-1} + SRG_{-2} + SRG_{-3})/3)\,\frac{S\hat{Z}G}{S\hat{Z}G_{REF}}$$

Oil:

$$\log\left(\frac{SRO}{1-SRO}\right) = \log\left(\frac{SRO_{REF}}{1-SRO_{REF}}\right)$$

$+\ WXO_{REF}[0.05521 + 0.02815DD1 + 0.02571DD2 + 0.0138DD3$
$\qquad\qquad (0.98)\qquad (1.09)\qquad\qquad (0.73)\qquad\qquad (0.69)$
$\qquad +\ 0.00208((PG_{-1} + PG_{-2} + PG_{-3})/3)$
$\qquad\qquad (0.80)$
$\qquad -\ 0.0378((PO_{-1} + PO_{-2} + PO_{-3})/3)]$
$\qquad\qquad (-1.27)$ (5)

$$R^2 = .043 \qquad S.E. = 3.7$$

where

$$SRO_{REF} = ((SRO_{-1} + SRO_{-2} + SRO_{-3})/3)\,\frac{S\hat{Z}O}{S\hat{Z}O_{REF}}$$

These equations follow the theory fairly closely, and the signs of the coefficients are all consistent with our expectations. For example, in equation (1) expected return appears with a positive coefficient while expected risk, drilling costs, and the interest rate all appear with negative coefficients. The positive coefficients for the depletion variable in the size equations are also correct, because the variable decreases in size as depletion occurs. Finally, in both the size equations and success ratio equations the price coefficients for gas and oil prices appear with opposite signs, which is to be expected if there is indeed directionality in oil and gas drilling.

These equations provide us with an important empirical result. As field prices of natural gas increase, additional drilling is done on average on the *extensive* margin. The size of gas discoveries for each successful well increases, while the success ratio for gas wells decreases, indicating that additional drilling has been undertaken in regions with lower probabilities of success but higher sizes of finds. Changes in the prices of oil also result in additional drilling directed on the whole toward the extensive margin.

The results also shed some light on the question of whether there has been "directional drilling." Increases in the price of gas seem to result in an increase in the success ratio for oil wells, and a decrease in the size of oil discoveries. That is, as the profitability of gas rises relative to the profitability of oil, producers shift to more extensive exploration for gas and more intensive exploration for oil. This does not mean that oil discoveries go down; they may in fact increase since the total amount of drilling activity is increasing. Finally, an increase in the price of oil, while resulting in more oil discoveries, will also result in some additional gas discoveries, both because the total amount of drilling has increased and because associated gas is found with the oil.

Extensions and Revisions. There is little economic explanation for extensions and revisions. Extensions of both natural gas and oil (XG, XO) should depend on lagged discoveries (DG_{-1}, DO_{-1}) and the number of exploratory wells drilled in the previous year (WXT_{-1}). Revisions of natural gas and oil reserves (RG, RO) should depend on past year-end reserves (YG_{-1}, YO_{-1}), changes in production $(\Delta QG, \Delta QO)$, and the depletion index. Our estimated equations are

Natural Gas Extensions:

$$XG = -38213 + 1.1307 \times 10^6 DD1 + 1.9595 \times 10^6 DD2$$
$$(-0.34) \quad (2.72) \qquad\qquad (6.18)$$
$$+ \ 16080.9 DD3 + 0.2942 DG_{-1} + 440.2 WXT_{-1}$$
$$(0.11) \qquad\quad (2.38) \qquad\quad (2.17)$$
$$R^2 = 0.44 \qquad S.E. = 2.87 \times 10^5$$

(6)

Oil Extensions:

$$XO = 4096.0 + 1.7852 \times 10^5 DD1 + 44092.7DD2 - 5192.7DD3$$
$$(0.79) \quad (10.31) \qquad\qquad (3.06) \qquad\qquad (-0.81)$$
$$+ \; 0.0924DO_{-1} + 33.928WXT_{-1}$$
$$(0.93) \qquad\qquad (2.86) \qquad\qquad\qquad (7)$$
$$R^2 = 0.69 \qquad S.E. = 1.9 \times 10^4$$

Revisions of Natural Gas Reserves:

$$RG = -712950 + 0.02007YG_{-1} + 0.3142\Delta(QG_{-1})$$
$$(-2.42) \quad (3.21) \qquad\qquad (0.52)$$
$$+ \; 930610DEPG_{-1}$$
$$(2.07) \qquad\qquad\qquad\qquad (8)$$
$$R^2 = 0.14 \qquad S.E. = 5 \times 10^5$$

Revisions of Oil Reserves:

$$RO = -133450 + 0.0483YO_{-1} + 3.501\Delta(QO_{-1})$$
$$(-2.38) \quad (5.80) \qquad\qquad (2.92)$$
$$+ \; 188210DEPO_{-1}$$
$$(2.33) \qquad\qquad\qquad\qquad (9)$$
$$R^2 = 0.56 \qquad S.E. = 1.02 \times 10^5$$

Production of Gas. Equations for production out of reserves were estimated separately for four different regions in the country. Explanatory variables are year-end reserves (YG) and the average wellhead price (PW). The regional breakdown is as follows:

1. Permian (New Mexico South, Texas 7C, 8, 8A)
2. Gulf Coast and Mid-Continent (Kansas, Louisiana South onshore, Oklahoma, Texas 1, 2, 3, 4, 10)
3. Other Continental (Colorado plus Utah, Louisiana North, Missouri, Mississippi, New Mexico North, Pennsylvania, Texas 6, Texas 9, West Virginia plus Kentucky, Wyoming)
4. Louisiana South offshore

Regression results for the three continental production regions are shown below while the production equation for offshore Louisiana is included in the offshore "submodel":

Permian:

$$QG = -6447700. + 1856700. \log (PW) + 0.1226 \, YG_{t-2}$$
$$(-2.35) \qquad (1.67) \qquad\qquad\qquad (5.24) \qquad (10)$$
$$R^2 = 0.925 \qquad S.E. = 1.42 \times 10^5$$

179

Gulf Coast and Mid-Continent:

$$QG = -169420. + 5881360. \, LX + 340752.$$
$$(-0.352) \quad (6.95) \qquad\qquad (2.00)$$
$$\log(PW) + 0.02638 YG_{t-1}$$
$$(6.78)$$
$$\qquad\qquad\qquad\qquad\qquad (11)$$
$$R^2 = 0.906 \qquad S.E. = 0.727$$

Remaining Continental Production:

$$QG = -9424.0 + 23034 \log(PW) + 0.05999 YG_{t-1}$$
$$(-0.22) \quad (1.65) \qquad\qquad\qquad (29.23)$$
$$\qquad\qquad\qquad\qquad\qquad (12)$$
$$R^2 = 0.968 \qquad S.E. = 0.785$$

Offshore Reserves and Production. Seven behavioral equations were estimated for the offshore "submodel." Wildcat wells drilled (WWT) is related to total acreage leased (ACT) and the field prices of gas and oil (PG, PWO):

$$WWT_t = -4333.4 + 162.8 \log(ACT_t + ACT_{t-1})/2$$
$$(-6.9) \quad (9.9)$$
$$+ 323.0 \log(1210.0 \, PG_{t-1} + 106.4 \, PWO_{t-1})$$
$$(3.5)$$
$$\qquad\qquad\qquad\qquad\qquad (13)$$
$$R^2 = .944 \qquad S.E. = 23.0$$

Discoveries per well (DG/WWT) is related negatively, through a depletion effect, to the cumulative number of wells drilled in the past ($CWWT$) and to the gas and oil field prices:

$$DG_t/WWT_t = -2.0 \times 10^5 - 2092.1 \log(CWWT_{t-1})$$
$$(-3.6) \qquad (-3.8)$$
$$+ 20895.7 \log(68967 \, PG_t + 3.2 \times 10^5 \, PG_t/PWO_t)$$
$$(3.8)$$
$$\qquad\qquad\qquad\qquad\qquad (14)$$
$$R^2 = .813 \qquad S.E. = 3.63 \times 10^3$$

Extensions and revisions are explained by the number of field wells drilled (FWT) and the number of producing acres (ACP) in the previous year:

$$XRG_t = -1.66 \times 10^6 + 4515.9 \, FWT_t + 0.405 \, ACP_{t-1}$$
$$(-5.1) \qquad (7.5) \qquad\qquad (2.5)$$
$$\qquad\qquad\qquad\qquad\qquad (15)$$
$$R^2 = .942 \qquad S.E. = 5.0 \times 10^5$$

The equation describing field wells (all offshore wells except wildcats) is a linear relationship between that variable, the number of offshore drilling rigs (DRO) and the long-term interest rate (INT):

$$FWT_t = 113.6 + 8.3 \, DRO_t - 21.0 \, INT_t$$
$$(1.2) \quad (7.0) \qquad\quad (-1.5)$$
$$\qquad\qquad\qquad\qquad\qquad (16)$$
$$RSQ = .821 \qquad S.E. = 72.2$$

Production of gas out of reserves (QG) is explained by the average wellhead price of gas (PWG) and total reserves (YT).

$$QG_t = 3.4 \times 10^6 + 2.3 \times 10^6 \log (PWG_t) + 0.116\ YT_{t-3}$$
$$(4.5) \qquad (5.1) \qquad\qquad (32.2)$$
$$R^2 = .992 \qquad S.E. = 9.0 \times 10^4 \tag{17}$$

Forfeited acreage $(ACRD)$ is explained by the amount of acreage leased (ACR) five years previously and an average of the acreage under supervision (ACT) five and six years previously:

$$ACRD_t = -1.26 \times 10^5 + 0.5\ ACR_{t-5} + .1\ ((ACT_{t-5}$$
$$(-2.3) \qquad (4.7) \qquad (4.7)$$
$$+\ ACT_{t-6})/2) \tag{18}$$
$$R^2 = .853 \qquad S.E. = 1.3 \times 10^5$$

Finally, new producing acreage $(ACPN)$ is explained by the amount of nonproducing acreage (ACN) one and two years previously, the amount of new discoveries (DG) in the previous year, and the cumulative number of acres leased $(CACR)$ since 1954:

$$ACPN_t = 27923 + 0.02ACN_{t-2} + .28DG_{t-1}\ (ACN_{t-1}/CACR_t)$$
$$(1.8) \qquad (1.9) \qquad (4.4)$$
$$R^2 = .92 \qquad S.E. = 3.2 \times 10^4 \tag{19}$$

Pipeline Price Markup. Economic and regulatory conditions lead us to expect that the pipeline price markup to wholesale buyers $(MARKUP)$ will depend on mileage (M), volumetric capacity of the pipeline (V), and an interest rate $(INTA)$. State dummy variables were also included in the final regression equation:

$$MARKUP = 9.528 + 0.00773M - 3.306 \times 10^{-4}V$$
$$(14.43) \quad (17.15) \qquad (-14.93)$$
$$+\ 1.109INTA_{-2} + 8.363NV + 7.394UT$$
$$(10.9) \qquad\quad (13.0) \qquad (4.61)$$
$$-\ 9.64CA + 7.384OH - 6.365WY + 4.013WV$$
$$(-9.28) \quad (5.80) \qquad (-8.34) \qquad (4.79)$$
$$-\ 5.475CO - 3.153IL + 5.476WI - 3.932FL$$
$$(-7.05) \quad (-7.27) \quad (6.04) \qquad (-3.12) \tag{20}$$
$$R^2 = 0.960 \qquad S.E. = 0.516$$

Wholesale Demand for Gas. The structural equations for wholesale demand for gas, whether residential, commercial, or industrial, explain the level of "new" demand, δQ, defined as

$$\delta Q_t = \Delta Q_t + rQ_{t-1} \tag{21}$$

where r is a depreciation rate for gas-burning appliances (estimated to be .07). Explanatory variables include the wholesale price of gas (PGW), the wholesale price of oil ($PFOIL$), the price of alternative fuels ($PALT$), population (NN), income (YY), capital investment (CAP), and value added in manufacturing (VAM). Two demand equations—one for residential/commercial demand ($TRCS$), and one for industrial demand ($TINS$)—were estimated for each of the five wholesale regions of the country. Dummy variables were used selectively; in the North Central region, for example, dummy variables were used for states such as Illinois, Iowa and Wisconsin since these states use natural gas to generate electricity which is transported to neighboring states for final consumption. The final regression equations are shown below:

Residential and Commercial Demand for Gas:

Northeast:

$$\delta TRCS = 13485 - 719.67PGW_{-1} + 1343.1PFOIL_{-1}$$
$$(0.89) \quad (-3.54) \qquad (1.36)$$
$$+ 42.85\delta NN$$
$$(8.77)$$
$$R^2 = 0.610 \qquad S.E. = 0.762$$

(22)

North Central:

$$\delta TRCS = 27968 - 1702.4PGW_{-1} + 90442PALT_{-1}$$
$$(1.94) \quad (-3.25) \qquad (3.27)$$
$$+ 60.30\delta NN + 38998IL + 8832.0IO + 10505WI$$
$$(6.57) \qquad (3.48) \qquad (2.69) \qquad (2.55)$$
$$R^2 = 0.409 \qquad S.E. = 0.690$$

(23)

Southeast:

$$\delta TRCS = 11642 - 790.4PGW_{-1} + 1918.6PFOIL$$
$$(0.74) \quad (-1.81) \qquad (1.80)$$
$$+ 1.240\delta YY - 5469.7FL$$
$$(1.03) \qquad (-2.06)$$
$$+ 7272.6GA + 7961.8KY - 4077.9SC$$
$$(3.21) \qquad (2.74) \qquad (-2.51)$$
$$R^2 = 0.394 \qquad S.E. = 0.649$$

(24)

South Central:

$$\delta TRCS = 42648 - 2355.0PGW_{-1} + 2912.0PFOIL_{-1}$$
$$(1.23) \quad (-3.48) \qquad (1.04)$$
$$R^2 = 0.158 \qquad S.E. = 0.819$$

(25)

West:

$$\delta TRCS = 5804.0 - 313.8PGW_{-1} + 593.4PFOIL_{-1} + 21.30\delta NN$$
$$(1.47) \quad (-6.51) \quad\quad (2.13) \quad\quad\quad (7.97)$$
$$+ 45642CA + 3077.0NV$$
$$(6.17) \quad\quad (4.36)$$
$$R^2 = 0.565 \quad\quad S.E. = 0.709 \tag{26}$$

Industrial Demand for Gas:

Northeast:

$$\delta TINS = 25092 - 589.2PGW + 25519PALT + 6.534CAP_{-1}$$
$$(3.32) \quad (-3.20) \quad\quad (1.37) \quad\quad\quad (1.85)$$
$$+ 35061\,OH + 23378\,PA$$
$$(6.16) \quad\quad (3.16)$$
$$R^2 = 0.570 \quad\quad S.E. = 0.467 \tag{27}$$

North Central:

$$\delta TINS = 11099 - 937.0PGW + 64174PALT + 2.818VAM$$
$$(0.629) \quad (-1.42) \quad\quad (1.23) \quad\quad\quad (6.85)$$
$$+ 11243IL - 5938.0IN + 1183.0IO + 86840MN + 9456.0WI$$
$$(0.77) \quad (-1.10) \quad (3.14) \quad\quad (1.69) \quad\quad (1.99)$$
$$R^2 = 0.760 \quad\quad S.E. = 0.461 \tag{28}$$

Southeast:

$$\delta TINS = 65234 - 2145.0PGW + 97293PALT + 14.37CAP_{-1}$$
$$(4.53) \quad (-4.70) \quad\quad (5.45) \quad\quad\quad (2.51)$$
$$- 16681NC - 17735SC$$
$$(-9.28) \quad (-5.96)$$
$$R^2 = 0.897 \quad\quad S.E. = 0.460 \tag{29}$$

South Central:

$$\delta TINS = 73360 - 5642.0PGW + 191595POIL$$
$$(1.52) \quad (-2.85) \quad\quad (2.16)$$
$$+ 158.7CAP_{-1} + 56895LA$$
$$(5.51) \quad\quad\quad (3.08)$$
$$R^2 = 0.649 \quad\quad S.E. = 0.507 \tag{30}$$

West:

$$\delta TINS = 9361.0 - 465.4PGW + 51805PCOAL$$
$$(4.00) \quad (-4.22) \quad\quad (3.76)$$
$$+ 16.99CAP_{-1} + 108575CA$$
$$(3.21) \quad\quad\quad (8.08)$$
$$R^2 = 0.513 \quad\quad S.E. = 0.459 \tag{31}$$

Lease and plant fuel demand (FS) must still be accounted for. This is the demand for gas as an energy source for extracting and pressurizing gas at the field site, and it is largely a function of the total quantity of gas produced. The equation for this demand is estimated by a pooling of data over the years 1968 to 1972 for all gas-producing states, and the use of a dummy variable for the state of Texas to account for the fact that Texas has a larger fraction of older fields that probably require more than the average amount of extraction fuel in their operations. The resulting equation is

$$FS = 1525.0 + 0.0434QG + 0.04993TX \cdot QG \qquad (32)$$
$$\quad\;\; (1.99) \quad\; (15.14) \qquad\quad (8.18)$$
$$R^2 = 0.847 \qquad S.E. = 0.538$$

Wholesale Demand for Fuel Oil. Oil demand is modeled for the residential/commercial and industrial sectors where oil can be used as a substitute for natural gas. Within the residential/commercial market, No. 2 distillate home heating oil (QO) is the major competitor with natural gas, while in the industrial market, No. 6 residual fuel oil (RSID) is the major competitor with natural gas. The oil demand equations should be compatible with the equations for gas demand, and the structural equations used were therefore of the same form as the structural equations for gas:

Residential/Commercial Demand for Oil:

Northeast:
$$\delta QO = -5829.8 + 237.2PGW_{-1} - 364.3PFOIL_{-1} + 0.5372\delta YY$$
$$\quad\quad (-0.6843)\,(1.90) \qquad\quad (-1.13) \qquad\qquad (8.64)$$
$$\quad\; -375.3TDUM(1970) + 3969.9NEW + 2497.1NJ$$
$$\quad\quad (-0.83) \qquad\qquad\quad (2.06) \qquad\quad (8.52) \qquad\quad (33)$$
$$R^2 = 0.88 \qquad S.E. = 0.52$$

North Central:
$$\delta QO = -1695.0 + 92.52PGW_{-1} - 148.2PFOIL_{-1} + 0.4706\delta YY$$
$$\quad\quad (-2.00)\;\;(4.58) \qquad\quad (-1.78) \qquad\qquad (10.06)$$
$$R^2 = 0.34 \qquad S.E. = 0.67 \qquad\qquad\qquad\qquad (34)$$

Southeast and South Central and West ("South"):
$$\delta QO = -152.8 + 15.18PGW_{-1} - 11.27PFOIL_{-1}$$
$$\quad\quad (-0.89)\;(5.11) \qquad\quad (-0.60)$$
$$\quad\; -221.1AZ + 356.6SC - 177.3NM$$
$$\quad\quad (-4.09) \quad\;\; (1.22) \qquad (-2.97) \qquad\qquad (35)$$
$$R^2 = 0.18 \qquad S.E. = 0.71$$

Industrial Demand for Oil:

Northeast:

$$\delta RSID = -23405 + 781.8 PGW_{-1} - 10498 POIL_{-1}$$
$$(-2.70) \quad (4.45) \qquad\qquad (-3.03)$$

$$+ 0.4002 \delta YY$$
$$(1.47)$$

$$R^2 = 0.45 \qquad S.E. = 0.90$$

(36)

North Central:

$$\delta RSID = -634.9 - 502.2 POIL_{-1} + 0.65888 YY + 142.1 IO$$
$$(-2.06) \quad (-1.48) \qquad\qquad (6.97) \qquad\quad (1.22)$$

$$+ 512.3 NB + 891.8 SD + 336.5 IN$$
$$(2.66) \qquad (4.71) \qquad (0.72)$$

$$R^2 = 0.51 \qquad S.E. = 0.65$$

(37)

Southeast and South Central and West ("South"):

$$\delta RSID = -168.5 + 11.49 PGW_{-1} - 413.2 POIL_{-1}$$
$$(-1.21) \quad (2.78) \qquad\qquad (-3.58)$$

$$+ 0.67228 VAM + 84.77.0 FL$$
$$(6.82) \qquad\qquad (1.41)$$

$$+ 4932.0 CA + 321.0 WY + 1352.0 LA$$
$$(2.96) \qquad\quad (2.18) \qquad\quad (3.25)$$

$$R^2 = 0.19 \qquad S.E. = 0.57$$

(38)

Interregional Flows of Gas. Interstate gas production is allocated from eight producing regions to forty demand regions through a set of static input-output coefficients f_{ij} and g_{ij} which determine, respectively, the fraction of state i's gas which comes from supply region j, and the fraction of district j's production which is supplied to state i. The only further allocation is between intrastate and interstate markets; this allocation is made through a price-dependent distribution equation. The input-output coefficients were calculated from data for 1971. They are shown in Table A-1 for the eight producing regions and the five aggregated demand regions.

The fraction of gas allocated to intrastate sales in gas-producing states (PCT) is a function of the ratio of the intrastate and interstate prices, P_{in}/P_{out}. A linear regression equation was estimated for two regions: the first over the Midcontinent, Permian, Mid-Texas, and Rocky Mountain production regions (but including regional intercept

Table A-1

U.S. NATURAL GAS FLOWS FOR 1971, BY REGION

Region	Producing Area [a]								Regional Total [b]
	Midcontinent	Permian	Mid-Texas	Gulf	Rocky Mountain	Canada	California	Appalachian	
Northeast	151 / .039 .040	0 / .000 .000	0 / .000 .000	3391 / .867 .292	0 / .000 .000	0 / .000 .000	0 / .000 .000	369 / .094 1.000	3911 / .186
North Central	1691 / .404 .447	457 / .109 .150	56 / .013 .143	1856 / .443 .160	80 / .019 .133	45 / .011 .072	0 / .000 .000	0 / .000 .000	4185 / .199
Southeast	0 / .000 .000	0 / .000 .000	0 / .000 .000	1382 / 1.000 .119	0 / .000 .000	0 / .000 .000	0 / .000 .000	0 / .000 .000	1382 / .066
South Central	1725 / .217 .456	900 / .113 .294	338 / .042 .857	4990 / .628 .429	0 / .000 .000	0 / .000 .000	0 / .000 .000	0 / .000 .000	7952 / .378
West	218 / .062 .057	1694 / .480 .555	0 / .000 .000	0 / .000 .000	467 / .132 .774	580 / .164 .928	572 / .162 1.000	0 / .000 .000	3529 / .168
Producing Area Total [b]	3785 / .180	3050 / .145	394 / .019	11619 / .553	603 / .029	625 / .030	572 / .027	369 / .018	21016

a Format is $\begin{bmatrix} \text{Quantity} & \\ f_{ij} & g_{ij} \end{bmatrix}$

All volumes 10^9 cubic feet.

b Numbers might not always add to totals due to rounding.

dummy variables), and the second over the Gulf region only. The estimation results are shown below:

$$PCT = -0.463 - 0.101DPERM - 0.252DTEX + 0.499DMTN$$
$$(-1.39)\ (-2.62) \qquad\quad (-4.10) \qquad\quad (11.61)$$
$$+\ 0.841(P_{in}/P_{out})$$
$$(2.50) \tag{39}$$
$$R^2 = .962$$

$$PCT = -0.202 + 0.507(P_{in}/P_{out})$$
$$(-0.49)\ (1.28) \tag{40}$$
$$R^2 = .290$$

Model Simulation. There are a total of only thirty-nine estimated behavioral equations, but a much larger number of equations must be solved simultaneously when the model is simulated. This larger number results from the regional structure of the model, and the fact that equations were estimated through the pooling of cross-section and time-series data. For example, although a single equation is given for the pipeline price markup, forty equations must be written to explain the wholesale price in each of forty demand regions when the model is simulated. Similarly, the nine equations for reserves become 180 equations that apply to twenty production districts; the six wholesale oil demand equations become eighty equations that determine (separately) residential/commercial and industrial oil demand in each of the forty demand regions, and so on.

In addition to this "multiplication" of the behavioral equations, all of the accounting identities in the model are "multiplied"; that is to say equations defining cumulative wells drilled, total reserves, and so on, must be written for each production district. Finally, the input-output matrix must be expressed as a set of simultaneous equations that determine gas flows from producing to consuming regions. As a result the model, in its simulation format, contains some 1,250 equations (or "statements") that must be solved simultaneously.

Evaluation of the Model

The statistical fit of the individual equations varies from block to block, but on the whole the fit is good, particularly when we consider the degree of structural and regional detail in the model. The equations for reserves have the weakest fit and contain a considerable amount of unexplained variance, reflecting stochastic elements in the discovery process that do not conform to economic laws. The production, offshore, markup, and demand equations all fit the data well. The equations for reserves, besides having considerable unexplained variance, are also the most nonlinear part of the model, so that errors in these equations, as they are squared and multiplied, may become magnified during simulation of the model. Since it is the level of reserves rather than reserve additions that affects production in the model, errors in the equations for reserves should not accumulate across other blocks of equations.

The most important test of model performance is the historical simulation. By simulating the model over a period in the recent past and comparing the simulated with the actual historical values of the endogenous variables in the model, we can see how well the model reproduces the behavior of the industry. This will provide one measure of model validation. If, for example, the simulation shows no upward or downward bias in production over time, it might be expected that the model's predictions for future excess would show no bias when they are compared to actual values five years hence. On the other hand, any bias in the historical simulation might be expected to be repeated in forecasting.

The historical simulation was performed by the use of actual values for 1966–1972 for the exogenous variables and actual 1966 values for the endogenous variables to "start up" the model so it could be solved for the 1967–1972 values of the endogenous variables. The computed values are shown for the most important endogenous variables of the model in Tables A-2 through A-5. In addition to listing the simulated values, actual values, and errors for each variable, we indicate the mean and root-mean-square (RMS) simulation errors.

The simulated values for total reserves are somewhat high—by about 6 percent in 1970 and 9 percent in 1971—but the simulated values for production in 1971 and 1972 are almost exactly equal to the actual values. Although this is in part a result of the fact that the production model emphasizes variables other than reserves, in part it is a result of too-high predictions of reserves-to-production ratios.

It is not possible to say that policy analysis of the 1960s would have been much affected by upward bias in historical simulations of reserves, and downward bias in reserve-production ratios. Policy analysis is focused on gas production and demand, and the dependence of these on regulated prices. In evaluating the model we thus place greater emphasis on its ability to reproduce past behavior of production, demand, and prices.

As can be seen in Table A-4, gas production is simulated with an RMS error about 2 percent of the average actual value. Average well-

Table A–2

HISTORICAL SIMULATION OF GAS AND OIL ADDITIONS TO RESERVES

Year	Gas Additions to Reserves [a]			Oil Additions to Reserves [b]		
	(1) Simulated (Tcf)	(2) Actual (Tcf)	(3) Error (1) − (2)	(4) Simulated (billion bbls.)	(5) Actual (billion bbls.)	(6) Error (4) − (5)
1967	17.6	20.6	− 3.0	2.85	2.69	0.16
1968	19.2	11.6	7.6	2.27	2.11	0.16
1969	17.8	8.0	9.8	2.14	2.03	0.11
1970	15.1	11.0	4.1	1.87	2.76	− 0.89
1971	14.4	10.5	3.9	1.70	2.04	− 0.34
1972	15.3	8.8	6.5	1.53	1.35	0.18

a Mean Actual: 11.8; Mean Error: 4.8; RMS Error: 6.3.
b Mean Actual: 2.16; Mean Error: − 0.10; RMS Error: 0.41.

Table A–3

HISTORICAL SIMULATION OF GAS AND OIL RESERVES

Year	Gas Reserves [a]			Oil Reserves [b]		
	(1) Simulated (Tcf)	(2) Actual (Tcf)	(3) Error (1) − (2)	(4) Simulated (billion bbls.)	(5) Actual (billion bbls.)	(6) Error (4) − (5)
1967	285	289	− 4	29.5	24.0	5.5
1968	285	282	3	29.2	28.4	0.8
1969	282	269	13	28.9	27.5	1.4
1970	276	259	17	28.3	27.2	1.1
1971	269	246	23	27.7	26.3	1.4
1972	261	234	27	26.9	24.6	2.3

a Mean Actual: 263; Mean Error: 13; RMS Error: 17.
b Mean Actual: 26.3; Mean Error: 2.1; RMS Error: 2.6.

Table A-4

HISTORICAL SIMULATION OF U.S. GAS PRODUCTION, AVERAGE WELLHEAD PRICE, AND AVERAGE WHOLESALE PRICE

Year	Production[a]			Average Wellhead Price[b]			Average Wholesale Price[c]		
	(1) Simulated (Tcf)	(2) Actual (Tcf)	(3) Error (1) − (2)	(4) Simulated (¢/Mcf)	(5) Actual (¢/Mcf)	(6) Error (4) − (5)	(7) Simulated (¢/Mcf)	(8) Actual (¢/Mcf)	(9) Error (7) − (8)
1967	18.9	18.9	0.0	17.3	17.3	0.0	30.7	30.7	0.0
1968	20.1	19.9	0.2	17.4	17.5	−0.1	31.3	30.7	0.6
1969	20.9	21.3	−0.4	17.8	17.9	−0.1	31.8	31.5	0.3
1970	21.8	22.6	−0.8	18.5	18.3	0.2	33.2	33.1	0.1
1971	22.8	22.8	0.0	19.7	19.5	0.2	35.3	37.4	−2.1
1972	23.6	23.3	0.3	d	d	d	d	d	d

a Mean Actual: 21.5; Mean Error: 0.1; RMS Error: 0.4.
b Mean Actual: 18.1; Mean Error: 0.05; RMS Error: 0.15.
c Mean Actual: 32.7; Mean Error: −0.19; RMS Error: 0.95.
d Data not available for 1972.

Table A–5

HISTORICAL SIMULATION OF NATIONAL GAS DEMAND

	Residential and Commercial Demand [a]			Industrial Demand [b]		
Year	(1) Simulated (Tcf)	(2) Actual (Tcf)	(3) Demand Error (1) − (2)	(4) Simulated (Tcf)	(5) Actual (Tcf)	(6) Demand Error (4) − (5)
1967	6.57	6.67	− 0.10	11.02	11.02	0.00
1968	6.81	7.29	− 0.48	11.68	11.75	− 0.07
1969	7.05	7.71	− 0.66	12.17	12.51	− 0.34
1970	7.24	8.01	− 0.77	12.69	13.34	− 0.65
1971	7.45	8.05	− 0.60	13.22	12.98	0.24

[a] Mean Actual: 7.55; Mean Error: − 0.52; RMS Error: 0.57.
[b] Mean Actual: 12.32; Mean Error: − 0.16; RMS Error: 0.35.

head and wholesale prices are simulated with RMS errors that are respectively 1 percent and 3 percent of average values, so that the field price "roll-in" mechanism is being accurately represented, as is the price markup charged by pipeline companies.

Simulated values for the demand for gas in all regions are close to the actual values, with average RMS errors that range from 1 percent to 6 percent. The larger errors occur in the South Central region, which is not surprising when we consider the poor statistical fits of the demand equations estimated for that region.

In summary, the historical simulation shows a small upward bias in the prediction of reserve levels, but this bias is counterbalanced by an over-prediction of the reserve-production ratio, so that there is no net bias in predictions of natural gas supply. This would suggest that our policy analyses and estimates of future gas shortages are, if anything, somewhat conservative.

**PERFORMANCE OF THE
FEDERAL ENERGY OFFICE**
Richard B. Mancke

PERFORMANCE OF THE
FEDERAL ENERGY OFFICE
Richard B. Mancke

Introduction

Roughly 17 percent of the oil supplies for the United States were
coming from Arab sources in late October 1973, when full-scale
warfare again erupted on Israel's Egyptian and Syrian borders.
Seeking to aid their Arab brethren, members of the Organization
of Arab Petroleum Exporting Countries (OAPEC) unanimously agreed
to reduce sharply—and, in the case of the United States and the
Netherlands, eliminate totally—oil exports to countries that failed to
adopt a "pro-Arab" foreign policy.[1] Because there were no substitutes
for Arab oil readily available, the shortages precipitated by these
actions threatened economic crisis.[2] In response, President Nixon

---

Discussions with Edward J. Mitchell, director of the AEI National Energy Project,
and the comments and criticisms of three referees have helped to clarify several
issues addressed in this paper. Responsibility for all conclusions remains the
author's.

[1] OAPEC is composed of the Arab members of the Organization of Petroleum
Exporting Countries (OPEC), which embraces all the major oil-exporting countries except Canada. Members of the OAPEC subgroup accounted for roughly
60 percent of OPEC's sales immediately before the start of the Arab embargo.
The OAPEC members never explicitly defined a "pro-Arab" foreign policy.
Their decision to embargo all sales to the United States and the Netherlands was
apparently premised on the belief that these two countries were Israel's strongest
supporters.

[2] Enormous geological variations distinguish oil and gas fields located in different
parts of the world. Huge regional differences in the likely size, incidence, and
productivity of petroleum sources explain the differences in the speed with which
previously unplanned expansions in a region's oil output can take place. Specifically, because huge but undeveloped reserves of low-cost oil have already been
discovered in such Persian Gulf countries as Iran, Kuwait, and Saudi Arabia,
their output can be expanded merely by drilling the necessary additional wells
and installing the appropriate surface gathering and storage facilities. Because of

195

issued an executive order establishing the Federal Energy Office (FEO), with instructions to initiate policies to alleviate the ill effects from domestic oil shortages. OAPEC officially ended its embargo of oil sales to the United States in mid-March 1974, and by mid-April U.S. petroleum supplies had been restored to adequate levels. The immediate crisis over, the FEO was replaced by the congressionally chartered Federal Energy Administration in early May.

The Federal Energy Office enjoyed a glamorous, hyperactive six-month existence. This paper constitutes a brief but comprehensive obituary evaluating its short lifetime. It deliberately departs from the customary eulogy in an effort to glean lessons for dealing with any future sudden interruptions in the supply of a key productive resource. Specifically, this evaluation concludes that, on balance, the measures taken by FEO actually exacerbated the nation's oil-supply problems. From this probe of the underlying causes of the FEO's policy failures, the most important lesson that emerges concerns planning. The oil shortages caused by the OAPEC embargo were severe enough that Americans somehow had to be persuaded to reduce their oil consumption. Even if the FEO had made no policy mistakes, cutbacks in oil consumption of the necessary magnitude inevitably would have been painful. Prior to the OAPEC embargo, the United States government had only the vaguest plans for dealing with such a contingency. Thus, both Congress and the White House panicked when it occurred. Good decision making is at best difficult in such a crisis atmosphere. It becomes nearly impossible when the organization responsible for making speedy decisions lacks adequate staff, administrative traditions, and a well-defined decision-making hierarchy, and is subject to political pressures from a plethora of interest groups. The blame for these deficiencies cannot be placed on the FEO. They were in fact inherent in its situation as a newly

---

the size and accessibility of these oil fields, only a one-year lag lies between a decision to expand future output from these sources and the production of significant quantities of that new output. In contrast, the location of large undeveloped oil fields in most non-Persian Gulf oil-producing countries is simply unknown. Hence, extensive exploration, which will take at least several years, is a necessary prerequisite for a large expansion of new oil supplies from these areas. In addition, because newly discovered oil fields in these areas will usually be much smaller, less productive, and less accessible than the new Persian Gulf fields, the time to develop them commercially is necessarily longer. For these reasons, the minimum lag between a decision to raise future crude-oil output appreciably above currently planned levels and the date when large amounts of this output will become available is now three to five years in areas like the U.S. Gulf of Mexico or the British North Sea and up to ten years in the Alaskan North Slope or northwestern Canada. Hence, worldwide oil shortages were an inevitable corollary of the OAPEC embargo.

established agency. It lies with Congress and, especially, the President, for failing to make adequate preparations to meet an oil embargo. Perhaps the government will have learned from the FEO's problems and formulate policies now for dealing with potential future interruptions of petroleum supplies.

1. Closing the Oil-Supply Gap

At birth, the most important problem facing the FEO was the need to prevent the United States from running out of oil. Realizing that substitutes for oil were not at hand, and not wishing to draw down inventories and bring on even worse shortages, the FEO responded with a conservation program initially designed to persuade, and if necessary to force, Americans to reduce their daily oil consumption by the entire 2.8 million barrels of crude oil or refined-product equivalents thought to come from Arab sources. The FEO pursued a two-pronged strategy. First, facing the possibility that other measures would fail, it started the extensive spadework for a rationing program that could force Americans to reduce their oil consumption by whatever amount might ultimately be necessary. Throughout December 1973 and early January 1974 this facet of the FEO's operations received the most public attention. It unleashed a flood of newspaper and television "special" reports detailing the difficulties commuters would suffer if rationing were imposed. Fortunately, the oil shortages were neither so prolonged nor so severe as to warrant rationing.

The second tactic employed by the FEO was to plead with consumers to accept voluntarily some hardship (in the form, for example, of lower temperatures in homes and offices and less pleasure driving) in order to reduce their petroleum demands. To put teeth into its pleas for "voluntary" conservation, the FEO persuaded Congress to force the states to return to daylight-saving time and (much more important) to cut maximum motor vehicle speeds.[3] It also relied on a mixed policy of persuasion and allocation regulations designed to result in sharp cutbacks in the quantities of oil products—especially gasoline—refiners could sell.

In late December, motorists in many urban areas began to endure hour-long waits to buy gasoline. Long lines at gas stations were to become the most visible and noxious symptom of the energy crisis in

---

[3] Year-round daylight-saving time directly conserved no appreciable amount of energy. However, it did serve to dramatize the severity of the energy crisis and thus probably encouraged greater voluntary conservation.

the United States.[4] In December the primary cause was panic buying. Many customers began "topping-out" their tanks with purchases of $1 or less because they feared more severe future shortages. As the lines began to lengthen, other motorists decided that they too should get into line. The panic was on.

The gas station lines were even longer and more widespread at the end of January and February 1974. By then, the reason was not topping-out, which most motorists realized was wasteful and time consuming, but the genuine shortages of gasoline at stations throughout the country. Misguidedly severe FEO policies imposed this painful, costly, and largely unnecessary symptom.

Table 1 presents monthly data on year-to-year changes in U.S. stocks of crude oil and refined products. These data establish that, on balance, the FEO's policies induced an overreaction to the Arab embargo. On the eve of the embargo (5 October 1973), although U.S. stocks of crude oil and all refined products except gasoline were slightly lower than the year before and most petroleum products were in tight supply,[5] no important sector of the economy was suffering from a severe shortage of petroleum products. Because U.S. petroleum consumption during the embargo averaged roughly 10 percent less than the year before, the FEO would not have been taking unnecessary risks if it had adopted measures that allocated petroleum products so that stocks always remained slightly below year-earlier levels.[6] Unfortunately, as Table 1 reveals, the FEO did not do this. Instead, by late April, when the embargo was lifted, stocks of every product except kerosene had registered significant improvement relative to the year before.

It is easy to calculate a rough quantitative estimate of the reduction in available petroleum supplies because higher stocks were accumulated. U.S. petroleum stocks totaled 848 million barrels at the onset of the OAPEC embargo, 27 million barrels, or 3 percent, below the year-earlier level.[7] However, by late April total stocks of

---

[4] See "FEO Seeks Relief on Crude Allocation," Oil and Gas Journal, 25 February 1974, p. 28.

[5] U.S. petroleum supplies had been tight throughout 1973. Prior to the Arab embargo too little refinery capacity was the cause of the supply stringency. For elaboration, see Richard B. Mancke, "Petroleum Conspiracy: A Costly Myth," Public Policy, Winter 1974, pp. 1–13.

[6] The use of year-to-year comparisons automatically takes account of the seasonal variations in inventories of most important petroleum products. To illustrate, oil companies typically build up large inventories of the distillate fuel oils used in space heating during the summer and draw them down during the winter.

[7] From the American Petroleum Institute's weekly refinery report, as reported in Oil and Gas Journal, 15 October 1973, pp. 180–81.

Table 1

YEAR-TO-YEAR CHANGES IN U.S. STOCKS OF CRUDE OIL AND REFINED PRODUCTS

(millions of barrels; percentage change in parentheses)

Period	Crude Oil (1)	Gasoline (2)	Jet Fuels (3)	Kerosene (4)	Distillate Fuel Oils (5)	Residual Fuel Oils (6)	Total Crude Oil and Products [a] (7)
Oct. 6, 1972 to Oct. 5, 1973	−10.80 (−4.2)	1.28 (0.6)	−5.95 (−19.7)	−0.73 (−3.3)	−0.29 (−0.1)	−7.90 (−12.3)	−26.87 (−3.1)
Nov. 3, 1972 to Nov. 2, 1973	−10.96 (−4.3)	2.92 (1.4)	−4.38 (−15.2)	1.86 (8.8)	6.81 (3.5)	−6.89 (−11.0)	−13.67 (−1.5)
Dec. 8, 1972 to Dec. 7, 1973	0.64 (0.2)	−6.72 (−3.1)	0.60 (2.2)	4.80 (24.1)	29.89 (16.8)	−0.83 (−1.5)	28.91 (3.4)
Jan. 12, 1973 to Jan. 11, 1974	1.23 (0.5)	−9.78 (−4.5)	3.35 (12.7)	4.20 (24.0)	44.66 (29.9)	−2.88 (−5.2)	43.69 (5.5)
Feb. 2, 1973 to Feb. 1, 1974	−4.96 (−2.1)	−3.83 (−1.7)	3.39 (13.4)	4.41 (27.5)	50.64 (38.4)	−2.85 (−5.8)	52.64 (6.8)
Mar. 2, 1973 to Mar. 1, 1974	0.89 (0.4)	9.79 (4.5)	4.42 (17.8)	2.16 (14.2)	36.54 (31.5)	−1.15 (−2.5)	58.22 (7.8)
Mar. 30, 1973 to Mar. 29, 1974	2.97 (1.2)	14.54 (6.8)	5.17 (19.6)	−1.21 (−6.9)	21.58 (19.5)	−1.47 (−3.2)	47.06 (6.2)
Apr. 27, 1973 to Apr. 26, 1974	7.39 (3.0)	20.48 (10.0)	4.30 (15.8)	−2.80 (−15.4)	18.36 (16.6)	1.76 (3.8)	51.85 (6.8)

[a] Includes aviation gas and unfinished oils, not shown separately.

Source: Raw data are from the American Petroleum Institute's weekly reports on stocks of crude oil and refined products as reported in the *Oil and Gas Journal*, October 1973–May 1974.

crude oil and refined products were up by nearly 7 percent, or about 52 million barrels, compared with a year earlier (see Table 1, column 7). This means that, precisely during the months of the Arab embargo, total U.S. petroleum inventories improved by about 80 million barrels when compared with the year-earlier date. The reduction in U.S. oil imports attributable to the embargo (assuming that they would have continued at October 1973 levels in its absence) was about 130 million barrels. However, because of the inventory build-up precipitated by the FEO's "successful" efforts to reduce the quantity of petroleum products available for sale, the effective short-fall suffered by American consumers was roughly 1.6 times that level—approximately 210 million barrels.

What might have happened if the Federal Energy Office had forced refiners to produce and offer for sale an additional amount of gasoline equivalent to the 80 million barrel net build-up of crude oil and refined product inventories that its actual policies fostered? According to Table 2, available U.S. gasoline supplies would have

Table 2

AVERAGE DAILY AVAILABLE SUPPLY, POTENTIAL SUPPLY, AND POTENTIAL DEMANDS OF GASOLINE IN THE UNITED STATES, JANUARY–APRIL 1974

(millions of barrels)

Month	Actual Available Supply[a]	Potential Available Supply[b]	Potential Demand Assuming No Embargo[c]	Excess of Potential Supply over Potential Demand
January	5.880	6.547	6.363	0.184
February	5.846	6.513	6.529	−0.016
March	6.178	6.845	6.633	0.212
April	6.484	7.151	7.027	0.124

[a] Assumed to be equal to the sum of (1) average daily gasoline production by U.S. refiners, (2) average daily gasoline imports, and (3) the net reduction in gasoline inventories.

[b] Assumes that petroleum inventories were not built up relative to the preceding year during the embargo, and that, instead, refiners were forced to produce an additional 80 million barrels of gasoline which they made available for sale in January–April 1974.

[c] Assumes no shortages and prices remaining at pre-embargo levels. Calculated as equal to gasoline consumption in the corresponding month of 1973 plus 5 percent, the amount by which gasoline consumption in the first nine months of 1973 exceeded that in the corresponding period of 1972.

Source: Compiled from the weekly refinery reports of the American Petroleum Institute as reported in the *Oil and Gas Journal*, January 1974–May 1974.

averaged nearly 11 percent higher during January–April 1974, when gasoline was in tightest supply, if the FEO had encouraged oil refiners to maximize gasoline supplies while holding inventories of all petroleum products at their year-earlier levels. This "no-risk" allocation strategy would have totally eliminated the gap between potential gasoline demand (estimated assuming no embargo) and available supplies. In other words, the long lines at gas stations were not neccessary.

Why did the Federal Energy Office overreact to the OAPEC embargo? A key reason was its focus on the wrong variable—the anticipated reduction in U.S. oil imports—rather than on the level of U.S. petroleum stocks. Its anticipations proved to be exaggerated for two reasons. First, during the embargo the daily level of U.S. petroleum imports averaged more than 1 million barrels higher than the 2.8 million barrel cutback initially predicted, primarily because the international oil companies undertook the massive task of redirecting the world oil trade. In order to circumvent OAPEC's announced intention to impose the brunt of the embargo on the Netherlands and the United States, these companies began shipping to this country large quantities of non-Arab crude oil that normally would have gone elsewhere.[8] Moreover, because U.S. oil companies offered higher prices for them, imports of refined products did not fall by the amount predicted. In fact, for the first time in recent memory, high prices even pulled some gasoline and kerosene from the Soviet Union to the United States.

In addition to overestimating the cut in U.S. oil imports, the FEO did not take into account the indirect oil savings from the voluntary reduction in U.S. demand for two substitutes, coal and natural gas. For reasons elaborated upon shortly, substitution of the "saved" coal and natural gas curtailed demand for both distillate and residual fuel oils, which in turn staunched the drain on U.S. petroleum stocks.

2. Allocation Problems

The FEO correctly realized that the American people would embrace its voluntary conservation measures only if its allocation of the costs of the oil crisis was demonstrably fair. Hence, besides making sure that the United States did not run out of oil, the FEO's major duty

---

[8] At the start of the embargo some OAPEC members (notably Libya) continued to ship some oil to the United States. Unfortunately, this information was leaked to the press by government officials, after which the flow of "hot" OAPEC oil dried up immediately. Source: interviews with former FEO officials.

was to develop and implement policies to spread the burdens of petroleum shortages in an efficient and equitable way.[9] Seeking to do this, the FEO introduced allocation measures designed to place a heavier burden on users thought to be better able to reduce their consumption without severe economic disruption (for example, most industries, but apparently not petrochemicals and trucking) or in some vague ethical sense less deserving (for example, motorists).[10] Unfortunately, even ignoring the complaints from each group that believed its share of the burden was unconscionably high, the FEO soon found that just and efficient allocation was no easy task. Four of its allocation problems are discussed below.

Allocation between Gasoline and Distillate Fuel Oil. Gasoline and distillate fuel oils are quantitatively the two most important refined-oil products. Most gasoline is used to power motor vehicles; most distillates are consumed either in industrial and home heating or in fueling diesel engines. U.S. gasoline consumption averaged 6.6 million barrels per day in 1973; the consumption of distillates averaged 3.2 million barrels.

Because, during winter, adequate home heating is obviously much more important to human life than most automobile travel, the FEO concluded that Americans would find it least disruptive to reduce their consumption of gasoline proportionately more than their consumption of distillate fuel oils. Hence, it repeatedly exhorted refiners to produce more distillate oils and less gasoline. Besides exhortation, it employed the price-setting powers delegated to it by the Cost of Living Council to skew allowable refined-product prices so that distillate sales were more profitable than gasoline sales. Table 1 confirms that by early December 1973 stocks of distillate fuel oils far exceeded year-earlier levels. But simultaneously, those notorious gasoline lines were beginning to form. The FEO had overestimated

---

[9] For reasons discussed below, the legislation authorizing petroleum allocation was actually written several months before the OAPEC embargo. Hence, a reading of the legislation does not suggest that the goal of allocation was to spread the burdens of the petroleum shortage in an efficient and "equitable" way. Nevertheless, after the embargo, this should have been the FEO's goal.

[10] No objective definition of an equitable distribution of the burdens of petroleum shortages is possible. Most individuals define as equitable all redistributions that benefit them. During the OAPEC embargo those interest groups with the most political clout tended to receive favored treatment. Thus, farmers and truckers were awarded higher allocations of petroleum products than less vocal consumers, and some refiners were subsidized by being granted the right to buy "cheap" crude oil from their competitors (of which more below). See "FEO Revises Allocation Rules Again," *Oil and Gas Journal*, 21 January 1974, p. 38.

the supply problems for distillate fuel oil and underestimated those for gasoline.

Even so, until late January 1974, the FEO continued to urge refiners to produce more distillates at the expense of gasoline, and until mid-February it manipulated price ceilings to achieve this end. The burgeoning distillate inventories—they had soared to more than 38 percent above year-earlier levels by early February—spurred by this policy are plainly illustrated in Table 1. If the FEO had instead adopted policies that required refiners to maintain distillate stocks at corresponding year-earlier levels, daily U.S. gasoline production could have averaged 403,000 barrels (or 6.5 percent) higher during the first four months of the OAPEC embargo (see Table 3).

Three factors explain why the FEO's emphasis on distillate fuel oils proved to be misplaced. First was a fortuitous warm winter in the more populous eastern half of the country. Second, in our car-dependent society, most motorists were unwilling to make the significant changes in life style that would have brought about immediate reductions in car miles traveled until they were forced to do so by "gasless" Sundays, alternate-day rationing, and the impossibility of

Table 3

AVERAGE DAILY U.S. PRODUCTION OF GASOLINE, ACTUAL AND POSSIBLE, OCTOBER 1973 THROUGH JANUARY 1974

(millions of barrels)

Month	Actual [a]	Possible [b]	Excess of Possible over Actual (percent)
October	6.551	6.794	3.7
November	6.395	7.055	10.3
December	6.080	6.502	6.9
January	5.883	6.168	4.8
Four-month average	6.227	6.630	6.5

[a] Given FEO policies.

[b] Calculated by assuming that without the special encouragement that distillate production received from FEO policies, U.S. refiners would have produced sufficient amounts of distillate fuel oils to maintain stocks at corresponding year-earlier levels, and that any crude oil made available as a result of this decision was refined into gasoline.

Source: Compiled from the American Petroleum Institute's weekly refinery reports as reported in the *Oil and Gas Journal*, October 1973–February 1974.

finding fuel. Even when they were willing, changing ingrained driving habits that resulted in high gas consumption required constant vigilance. In contrast, significant reductions in demands for distillate fuel oils followed directly from some extremely simple moves. Most obvious, in northern climes use of fuel oil for heating could be cut back 6 to 10 percent merely by turning down thermostats 6 degrees. Third, because Americans voluntarily reduced their demands for coal and natural gas (which together supply roughly 50 percent of total U.S. energy needs) by about 10 percent below predicted nonembargo levels, some industrial consumers who normally used distillate fuel oil could turn to these other fuels. To illustrate, in recent years U.S. supplies of natural gas have been inadequate to satisfy winter heating demands.[11] Therefore, many industrial, commercial, and institutional users buy natural gas on interruptible contracts and expect their supplies to be stopped during winter. When this happens, most do not shut down but, instead, begin burning other fuels, including distillate or residual fuel oils. The voluntary cutbacks by natural-gas users during winter 1973–74 reduced the number and duration of natural-gas interruptions, thus lightening demands for distillate fuels. Because most automobiles are powered by gasoline, no comparable reduction was experienced in gasoline demand.

Interregional Allocation of Gasoline. Some sections of the country are much more dependent on oil imports than others. On the eve of the OAPEC embargo, well over half of the Northeast's oil demands were being supplied from foreign sources other than Canada. In stark contrast, the Gulf Coast states and their immediate neighbors had access to domestic supplies sufficient to meet all their needs. Obviously, after the onset of the embargo, both efficiency and equity made it desirable to reallocate large quantities of oil from relatively oil-rich to relatively oil-poor regions.[12]

Gasoline was the petroleum product in tightest supply throughout the Arab embargo. In order to ensure that the available supplies would be distributed equitably around the country, the FEO issued

---

[11] Inadequate natural gas supplies are the direct result of wellhead price regulation of natural gas sold in interstate markets by the Federal Power Commission. Most oil economists agree that holding the price of natural gas below market-clearing levels is one of the most costly of U.S. energy policies. For elaboration see Edward Mitchell, *U.S. Energy Policy: A Primer* (Washington, D. C.: American Enterprise Institute, 1974), pp. 53–69.

[12] Congressional representatives of the oil-poor regions used every political resource at their command to force the FEO to get them a larger share of the total U.S. petroleum supplies.

regulations requiring that, after meeting certain priority needs (trucking and farming, for example), oil companies had to allocate their gasoline among their dealers according to sales in the corresponding month of 1972. (The reasons for basing allocations on 1972 sales will be discussed shortly.)

The FEO regulations did not, however, achieve equitable interstate distribution of gasoline supplies. As Table 4 shows, in February, when gasoline shortages were most severe, initial allocations for the states ranged from a low of 63 percent of projected needs in both New Hampshire and Virginia to a high of 122 percent of projected needs in Wyoming. States that produced large quantities of oil or bordered oil-exporting western Canada had the most gasoline so that most of their residents suffered no direct discomfort from the embargo. Hardest hit were five eastern states (New Hampshire, New Jersey, Vermont, Virginia, and West Virginia), whose initial allocations averaged only 66 percent of their projected needs. Even after these states were awarded emergency supplementary allocations in late February, their available supplies averaged only 73 percent of projected needs. Obviously, in these and similarly situated states, stringent belt-tightening was necessary to reduce gasoline consumption to the low level of available supplies. And even that was not enough; large areas of most of these states completely ran out of gasoline at the end of both January and February.

Transportation bottlenecks were probably the chief cause of the large interstate differences in gasoline supply: the network of petroleum-product pipelines in the United States did not have sufficient extra capacity to ship the necessary quantities of gasoline from relatively gasoline-rich to relatively gasoline-poor regions. Apart from this physical limitation, the allocation regulation itself helped to exaggerate shortages in three ways:

1. Basing allocations on 1972 sales disproportionately hurt fast-growing regions such as Arizona, Florida, and Nevada.[13]

2. In 1972 major oil companies (British Petroleum, Gulf, Phillips) began consolidating retailing operations by closing several

---

[13] The FEO allowed gas stations that desired more gasoline than they were allotted by the general allocation rule because of special circumstances (for example, a sharp jump in their sales volume had occurred since the 1972 base period) to file "Form 17s." Thousands were filed. Unfortunately, inadequate staffing prevented the FEO from processing most of them. Hence, few exceptions were granted prior to March. The FEO decided to honor all Form 17 requests in March. As a result, by April the interregional allocation program for gasoline stations had been effectively gutted. Since the gasoline shortage was over, this was a desirable result. Source: interviews with former FEO officials.

Table 4

FEBRUARY GASOLINE ALLOCATIONS, BY STATE

(millions of gallons)

State	Projected February Need	Initial February Supply	Supply as Percent of Need	Emergency February Allocation	Initial plus Emergency Allocation as Percent of Need
Wyoming	17.6	21.5	122	—	—
Louisiana	141.3	154.0	109	—	—
Kansas	99.0	106.9	108	—	—
Minnesota	159.9	164.7	103	—	—
Oklahoma	118.9	121.3	102	—	—
Texas	548.2	542.7	99	—	—
Hawaii	22.3	21.4	96	—	—
Arkansas	86.2	82.8	96	—	—
New Mexico	48.9	46.5	95	—	—
Colorado	105.4	99.1	94	—	—
Alaska	8.8	8.3	94	—	—
North Dakota	25.1	23.3	93	—	—
Idaho	32.5	29.9	92	—	—
Maine	37.5	34.1	91	3.4	100
Washington	123.1	112.0	91	—	—
Nebraska	66.8	59.5	91	—	—
Delaware	22.8	20.3	89	2.0	98
D.C.	18.7	16.6	89	1.7	98
Massachusetts	184.9	162.2	88	16.2	97
New York	465.1	409.3	88	40.9	97
Michigan	343.4	295.3	86	—	—
Utah	44.7	38.0	85	—	—
California	791.4	672.7	85	—	—
South Dakota	31.0	26.4	85	—	—
Ohio	397.9	319.1	84	—	—
Tennessee	176.2	148.0	84	14.8	92
Wisconsin	162.9	135.2	83	—	—
Montana	33.0	27.4	83	—	—
Kentucky	126.2	103.5	82	10.4	90
Rhode Island	35.7	29.3	82	1.9	87
Florida	362.0	293.2	81	17.6	86
Iowa	123.5	100.0	81	—	—
Mississippi	97.2	78.7	81	7.9	89
South Carolina	112.1	90.8	81	9.0	89
North Carolina	214.9	171.9	80	17.2	88
Indiana	210.6	166.4	79	16.6	87
Missouri	199.0	155.2	78	15.5	86
Connecticut	112.4	87.7	78	8.8	86
Illinois	407.3	313.6	77	31.4	85
Pennsylvania	401.7	305.3	76	30.5	84
Maryland	146.8	110.1	75	11.0	82

Oregon	91.5	67.7	74	6.8	81
Alabama	143.4	104.7	73	10.5	80
Arizona	101.5	73.1	72	7.3	79
Georgia	242.9	174.9	72	—	—
Nevada	27.4	19.2	70	1.9	77
New Jersey	307.8	212.4	69	21.2	76
Vermont	19.6	13.5	69	1.4	76
West Virginia	58.6	39.3	67	3.9	74
New Hampshire	31.1	19.6	63	2.0	69
Virginia	233.0	146.8	63	14.7	69

Source: *National Journal Reports*, 9 March 1974. From data used by the Federal Energy Office.

thousand stations in regions of the country where inadequate or obsolete refining capacity made retailing relatively less profitable. Normally these oil companies might have been expected to build new refineries to supply these markets at less cost. However, because oil import quotas were still in effect, builders of new refineries had no guarantee of securing the necessary supplies of crude oil; prudence thus dictated that no new refineries be built.[14] Abandonment of gas stations was especially prevalent in the Southeast and Midwest. Since each oil company's available gasoline was to be allocated on the basis of its dealers' 1972 sales, these areas suffered a disproportionate fall in gasoline supplies.[15]

3. Like states, oil companies relied on imported oil in widely varying degree. Domestic crude-oil supplies of companies like Exxon, Getty, Gulf, and Marathon were sufficient to supply most of their refineries' needs. In contrast, the embargo led to proportionately larger falls in output for companies like Ashland and Sohio. Those states (chiefly on the East Coast) with heavy concentrations of stations supplied by these refineries thus suffered more than others.

In addition to failing to correct the sharp inequities among states, the FEO's program also led to misallocation of gasoline supplies within states. The long lines that were commonplace in most major eastern urban centers from late December 1973 through February 1974 were unknown in many rural and vacation areas located in the same states. Urban areas suffered most because throughout the

---

[14] This disincentive was eliminated in May 1973, when the President issued an executive order abolishing the United States's Mandatory Oil Import Quota Program. By this time, several oil companies had already closed down retailing operations in large regions of the country.

[15] Some dealers who had gone out of business after 1972 found that it was profitable to reopen during the OAPEC embargo. The allocation regulations required their former suppliers to resupply them. Source: interviews with former FEO officials.

embargo drivers tended to fill their tanks close to home or work. The sharp reductions in pleasure driving and weekend trips meant that far fewer fill-ups took place in outlying rural and vacation areas.

Despite the good intentions of the FEO program to allocate available gasoline supplies equitably among regions, it failed. Enormous interregional differences in gasoline supplies persisted throughout the embargo. A better policy would have allowed oil companies to charge slightly higher prices on sales to dealers in areas classified by the FEO as gasoline-short. Since the FEO's price controls on petroleum products did take account of interregional differences in gasoline production and delivery costs, allowing oil refineries to impose a surcharge of about 1¢ per gallon on sales in gasoline-short areas should have provided ample incentive for the elimination of the costly regional shortages.

Intertemporal Allocation of Gasoline. One of the most frustrating problems posed by the Arab embargo was the worsening of gasoline shortages near the end of the month. These intertemporal supply inequities created wasteful end-of-the-month transportation bottlenecks in most regions of the country. Paradoxically, these cyclical shortages arose largely from one of the FEO's pricing regulations: the decision to allow refiners and dealers to raise prices to offset higher costs only at the start of each month. With costs of gasoline production soaring, this rule gave refiners a strong incentive to withhold gasoline at the end of a month for sale at the beginning of the new month, when they could charge the new higher price.[16]

The gasoline shortages were especially severe at the end of February, when many eastern motorists found it impossible to purchase any gasoline.[17] The blame rests squarely on the FEO announcement in mid-February that gas stations would be allowed to raise their margins from 8¢ to 10¢ on each gallon sold after 1 March. A dealer's profit-maximizing response to such an announcement would be to lock up his station until March. Many did just that.

The American motorists' monthly cycle of relative feast followed by absolute famine could have been largely eliminated by allowing oil companies to pass through higher costs as they occurred and by allowing dealers to raise their margins on the date the rule change was announced.

---

[16] To illustrate, because of higher raw material costs, most refiners were allowed to raise their prices by about 4¢ per gallon on 1 March. Therefore, they held back on late February deliveries.

[17] Source: interviews with former FEO officials.

Interrefinery Allocation of Crude Oil. American oil companies depend on Arab crude in widely varying degree. Those that were most dependent, and therefore faced the severest shortages, persuaded Congress that this situation was not equitable. The Federal Energy Office was therefore instructed by Congress to establish a program requiring relatively crude-rich refiners to share supplies with their less fortunate competitors. To implement this directive, the FEO (as of 1 February 1974) ordered refiners with crude-oil supplies that exceeded the industry average to sell some of their "surplus" to crude-poor competitors. The maximum price a refiner could charge for its "surplus" was set equal to the weighted average of its total crude-oil costs from all sources. Because most price-controlled domestic crude cost several dollars less per barrel than foreign crude, crude-poor refiners like Ashland and Sohio found that they could reduce their costs by curtailing their own imports of non-Arab oil at $10.00-plus per barrel and, instead, buying "surplus" from crude-rich refiners like Exxon and Gulf for about $7.00. For the same reason, crude-rich refiners realized they would lose several dollars on every barrel of oil imported and then sold at the maximum average price. The regulation thus had the perverse effect of encouraging both crude-short and crude-rich refiners to cut back their oil imports.

To soften the impact on crude-rich refiners who were forced to sell crude to others, the FEO issued three regulations. First, the "84¢ provision" allowed them to raise their refined-product prices enough to capture an additional 84¢ of revenue for each barrel they sold. Second, they could add a 6 percent selling fee to their average crude-oil costs before making any sales to their crude-short competitors. Third, they could raise their prices for petroleum products by an amount equal to the reduction in their profits caused by the forced sale.[18] Taken together, these three supplementary regulations allowed crude-rich refiners to more than recover their total "losses" (that is, their potential but unrealized profits) due to forced sales. As a result, imports did not decline appreciably because of the FEO's interrefinery allocation regulations. In September 1974, John Sawhill, then head of the Federal Energy Administration, accused the crude-rich refiners that took advantage of all three supplementary regulations of "double-dipping" because they recovered more than 100 percent of the reduction in their profits due to the forced sales of their crude oil and in

---

[18] This clause read: "Refineries required to sell crude oil under this program shall be allowed to increase their product prices to reflect increased crude oil cost of all available crude prior to making crude oil sales to comply with this program." Reprinted in "Double-Dipping Oil Companies?" *Wall Street Journal*, 17 September 1974, p. 22.

the process overcharged consumers by $100 million to $300 million.[19] Sawhill's criticism was too strong. First of all, the FEO staff became aware of the possibility of double-dipping only when top officials of several major oil companies told them about it.[20] Second, many oil companies refrained from exercising their legal right to double-dip, so that the "overcharge" was probably far less than Sawhill's initial estimate.[21] Third, the possibility of double-dipping arose only because the FEO established a cumbersome, poorly designed interrefinery allocation program that required complicated special exemptions to forestall severe disincentives to import oil.

Who Was Responsible for the Allocation Failures? The policies of the FEO did not achieve a just and efficient petroleum allocation among products, regions, refiners, or time periods. Many have charged the oil companies with the responsibility for these failures. After all, their indictment reads, if the companies had not reached greedily for higher profits, the observed misallocation of petroleum supplies need not have been so severe. As the foregoing discussion amply documents, however, if the oil companies were at fault, it was because they responded in accordance with the price controls, the regulatory constraints, and the repeated public pleas of the FEO. Indeed, they would have deserved the strongest public censure if they had done otherwise during a period of national economic crisis.

At least some of the responsibility for the FEO's misguided allocation measures rests with the Congress whose Emergency Petroleum Allocation Act called for a comprehensive allocation program within thirty days of its passage. Though passed in November 1973, after the OAPEC embargo was imposed, this act had been drafted six months earlier. At that time Congress perceived two chief energy problems: (1) inadequate supplies of crude oil for independent refiners, who bought most of their crude oil inputs, and (2) inadequate supplies of petroleum products for independent dealers, who since early 1973, had been cut off by refiners suffering from a shortage of refinery capacity. In order to satisfy the intent of Congress to aid the independent dealers and its instructions to base allocations on more "normal" 1972 conditions, the FEO geared its gasoline allocation

---

[19] See "Allocation Bungle Triggers FEA Probe," *Oil and Gas Journal*, 23 September 1974, p. 112.

[20] Source: interviews with former FEO officials and "FEA Bungling," *Wall Street Journal*, 8 October 1974, p. 28.

[21] A subsequent estimate of the actual overcharge was $40 million. See "FEA Bans Costs Pass-through via 'Double Dip,'" *Oil and Gas Journal*, 7 October 1974, p. 54.

measures to customer-supplier relationships in that year. Unfortunately, these had changed drastically by early 1974 because many independents, unable to get adequate supplies, had lost sales, acquired new suppliers, or left the business. Given the haste with which the FEO was created, its staff lacked both the size and the expertise to implement the complex and highly detailed measures necessary for adjusting to these changes. Many of these administrative problems persisted until April, when the embargo was over. If Congress had given the FEO greater administrative flexibility, many could have been avoided and the allocation measures might have proven more successful.[22]

3. Price Controls

No evidence has been presented to support the widely held belief that the large oil companies engineered the petroleum shortages during the OAPEC embargo in order to reap sharply higher profits. Nevertheless, the mere fact that so many Americans held it meant that their cooperation with the FEO's voluntary conservation plans depended on confidence in FEO's efforts to prevent profiteering from the shortage. The FEO used the price-setting powers delegated to it by the Cost of Living Council in this effort. They failed. Understanding how and why requires some background.[23]

Multi-tiered Prices for U.S. Crude Oil. Domestic crude-oil prices were rising in early 1973. As part of its program to combat inflation and to prevent owners and producers of previously developed supplies from reaping windfall profits, the Cost of Living Council set ceiling prices on all crude oil classified as "old"—that from leaseholds producing prior to 1973. The council believed that this action would not lead to reduced production of old oil because the out-of-pocket costs of exploiting most developed sources were far lower than the ceiling price. However, responding to pressure from politically powerful owners, Congress exempted the oil from low-productivity stripper wells that produced less than 10 barrels of crude oil per day. Stripper oil pro-

---

[22] One caveat is necessary. Some lawyers familiar with the Emergency Petroleum Allocation Act have told the author that they feel the FEO's interpretation of its powers was far too narrow.

[23] A more comprehensive discussion of price controls on oil may be found in William A. Johnson, "The Impact of Price Controls on the Oil Industry: How to Intensify an Energy Crisis," George Washington University, 1974 (unpublished).

duction costs were already near the May ceiling price and rising sharply due to the rapid price inflation of drilling equipment and supplies. Hence, the justification for the exemption ran, imposition of effective price ceilings would perversely discourage output, precisely at a time of tight supply, by making it unprofitable to continue producing from marginal fields, to rework closed fields, and to make the investment necessary for boosting output from stripper wells already in operation.

The Cost of Living Council also recognized that higher crude prices would encourage oil companies to expand greatly their investments for exploration and for developing and producing oil from new sources. Hence, "new" crude—production from a leasehold above the level achieved in 1972—was also exempted from the price ceilings. To reinforce these incentives, a barrel of "released" crude was also exempted from the price ceilings each time a barrel of new crude was produced. As of mid-June 1974, approximately 40 percent of all U.S.-produced crude oil was exempt from price controls.

Before the imposition of price controls, the price paid by oil refiners for any specified barrel of crude oil corresponded directly with its economic value. Thus, premiums were paid for (1) higher-gravity crudes because they yield proportionately more gasoline, (2) low-sulphur crudes because they are cheaper to refine and their products contain fewer pollutants and therefore are more valuable, and (3) crudes located relatively close to major refining and consuming centers. Since the imposition of controls, the price paid for a barrel of crude oil delivered to any specified American refinery has also depended on whether it is classified as old, exempt (that is, new, released, or stripper oil), foreign, or some combination of the three. Old oil is cheapest. Its average wellhead price has been $5.25 per barrel since late 1973. In sharp contrast, exempt oil of similar quality has been selling for about $10.00, and in early 1974 most foreign oil delivered to U.S. refineries ranged between $10.00 and $15.00 per barrel.[24]

Unlike stripper oil and new oil, production of discovered and developed old oil is not likely to be very price-responsive (in the vicinity of present prices) except over a span of several years.[25] Hence, assuming that the price controls on this product would be

---

[24] See "U.S. Exempt-oil Prices May Stall at $10/bbl. Level," *Oil and Gas Journal*, 4 February 1974, p. 34; "U.S. Crude Price Rollback Seen Certain," *Oil and Gas Journal*, 18 February 1974, p. 46.

[25] There is one exception to this rule. Large annual expenditures are necessary to maintain oil output from most oil fields where secondary recovery is being used. Hence, the supply of old oil from these fields is probably relatively price responsive.

short-lived, the Cost of Living Council (and subsequently the FEO) was probably correct in inferring that they would not lead to an appreciable reduction in supply.

Well before the start of the Arab embargo, the shortages that developed made it evident that the price ceilings on old oil had been set far below market-clearing levels. Crude-short refiners, desperate for refinery feedstocks, bid up the price of exempt crude. Desiring even more oil, they began seeking ways to circumvent the price controls of old oil. According to reports in the trade press prior to the OAPEC embargo, some succeeded by agreeing to tie together purchases of old and new oil from a given source: they bought old oil at the controlled price, but bought new oil at a price so high that the weighted average price for the total purchase rose to near the market-clearing level.[26] Thus, the price controls on old oil had the undesirable consequence of accelerating the inflation of prices of new oil.

U.S. petroleum supplies became much tighter after the OAPEC embargo. Realizing that producers of old oil would almost certainly require tie-in purchases in order to circumvent the price controls, the FEO froze all buyer-seller arrangements on old oil as of 1 December 1973. This ruling eliminated the possibility of tie-in sales and thereby saved the controls on crude-oil prices from total emasculation.

Some refiners process much greater proportions of old crude than others. In order to prevent these fortunate refiners from reaping vast windfall profits, the FEO had to enforce differential ceilings on the prices refiners could charge for their products. The method was to allow each refiner a specified markup over its full unit production costs. Even within well-defined geographical markets, the price controls on old crude led to intercompany differences of as much as 12¢ per gallon in retail gasoline prices.

All petroleum products were in short supply during the Arab embargo. Hence, even companies whose products carried prices as much as 20 percent above those of their competitors because they processed proportionately more of the high-priced new and foreign crude did not lose sales. However, once the embargo ended and the shortages eased, these companies confronted the dilemma of maintaining their prices and watching their sales plummet or cutting prices and incurring huge losses. This situation was neither "fair" nor economically desirable. However, given multi-tiered pricing for crude oil, the unhappy choice could be avoided only by requiring relatively

---

[26] See "NPRA Complains about Two-Tier Crude Pricing," *Oil and Gas Journal*, 24 September 1973, p. 82.

crude-rich refiners to sell (at controlled prices) some of their cheap crude to crude-short refiners. Disregarding the vigorous protests of the crude-rich refiners, who felt (correctly) that they were being asked to subsidize their less fortunate competitors, the FEO and its successor, the Federal Energy Administration, enforced the interrefinery allocation rules discussed earlier.

The Failure of Price Controls on Crude Oil. The foregoing discussion provides a taste of the complexities of the price regulations on crude oil and of the problems arising from their enforcement. The FEO was aware of most of these problems. It used much of its scarce manpower trying to make the controls more efficient and equitable and to enforce them properly, but to no avail. Unfortunately, because crude oil was in such short supply, inequities and inefficiencies were inherent in any system of effective price controls. Perhaps even worse than the myriad problems that the controls caused was their failure to achieve one of their main goals, restraint on profits.[27] To illustrate, in the first quarter of 1974, in the aftermath of the OAPEC decision to embargo oil sales, earnings of thirty of the largest U.S.-based oil companies soared 78.4 percent over the same period in 1973.[28]

The FEO never questioned the desirability of preventing the oil industry from reaping windfall profits due to the OAPEC embargo. Recognizing the need for voluntary public support for its energy conservation plans and the enormous public distrust of the oil industry, I concur with this decision. But controlling windfall profits is not without problems. Most important, it places the government in the difficult position of defining acceptable profit levels. Judged by the most common measure—the rate of return on equity investments—profits of most U.S. oil companies were below the average for all U.S. industry for the ten years prior to the OAPEC embargo.[29]

---

[27] Slowing inflation was the initial motivation of the Cost of Living Council for enforcing petroleum price controls. However, after the onslaught of the OAPEC embargo, the goal of preventing windfall profits assumed at least equal importance.

[28] "U.S. Oil Sees Possible Profit Slowdown," *Oil and Gas Journal*, 13 May 1974, pp. 40–41.

[29] A Federal Trade Commission report cited by the *Oil and Gas Journal*, 18 February 1974, p. 38, shows that, for the twelve months ending September 1973, oil refiners earned a return on equity of 10.5 percent compared with 12.4 percent for all U.S. manufacturing. Because the oil industry enjoys special tax treatment (the oil depletion allowance and quick expensing of many development costs), a comparison of unadjusted returns on equity may understate slightly the industry's profitability vis-à-vis other industries. However, it is unlikely that these adjustments would be sufficient to explain away the entire difference in average returns on equity.

When profits of twenty-five leading oil companies rose nearly 53 percent in 1973, their rate of return on equity was 15.1 percent against more than 14 percent for all U.S. manufacturing.[30] These comparisons do not establish that profits in the American oil industry were "excessive" and needed to be controlled.

The price controls failed to limit the post-embargo profits of oil companies for three reasons. First, the sharp rise in the price of foreign oil roughly doubled the value of stocks of foreign crude. Large inventory profits were realized when crude bought at pre-embargo world prices was sold at post-embargo prices. Price controls on domestically produced crude oil could not limit this source of approximately half of the higher profits attributable to the embargo. Second, because they did not wish to worsen shortages, the designers of the price controls exempted new, released, and stripper oil, which accounted for roughly 40 percent of all domestic crude. This was a wise decision. However, the shortage pushed prices of exempt domestic crude from less than $6.00 per barrel on the eve of the embargo to nearly $10.00 by late December; roughly three-fourths of the higher revenues due to this price rise accrued as higher profits to the owners of exempt crude.[31] Third, the FEO, wanting to maintain output in the face of escalating production costs, granted producers of old oil a price rise of $1.00 per barrel.

It should be stressed that the inefficiencies and inequities of price controls, and their ultimate failure to limit oil-company profits, were not the fault of the FEO. It made repeated attempts to remedy these deficiencies. Rather, the fault lies with the basic policy of controlling the price of a product at a level so low that its demand far exceeds its supply.[32]

A Remedy. The United States may experience renewed interruptions in oil supplies. In that event, it may once again seek to limit the profits of oil companies to gain public acceptance of the necessary austerity measures. The unsatisfactory experience with price controls

---

[30] See "Treasury Cites 1968–72 U.S. Profits Dip for Oil's Top 22," *Oil and Gas Journal*, 18 February 1974, pp. 38–39; and "Top Oil Firms 1973 Profits Jump 52.7%," *Oil and Gas Journal*, 18 February 1974, pp. 32–33.

[31] Royalties and severance taxes typically take up about 20 percent of any rise in oil revenues. Inflation-caused higher production costs probably ate up another 5 to 10 percent of the $4 hike in the price of exempt crude.

[32] The FEO also could have avoided several problems in gasoline allocation if there had been no petroleum price controls. For example, gasoline prices would have been relatively higher in the Northeast, giving refiners an incentive to eliminate regional disparities in supplies. Similarly, the FEO would not have had to adopt interrefinery allocation rules.

prompts me to suggest an alternative policy to meet any new crisis in petroleum supply. First, prices of crude oil and refined products should be allowed to rise freely both to discourage their consumption and to facilitate the allocation of scarce supplies to their most important uses. However, the government should have ready for quick implementation a rationing program designed to restrict demands to the supplies available—if, and only if, the petroleum shortage is so great that it threatens to push prices up to politically intolerable levels. Second, to prevent the oil companies from reaping windfall profits from crisis-bred higher prices, Congress should pass legislation that requires the President to impose a temporary excise tax on sales of petroleum products after a formal finding of an energy crisis by the Federal Energy Administration. (It is tempting to recommend the inclusion of a tax on excess profits in this legislation as an alternative presidential option. But I suspect that, as was the case with price controls recently, an efficient and equitable excess-profits tax is impossible to devise. Furthermore, in practice, companies find many ways to avoid this type of tax.) The temporary excise tax should be set nearly equal to the maximum hike in the prices of petroleum products that Congress feels Americans would tolerate under the circumstances. If Congress feels that poor Americans would suffer a disproportionate burden from a temporary petroleum excise tax, it should also require that its imposition be coupled with offsetting income tax credits or some other type of tax reduction.

4. The FEO's Staffing Problems

This paper has explained how many of the FEO's policies actually exacerbated the U.S. energy crisis. Should blame for the ultimate failure of these policies be placed on the FEO's leadership and staff?

The FEO was created after the energy crisis was already in full force. No well-considered plans awaited it, and from all sides— congressional, executive, and public—came urgent calls for bold new policies. Even a well-established agency can flounder in a crisis atmosphere. But FEO was brand new and was, of necessity, in the throes of a massive expansion.

In its new and still unsettled state, the agency especially needed strong day-to-day supervision from the top. Unfortunately, its two top officials—Administrator William Simon and Deputy Administrator John Sawhill—could not supply it because they had to spend most of their time testifying before congressional committees, pleading with various interest groups, or appealing directly to the American people to conserve energy.[33] Because Simon and Sawhill were nearly exhausted by these public relations activities, the direction of day-to-day operations was frequently left to seven assistant administrators and the general counsel. Most of these men were not accustomed to exercising such significant administrative power and responsibility. Several knew little about energy problems. In the absence of top-level leadership and of established decision-making traditions, these assistants and their nascent staffs inevitably spent considerable time jockeying for internal power.[34]

The FEO's rapid rate of growth also led to staffing problems at lower levels. Even after raids on other governmental agencies, few of the important staff positions were filled with people versed in petroleum matters. Almost no one on the staff had the first-hand experience in the oil industry that might have prevented FEO's complex pricing and allocation regulations from having their frequently undesirable consequences. The obvious way to remedy this particular staff weakness would have been to hire experienced people from the oil industry. However, because both Congress and the FEO's top leadership feared that such employees would unavoidably appear to have conflicts of interest, this alternative was not politically feasible.

In sum, the FEO did suffer severe staffing problems. Nevertheless, it would be fatuous to blame these for the ultimate failure of the FEO's regulations. Given the lack of preparation for dealing with any significant interruption in petroleum supply and the impossibility of insulating the FEO from the belligerent demands of politically powerful interest groups, severe staffing problems were unavoidable. In fact, taking account of the conditions under which the staff had to operate, I believe that it deserves high marks.[35]

5. Lessons

In addition to dramatizing the need for long-term policies to reduce U.S. dependence on insecure oil supplies, the largely unsuccessful

---

[33] Source: newspaper reports and interviews with former FEO officials.

[34] Source: interviews with former FEO officials.

[35] Other independent observers of the FEO appear to concur with this conclusion. For example, after attending the first meeting of the FEO's blue-ribbon Evaluation Panel on the Short-term Energy Situation, Walter Heller, chairman of the Council of Economic Advisers under President Kennedy, wrote in a letter (dated 5 January 1974): "With respect to personalities, both Simon and Sawhill make a very good impression. They were aware of the pitfalls in their data and in their public posture. As to the staff, their economists also made a good impression, but they are distinctly shorthanded for the huge job they have to do."

efforts of the FEO in the crisis of 1973–74 suggest four lessons for mitigating the impact should the nation become the target of another petroleum embargo.[36]

First, the Federal Energy Administration should not be swayed by shrill threats of the magnitude of the petroleum shortages in a new crisis. The embargoing countries have an obvious interest in exaggerating these cutbacks to induce swift and total compliance with their demands. The Federal Energy Administration must also carefully discount the exaggeration arising because each oil-importing country (and each interest group within that country) prepares for the worst by assuming—and claiming—that it will suffer especially severe interruptions. It is useful to remember that not *all* countries (and *all* interest groups) can suffer more than the average. Recent experience confirms that the FEO would have had a better appreciation of the real magnitude of the U.S. petroleum shortage if it had examined trends in oil inventories rather than relying on self-serving claims by the embargoers and domestic oil consumers, or on the too anxious predictions of its own staff.

Second, the Federal Energy Administration should declare publicly that, in future petroleum-supply crises, it will not adopt policies that prevent rising petroleum prices. Higher prices should be one of the administration's most powerful tools for obtaining necessary reductions in demand and for allocating scarce supplies to their most important uses. Assuming that Congress passes the appropriate enabling legislation, either excise taxes (or excess-profit taxes) should be used to prevent the oil companies from garnering higher profits from a petroleum embargo.

Third, every effort should be made now—in a crisis-free atmosphere that is favorable to careful design—to pass legislation that would allow the Federal Energy Administration promptly to implement rationing and taxing policies in a new emergency.

Fourth, to facilitate the third recommendation, the Federal Energy Administration should assign a small permanent staff to make ready to administer a comprehensive program of rationing should another embargo push oil prices to politically intolerable levels. Because any rationing system would be cumbersome to administer and would severely distort resource allocation, this plan should be implemented

---

[36] Several policies for eliminating U.S. dependence on insecure oil are discussed in Richard B. Mancke, *The Failure of U.S. Energy Policy* (New York: Columbia University Press, 1974), and in M.I.T. Energy Laboratory Policy Study Group, *Energy Self-Sufficiency: An Economic Evaluation* (Washington, D. C.: American Enterprise Institute, 1974).

only after the FEA has reached a formal finding of a likely supply interruption so large that no other policy will prove adequate for reducing demand quickly and sufficiently.

6. The Future of the Federal Energy Administration

U.S. energy policy has always emanated in bits and pieces from a variety of power centers. Prior to the establishment of the FEO, the most important were five executive departments—Interior, Treasury, State, Defense, and Commerce—and four administrative agencies or regulatory commissions—the Atomic Energy Commission, the Cost of Living Council, the Federal Power Commission, and the Environmental Protection Agency. Within many of these were several competing power centers, and all were subject, in varying degrees, to input from a plethora of congressional committees, presidential assistants, the Office of Management and Budget, the courts, industries, landowners, state governments, and the citizenry. By deliberate design as much as mere neglect, each of these power centers saw only a part of the total energy problem and each typically represented only a few of the legitimately concerned interests.[37]

Ideally, the Federal Energy Administration, the congressionally authorized successor to the FEO, should provide the coordination the United States needs for an effective and comprehensive energy policy. In actuality, because the major sources of U.S. energy policy making in the past have successfully defended their right to set policy in their historical bailiwicks, the creation of the new agency has not eliminated the problems stemming from a failure to coordinate U.S. energy policy. Instead, the mission of the Federal Energy Administration has been restricted to two principal concerns: running existing petroleum allocation programs and devising plans to achieve the amorphous goals of "Project Independence." Unless the scope of the Federal Energy Administration is expanded, it seems likely that U.S. energy policy will continue to languish for lack of coordination.

---

[37] For a more elaborate discussion of these problems, see Richard B. Mancke, "The Genesis of the U.S. Energy Crisis," in Joseph Szyliowicz and Bard O'Neill, eds., *The Energy Crisis and U.S. Foreign Policy* (New York: Praeger, forthcoming 1975).

**TOWARD ECONOMY IN
ELECTRIC POWER**
Edward J. Mitchell
Peter R. Chaffetz

This essay is a policy-oriented analysis of a 450-page report under-taken for the National Science Foundation's Office of Energy R and D Policy. The purpose of the full report is to explore the technical, economic, legal, and regulatory implications of a plan under which private industrial firms would generate electric power as a by-product of the steam they produce for industrial processes and central power stations owned jointly by utilities and industrial firms would supply steam to industry. The report, which is entitled *Energy Industrial Center Study*, addresses itself to two major policy questions:

(1) What are the potential economic benefits that may be real-ized by the nation and by consumers from implementing this plan?

(2) What are the legal and regulatory barriers that must be removed to expedite implementation of the plan?

The report indicates that the plan's economic benefits might be enormous. Over the next decade capital expenditures could be reduced by as much as $5 billion a year and total household electric bills could fall as much as $3.6 billion a year, without in any way curtailing U.S. consumption of electricity. The legal and regulatory modifications necessary to smooth the way for implementation seem, by com-parison, to be relatively modest.

The purpose of this essay is to introduce a broad readership to the technical concept, its potential economic benefits, and the legal and regulatory hurdles it faces. It is hoped that this will spur readers, especially policymakers, to give serious attention to this option for dealing with the impending power crisis.

The full report upon which this essay is largely based is the work of many people. The executive committee overseeing the effort con-sisted of Paul W. McCracken of the University of Michigan (chairman), Gerald Decker of Dow Chemical Company, and William Rosenberg of the Michigan Public Service Commission. The advisory committee was composed of James S. Grant of Toledo Edison, C. M. Laffoon of San Diego Gas and Electric Company, Richard J. Peterman of Gulf States Utilities Commission, Vernon Sturgeon of the California Public Utilities Commission, H. H. Woodson of the University of Texas, and myself.

The research and report writing were divided among several organizations:

- The technical work was done at the Dow Chemical Company under the direction of Robert S. Spencer.

- The environmental work was carried out at the Environmental Research Institute of Michigan by Robert E. Sampson and Virginia Prentiss.

- The economic work was done by Alan Greenspan (before he left for government service) and Lowell Wiltbank, both of Townsend-Greenspan and Company, and by Raymond Reilly and myself from the University of Michigan.

- The legal and regulatory work was done at Cravath, Swaine and Moore under the direction of David G. Ormsby.

This essay contains much that is included in the report's executive summary, which was drafted by Peter Chaffetz and myself.

EDWARD J. MITCHELL
Project Director,
National Energy Project

TOWARD ECONOMY IN ELECTRIC POWER

Edward J. Mitchell
Peter R. Chaffetz

Introduction

Despite increases in electric rates in many parts of the nation, some electric utilities find themselves unable to recoup still greater increases in fuel and capital costs. If electric rates are not sufficient to earn investors a normal rate of return on capital, power-generating capacity will not be built. Should this situation persist for several years, the prospect of sizable electric power shortages will become a reality.

This essay examines a modest first step toward reforming the electric power industry in order to reduce capital requirements and lower the costs of producing power. The creation of energy industrial centers (EICs)—facilities in which private industrial manufacturers would participate in the production of electric power—could save the nation billions of dollars over the next ten years. Specifically, the nation could save as much as $5 billion per year in capital investments during the next decade and household consumers as much as $3.6 billion per year in electric bills if this course were followed.

The rationale for establishing an industry-utility linkage is based on the fact that both manufacturing and power-generating facilities require large quantities of steam, although industries and utilities currently use this steam for different purposes. The role of steam in power generation is widely known; less widely known is the surprisingly large volume of steam employed directly in industrial processes, the production of which accounts for 17 percent of the nation's consumption of primary fuels (see Figure 1).

Energy industrial centers would take advantage of the fact that wherever industrial steam is generated, there is a potential for generating electricity as well. By raising the steam pressure and temperature above what is required for industrial use and bringing it back

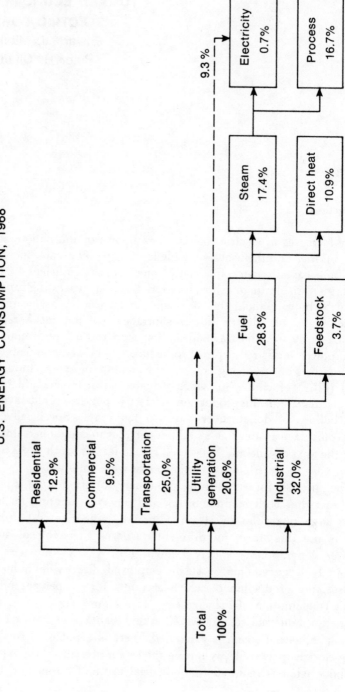

Figure 1

U.S. ENERGY CONSUMPTION, 1968

Source: *Energy Industrial Center Study,* p. 24.

226

down through a turbine coupled to a generator, an industrial plant can produce electric power. It has been known for many years that the additional fuel consumed in this process would be as little as half of what is required to produce the same amount of power at the most efficient central-station power plant. Similar fuel savings can be achieved by supplying steam from utility central-station power plants to industry.

Although some arrangements similar to the EIC system have been in effect for many years, these represent only a small fraction of the potential. This study explores the capital and operating economies available through the widespread adoption of the EIC concept.

1. The Crisis in the Electric Utility Industry: An Overview

The EIC idea is only one of many proposals for reforming the electric utility industry, a subject which itself has become a topic of emotional debate. Why has an industry that has been so strong over the years suddenly lost attractiveness for investors and come under bitter attack from consumers? What are the merits of various proposed reforms? To understand how the EIC concept relates to the general question of electric utility reform, it will be useful first to examine the issues which bear on the operation of the industry and then to delineate the dimensions of its current predicament.

There can be little question that the investor-owned electric utilities face staggering financial problems. Although they must finance an estimated $305 billion of new construction over the next ten years,[1] rate increases have already made the utilities a prime target for consumer protest. The problem of meeting increased demand while maintaining moderate rates presents an enormous challenge to the utilities at a time when business conditions—reduced earnings, high interest rates, declining bond ratings, and depressed stock prices—have increased the difficulty of funding needed expansion.

The Financing Problem. The most serious problem facing electric utilities is the low rate of return on capital. Some utilities can no longer earn sufficient rates of return to attract new capital. The result has been a precipitous decline in the construction of new generating facilities.

---

[1] See National Science Foundation et al., *Energy Industrial Center Study (EICS)*, (Washington, D. C., 1975), p. 273. The demand projections used in *EICS* are lower than those of several other major studies.

This situation has arisen because regulatory commissions have not allowed the utilities to set rates high enough to recoup the unprecedented increase in the cost of supplying electric power caused mainly by rising fuel prices and by the higher interest payments now required on the bonds that finance new construction.[2] Despite rate increases that have been generous by historical standards, electric rates have not kept pace with the costs of fuel, the costs of plant construction, and the cost of capital. Under these circumstances, there is growing doubt that the utilities will be able to meet anticipated future demand.

In a free, unregulated market such problems would be of short duration. The market would perceive the future scarcity of electric power at existing rates, and prices would rise sufficiently to compensate for higher operating and capital expenses. Investors, recognizing that they would receive higher prices by the time their plant came on-stream, would be willing to contribute capital for investment in new facilities.[3] But investor-owned electric utilities are regulated. Present and future prices are set not by the marketplace but by regulatory commissions. Although the economic forces of supply and demand play a role in rate-making policy, legal and political considerations also influence the outcome, and there is no automatic tendency for electric rates to equate supply and demand as they would in a free market.

The rationale for regulation is the assumption that electric utilities are "natural monopolies."[4] It is thought that in the absence of regulation, economies of scale—the lower costs associated with larger plants—would inevitably give rise to regional monopolies that could set prices above the costs of service, thus restraining consumption and creating monopoly profits. To avoid this, regulatory commissions offer exclusive franchises—that is, monopoly status—to private electric companies. The commissions then restrict the monopoly profits of the companies by setting electric rates at levels just sufficient to raise capital and to build the plants necessary to meet the demand for electricity. Justice Douglas, in his opinion in the *Hope* case, clearly

---

[2] Murray L. Weidenbaum, "Economic Policy and the Electric Utilities," Statement to the Joint Economic Committee, 93rd Congress, 2d session (4 December 1974), p. 1.

[3] For an explanation of why capital shortages cannot exist in a free market, see J. E. Hass, E. J. Mitchell, and B. K. Stone, *Financing the Energy Industry* (Cambridge, Mass.: Ballinger Publishing Co., 1974), pp. 25-27.

[4] See C. F. Phillips, Jr., *The Economics of Regulation* (Homewood, Ill.: Richard D. Irwin, 1969), pp. 21-23.

delineated the responsibility of the regulatory commissions to the utility:

> From the investor or company point of view it is important that there be enough revenue not only for operating expenses, but also, for the capital costs of the business. These include service on the debt and dividends on the stock. . . . By that standard the return to the equity owner should be commensurate with returns on investments in other enterprises having corresponding risks. That return, moreover, should be sufficient to assure confidence in the financial integrity of the enterprise so as to maintain its credit and attract capital.[5]

The prevailing view at this time is that electric utility regulation has been at least partially effective and has made a positive contribution to the public welfare. But even the most fervent supporters of the present regulatory system recognize that the serious economic and financial problems that face the industry are related to regulation. These problems will grow as political pressures make it harder for regulatory commissions to fulfill the prescription of the *Hope* decision. Even if rates are eventually set at appropriate levels, the lag in rate-setting will reduce interim earnings, internal capital availability, and the attractiveness of electric utility securities in the capital markets.

Although the financing problem in the electric utility industry is caused primarily by the low rates set by regulatory commissions, three characteristics of the industry exacerbate the problem: (1) Because electric utilities pay a large percentage of their earnings in dividends, they have traditionally relied heavily on external financing. For example, in 1972, 69 percent of the capital raised by private electric utilities came from the sale of stocks, from the sale of bonds, or from other loans. In contrast, U.S. nonfinancial corporations as a whole raised only 45 percent of their capital in this way.[6] The decline in the rate of return utilities offer in the capital market dramatically reduces their ability to raise capital. (2) The debt of most electric utilities (95 percent) is subject to indenture clauses requiring that earnings equal at least twice the amount of interest payments.[7] If earnings are not adequate to provide this coverage, new debt cannot be offered. (3) During the period from 1974 to 1978, $8.2 billion in utility bonds carrying interest rates of 4 percent or less will expire

---

[5] Federal Power Commission v. Hope Natural Gas Co., 320 U.S. 591, 603 (1944).
[6] Murray L. Weidenbaum, *Financing the Electric Utility Industry* (New York: Edison Electric Institute, 1974), p. 57.
[7] Ibid.

and will have to be replaced with debt at more than double the present interest cost.[8]

Proposed Remedies. Recognition of these constraints has prompted numerous proposals to alter the regulatory and fiscal environment of the utilities. On the more helpful side these include the following:

Changing accounting procedures. For example, regulatory commissions could allow utilities to include the costs of construction work in progress in the rate base if this would not delay the completion of new capacity. Also, it may be noted that many utilities have already improved their cash-flow situation by changing from a flow-through to a normalized accounting procedure.[9]

Reducing special utility taxes. State and local governments commonly tax utilities at a higher rate than they do other businesses. In a *New York Times* interview, the retiring chairman of the New York State Public Service Commission, Joseph C. Swidler, stated that New York City alone takes over twenty cents of every revenue dollar received by Consolidated Edison and that such taxes amount to more than 8 percent of all taxes collected by the city.[10]

Tax relief on the federal level. The President's Labor Management Advisory Committee recently recommended that utilities be granted a permanent 12 percent investment tax credit and a deferred tax liability on utility company dividends reinvested in the company's stock.[11] Although government awareness of the utility industry's problems is a hopeful sign, it would not be good policy to rescue the utilities from discriminatory tax treatment by creating an unduly favorable situation. Overly compensatory relief will merely lead to further economic distortions. Nonetheless, thoughtful reform in this area could be very useful and would require only simple adjustments in the existing regulatory and tax structures.

Some observers believe that more radical action will be needed to restore the health of the utility industry. There is support in some

---

[8] Ibid., p. 52.

[9] Hass, Mitchell, Stone, *Financing the Energy Industry*, p. 71.

[10] "Con Ed Troubles are Laid to City," *New York Times*, 2 June 1974.

[11] Testimony of Secretary of the Treasury William E. Simon before Committee on Ways and Means, U.S. House of Representatives, 8 July 1975.

230

quarters for direct government intervention, particularly in the form of federal guarantees of electric utility bonds. Proponents argue that this approach would reduce interest costs, thereby relieving one of the major sources of upward pressure on utility rates. Although the current economic and political climate tends to enhance the appeal of this approach, it would in fact be counterproductive for the economy as a whole. Professor Murray Weidenbaum has explained the economic objections to this proposal in the following terms:

> Boiled down to its basics, government guarantees of utility bonds really involve putting "the monkey" on someone else's back. They do not increase the amount of investment funds available to the economy. Rather, to the extent they succeed, they merely take capital funds away from other sectors of the economy and lead to similar requests for aid by those sectors. These government guarantees also tend to raise the level of interest rates in the economy, including the rates on Treasury debt which is a cost borne by the taxpayer. That added cost alone is estimated at $145 million a year.[12]

Because the loan guarantee plan does nothing to reduce the costs or amounts of capital or fuel required by the utilities, it ignores the two real causes of the problems it is meant to solve. Moreover, a policy of price subsidy, which is what federal loan guarantees would be in effect, cannot encourage the efficient use of the subsidized commodity. In fact, exactly the reverse would occur, because an artificially low price would distort the consumer's perception of the true cost of electricity. The result would be a waste of capital and natural resources consumed in power production.

The EIC Approach. It is the problems inherent in this and other subsidy approaches that establish the proper context for considering the idea of the energy industrial center. The EIC alternative to present methods of power generation merits attention not only because of the savings it promises, but also because it exemplifies the best kind of approach to the nation's energy problems; it is strongest in those areas where the subsidy approach is weakest. Instead of simply hiding or shifting existing costs, the EIC approach would actually reduce them. And instead of introducing greater inefficiency into the power industry, EICs would help the industry become more efficient in several important areas. Sections 2 and 3 of this essay explore and quantify

---

[12] Weidenbaum, *Financing the Electric Utility Industry*, p. 5.

the factors that give the EIC approach its great potential for capital and fuel savings.

However, these are only the direct benefits that could occur with widespread implementation of the EIC plan. There are additional indirect benefits to consider before turning to that discussion—benefits residing in the impact that EICs would have on the monopoly structure of the power industry. To put the matter in a nutshell, the EICs have the potential advantage of substantially increased competition.

The idea that more competition is desirable would seem to run directly counter to the assumptions that have always governed utility policy—namely, that the utilities are natural monopolies and that regulation is essential if the consumer is to have the advantages both of economies of scale and of reasonable power rates.

Regulation does serve an important purpose in certain aspects of utility operations—transmission and retail distribution, for example—but some economists have questioned whether electric power monopolies are really "natural" in their generating and wholesale operations and whether regulation has succeeded in restraining electric rates. Leonard Weiss has argued that economies of scale in the generation of electricity disappear at a level low enough to permit considerable competition in many areas if an appropriate antitrust policy is followed: "Most important regions could support enough generating plants to permit extensive competition if the plants were under separate ownership and had equal access to transmission and distribution." [13] The significance of this unrealized potential for competition becomes clear in light of the findings of Thomas Gale Moore and George Stigler that, historically, rates charged by unregulated electric utilities have not differed significantly from those charged by regulated electric utilities.[14] The probable reason for this is the inefficiency that almost inevitably characterizes regulated industries. Walter J. Primeaux, Jr. has concluded that "more reliance on the market system would probably make electric firms operate more efficiently, and produce fewer social costs than policies that protect the interests of inefficient utility firms to the detriment of consumers." [15]

---

[13] Leonard W. Weiss, "Antitrust in the Electric Power Industry," in Almarin Phillips, ed., *Promoting Competition in Regulated Industries* (Washington, D. C.: Brookings Institution, 1975), p. 136.

[14] See George Stigler and Claire Friedland, "What Can Regulators Regulate? The Case of Electricity," *Journal of Law and Economics*, vol. 5 (October 1962), pp. 1-16, and Thomas G. Moore, "The Effectiveness of Regulation of Electric Utility Prices," *Southern Economic Journal*, vol. 36 (April 1970), pp. 365-75.

[15] Walter J. Primeaux, "The Monopoly Market in Electric Utilities" in Phillips, *Promoting Competition*, p. 183.

As the following sections will demonstrate, successful implementation of the EIC plan would result in a proliferation of independently owned power sources, operating at costs significantly lower than those of the present regulated utilities. In addition to the savings inherent in the EIC itself, the increase in competitive pressure that might result from implementation could have further favorable effects on power costs to the consumer and capital costs to the utilities and the nation.

2. Technical and Industrial Considerations

At the turn of the century, most industrial plants generated their own electric power and their own steam. Although a high percentage of plants still produce their own steam, industry generated only 16.8 percent of its power needs in 1968 and only an estimated 14.2 percent in 1974.[16]

Behind this decline are certain economic factors, including utility rate structures designed to discourage industrial power generation and the reluctance of industries to become involved in a highly regulated activity. Moreover, the trend in industrial equipment has been from field-assembled, coal-fired boilers that are easily adapted for power generation to lower-cost oil or gas-fired "package boilers" that are suitable only for the production of steam and that are generally incapable of high fuel and operating efficiencies. Simultaneously, the development of more efficient central-power-station boilers, which can run economically only when steam condensate is recovered and reused, has led to a decline in the utilities' practice of selling steam for industrial use. These parallel trends have encouraged the evolution of two large and relatively independent steam systems. These systems could be integrated and resultant economies obtained through industrial power generation and through the creation of dual-purpose central power stations that would sell steam for industrial use.

Industrial By-product Power Generation. By-product power is electricity produced from steam that is required for industrial application and that is still suitable for the production of power after passing through a generating turbine. The most common process employs an extraction or back-pressure turbine that drives the generator.

The basic principle that makes by-product generation potentially attractive in comparison with central station power is illustrated

---

[16] *Energy Industrial Center Study*, p. 23.

Figure 2

RELATIVE WASTE HEAT PRODUCED IN CENTRAL POWER STATION AND BY-PRODUCT POWER GENERATION

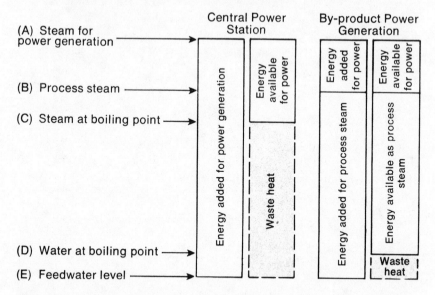

Note: In the central power station, sufficient energy must be added in the boiler to bring the temperature of the feedwater up to point (A). However, the condensing turbines that drive the generators can only utilize the amount of energy between points (A) and (C) to make electricity, leaving the large amount of energy between point (C) and the feedwater level (E) to be rejected into the environment. In by-product power generation, the energy between the feedwater level and point (B) is already needed for the generation of steam for process and other industrial needs. Energy is added to this to bring the steam up to point (A). Thus, the energy from (A) to (B) is available for power generation, that from (B) to (D) can be used for steam production, and only a small amount remains as waste heat.

in Figure 2. In the conventional central power station, much of the energy required for power generation is expelled into the environment as waste heat. In the generation of by-product power, the energy below the increment needed for power generation is used in the production of process steam. This has two clear advantages: (1) it greatly reduces consumption of fuel per kilowatt hour of electricity and (2) it alleviates the problem of so-called thermal pollution in power generation. Moreover, as will be seen, if adopted in operations of sufficient scale, by-product power generation should be an attractive investment for many industries. This should be especially true as continuing high fuel costs cause a reversal of the trend toward package boilers. It is likely that fuel costs alone will furnish a strong incentive for a general return to coal-fired boilers by 1980.

As field-assembled, coal-fired boilers again become common, the industrial steam base will again be suitable for the generation of by-product power. A simple and efficient industrial generating system could be based on a single coal-fired boiler, although this arrangement would be of limited reliability and limited flexibility. Typical utility rate structures, with high standby demand charges, would encourage the use of a more dependable system incorporating low-pressure package boilers for back-up steam production during periods of high power demand or main-boiler outages. Such a "mixed" system has been assumed in calculating the desirability of by-product power generation.

On the basis of a projected average 1980 cost of power to industry of 31.26 mills per kilowatt hour (kwh),[17] it is estimated that where existing steam systems produce above 400,000 pounds per hour, by-product power generation will achieve costs per kwh low enough to bring a return on investment (ROI) in the area of 20 percent or better before tax.[18] This return is generated by savings on power purchased from utilities and has been posited as a minimum level of return for by-product power generation to be attractive. Steam installations at or above the 400,000 pounds per hour minimum currently account for 43 percent of the industrial steam load.[19]

Although in 1967 industry consumed 82 percent more electric power than could be generated from its existing base,[20] it can be demonstrated that, for those 43 percent of the plants where by-product power generation is economically feasible, the installation of additional capacity utilizing the condensing end of the mixed-pressure turbine could increase power generation even beyond the point of electrical self-sufficiency, while still surpassing minimum ROI requirements.[21] This presents the possibility that industrial plants could generate surplus power for sale to the utilities.

While it seems likely that an industrial plant capable of economical by-product power generation would install condensing capacity needed to meet its own electrical requirements, it is not clear how much additional condensing capacity would be installed to produce power for sale, even if such sale were economically attractive. How-

---

17 Ibid., p. 45.
18 Ibid., p. 75.
19 Ibid., p. 86.
20 Ibid., p. 7.
21 Ibid., p. 81.

ever, if firms with 400,000-pound-per-hour installations invested at a level 20 percent above what was required for power self-sufficiency, industry could achieve an excess capacity of 57,178 megawatts in 1980—more than half of the projected national industrial requirement from electrical utilities for that year.[22] By 1985, the reduction in fuel use through by-product generation alone could be roughly equivalent to 680,000 barrels of oil a day.[23]

The viability of industrial generation of power for sale to utilities can be determined by comparing the cost involved with the projected value of power at the bus-bar (that is, the cost before distribution costs) for the utility's best alternative, which is assumed here to be an average-sized central power station operational in 1980. The National Science Foundation study makes such a comparison and, finding that the industrial generating plant would have a decided cost advantage, concludes that there is the potential for substantial capital savings for the utilities.[24]

This, of course, assumes that utilities would be willing to substitute industrial generating capacity for new capacity of their own. However, industrially generated power is of value to the utilities only to the extent that its availability is predictable. If it were not predictable, the utilities would have to duplicate the industrial capacity and would not pay a rate high enough to justify industrial investment in added condensing capability. Thus, for industrially generated power to become a salable commodity, industrial production and generator maintenance schedules must be adjusted to utility needs. One way around this problem would be to give wide distribution to industrially generated power, so that each utility could choose among several available industrial sources and not be dependent on one. The shifting of power among utilities is called wheeling, and provisions for extending wheeling services to industrial power sources would be essential. Wheeling would also be useful in cases where a utility wished to purchase surplus power from a distant industrial source.

Transmission systems designed to integrate industrial power sources with existing utility facilities could result in increased dependability for the system as a whole and overall transmission requirements lower than would obtain if all power were supplied by conventional central stations. The development of a large number of properly integrated and relatively small power sources could thus render unnecessary the adoption of other proposals currently under

---

[22] Ibid., pp. 44 and 88.
[23] Ibid., p. 88.
[24] Ibid., pp. 286-87.

236

consideration for the reduction of transmission and generating capacity requirements.

In discussing the integration of industrial power sources with utility systems, it must be considered that a long-term purchase contract, essential for the utility, might require a commitment longer than would be acceptable to the industrial producer. Another problem area that must be considered is the impact of business fluctuations on the reliability of the industrial power source.

Dual-Purpose Central Plants. The term "dual-purpose" plant describes a central power station, of a size and type typically constructed by the utilities, that also furnishes a significant amount of steam to one or more industrial customers. Such plants could be undertaken as a joint venture between the utility and a large industrial consumer of steam. The respective investments might be determined in proportion to what each partner would have to invest for separate facilities. The savings resulting from the joint venture would permit each partner a rate of return that would be higher than his standard rate. Savings beyond recovery of the standard ROI might be distributed in proportion to each partner's investment in the venture.

A conservative estimate is that one million pounds of steam per hour would be the minimum load that could attract utility interest. Twenty-three percent of the industrial steam load is currently generated in loads of that size or larger at single locations, giving a lower limit for the breadth of applicability for this approach.[25] According to projected implementation schedules, fuel savings under this approach could be equivalent to 535,000 barrels of oil per day by 1985.[26]

Factors that must be evaluated here include the life of the steam purchase contract that might be required of the industrial parent firm, whose plant will typically have a shorter life-span than the power station, and lack of space for the location of power stations near existing industry (long steamlines are prohibitively expensive and inefficient).

Environmental Issues. In the aggregate, industrial participation in power generation would have a highly favorable environmental impact. The expected 50 percent reduction in fuel use would bring about a corresponding 50 percent reduction in the total emission of pollutants. In addition, the use of the waste heat from power genera-

---

[25] Ibid., p. 114.
[26] Ibid., p. 116.

tion for industrial processes would alleviate the problem of thermal pollution (Figure 2).

On the other hand, implementation of the EIC approach would result in greater local concentration of fuel-burning operations, which could bring emission levels at specific locations above acceptable levels. For this reason, the environmental implications of integrated steam and power generation might require case-by-case determinations based on consideration of existing conditions at each prospective location.

3. Economic and Financial Implications

The economies of industrial power generation and dual-purpose central power plants may be translated into reduced capital demands for the nation, lower external financing requirements for the electric utilities, and lower electric rates for consumers. To project these economic benefits, the EIC study incorporated the economic and financial characteristics of the investor-owned electric utility industry into a computer program designed to compile balance sheets and income statements for the industry for each year from 1978 to 1985.[27] Aggregate financial statements for the years from 1956 through 1972 set the initial conditions for developing the computer model. Comparison of data produced by the model with known financial results for the investor-owned electric utility industry during 1973 and 1974 provided a check on the reliability of the model. A schematic representation of the model structure is shown in Figure 3.

By combining the data produced by the model with estimates of the impact of industrial power generation and dual-purpose operations on the industrial and utility participants in such ventures, it was possible to project the total capital savings to the nation that would be available at different levels of implementation. For this purpose, the EIC study defined four implementation cases, A through D (as illustrated in Figure 4), and compared each of these with the base case in which there was no implementation.

Description of the Cases. It should be noted that because each comparison assumed maximum implementation under the limits defining

---

[27] The economic and financial section of the *Energy Industrial Center Study* is by and large descriptive of the process by which the necessary computer programs have been constructed. The output of these programs forms the basis for the conclusions presented here.

Figure 3
THE UTILITY MODEL

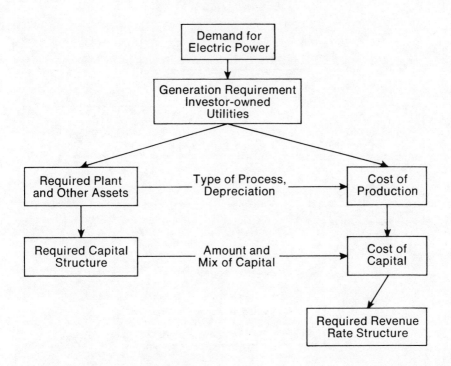

Source: *Energy Industrial Center Study*, p. 236.

the case, an ideal unlikely to be realized, the cases serve primarily a heuristic purpose, giving an idea of the range of additional benefits available from implementation.

The base case. Extrapolating from certain key trends and inter-relationships in the investor-owned electric utility industry, it is possible to project the probable course for the industry over the next ten years should there be a continuation of the present trend of declining industrial involvement in power generation.

Case A: Industrial generation for own use. In this case, indus-try is assumed to take advantage of all opportunities to generate by-product power and incremental condensing power wherever the installation of by-product alone would yield a before-tax return on investment greater than 20 percent. Each industrial plant would also invest in additional condensing capacity in an amount sufficient to meet all its own electrical requirements. Table 1 indicates the cumu-lative total by-product capacity that would accrue under these circum-

Figure 4
THE GENERATION CASES

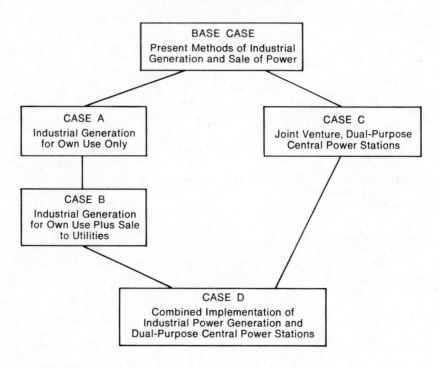

Source: *Energy Industrial Center Study*, p. 262.

stances through 1985 and shows that by 1985 the reduction in the utilities' industrial load would be 372 billion kwh. In this, as in all other calculations of load reductions, an 85 percent load factor is assumed.

Case B: Industrial generation for own use plus sale to utilities. In this case, each plant producing by-product and condensing power under Case A would increase its investment by 20 percent over the amount required for electrical self-sufficiency. The additional power produced would be sold to electric utilities in the amounts shown in Table 2.

Case C: Joint venture central power stations. This case assumes that coal-fired, dual-purpose central power stations displace the coal-fired plants that, in the base case, were assumed to have become operational from 1979 on. Similarly, dual-purpose nuclear stations replace all base case utility nuclear facilities beginning in 1981. Because this would constitute only a substitution of dual-purpose for

240

Table 1

CASE A GENERATION ASSUMPTIONS: INDUSTRIAL GENERATION FOR OWN USE

| Year | Capacity Added (mw) | | | Total, cumulative | Reduction in Utilities' Industrial Load (billions kwh) |
	By-product power	Condensing power	Total		
1978	8,165	4,083	12,248	12,248	91.20
1979	17,087	8,544	13,383	25,631	190.85
1980	26,806	13,403	14,578	40,209	299.40
1981	28,023	14,013	1,826	42,035	312.99
1982	29,283	14,643	1,890	43,925	327.07
1983	30,587	15,294	1,956	45,881	341.63
1984	31,937	15,969	2,025	47,906	356.71
1985	33,335	16,668	2,097	50,003	372.32

Source: *Energy Industrial Center Study*, p. 266.

Table 2

CASE B GENERATION ASSUMPTIONS: INDUSTRIAL GENERATION FOR OWN USE PLUS SALE TO UTILITIES

| Year | Capacity Added (mw) | | | Total, cumulative | Reduction in Utilities' Industrial Load (billions kwh) | Industrial Sales to Utilities (billions kwh) |
	By-product power	Condensing power	Total			
1978	8,165	9,252	17,417	17,417	91.20	38.49
1979	17,087	19,361	19,031	36,448	190.85	80.54
1980	26,806	30,372	20,730	57,178	299.40	126.35
1981	28,023	31,752	2,597	59,775	312.99	132.09
1982	29,283	33,179	2,687	62,462	327.07	138.03
1983	30,587	34,657	2,782	65,244	341.63	144.17
1984	31,937	36,186	2,879	68,123	356.71	150.54
1985	33,335	37,770	2,982	71,105	372.32	157.13

Source: *Energy Industrial Center Study*, p. 267.

Table 3

CASE C GENERATION ASSUMPTIONS: JOINT VENTURE, DUAL-PURPOSE CENTRAL POWER STATIONS

| Year | Capacity Added (mw) | | Total, cumulative | Generation (billions kwh) |
	Coal	Nuclear		
1979	13,706	—	13,706	65.44
1980	12,534	—	26,240	122.47
1981	7,572	15,887	49,699	267.93
1982	5,546	15,714	70,959	401.33
1983	6,319	17,054	94,332	548.43
1984	5,411	17,399	117,142	693.34
1985	4,130	17,775	139,047	835.90

Source: *Energy Industrial Center Study*, p. 270.

central power generation, capacity in Case C would be the same as projected base-case capacity each year.

It is further assumed here that dual-purpose projects operate as joint ventures financed with 50 percent debt. Equity would be contributed by the partners in proportion to the cost of separate steam and power facilities. The utility would provide 84 percent of the equity for coal-fired units and 92 percent of the equity for nuclear plants.[28] The prices paid by the utility for electricity and by the industry for steam would be set at levels that permitted each partner to save an amount sufficient to provide his standard return. The EICS technical section shows that returns would in fact be higher than the standard returns. As a comparison of Tables 1, 2, and 3 indicates, the total capacity and generation projections in this case are considerably higher than they are in cases A and B, because of the assumption that virtually all new capacity after 1980 would be installed in dual-purpose operations.

Case D: Combined implementation. This case assumes that industrial power generation replaces all coal-fired capacity due for completion during 1979/1980 and all nuclear capacity to be completed during 1981/1982. Joint ventures would provide the capacity of coal-fired plants and of part of the combined-cycle plants expected to come on-stream in the period 1981-85 and of nuclear plants scheduled to begin operation during the years 1983-85. Table 4 summa-

---

[28] *Energy Industrial Center Study*, p. 269.

Table 4

CASE D: COMBINED IMPLEMENTATION OF INDUSTRIAL POWER GENERATION AND DUAL-PURPOSE CENTRAL POWER STATIONS

| Year | Industry Capacity Added (mw) | Joint Venture Capacity Added (mw) | | Total Capacity Operational (mw) | Industrial Generation | | Joint Venture Generation Sold to Utility (billions kwh) | Total Utility Power Purchased (billions kwh) |
		Coal	Nuclear		For own Use (billions kwh)	For Sale to Utilities (billions kwh)		
1979	11,659	—	—	11,659	61.05	25.76	—	25.76
1980	8,914	—	—	20,573	107.73	45.46	—	45.46
1981	12,734	6,238	—	39,545	174.40	73.60	28.03	101.63
1982	12,239	4,761	—	56,545	238.47	100.65	47.75	148.40
1983	—	6,286	13,995	76,826	238.47	100.65	174.82	275.47
1984	—	6,357	14,332	97,915	238.47	100.65	303.99	404.64
1985	—	6,162	14,614	118,691	238.47	100.65	434.09	534.74

Source: *Energy Industrial Center Study,* p. 271.

rizes the impact of implementation under these assumptions. (There are, of course, many other possible combined implementation scenarios.)

Potential Savings. Estimates of the potential savings to the utility industry and to the nation as a whole have been derived by reducing projected demand on the electric utilities by the amount generated by industry under each of the four implementation cases and calculating the corresponding reduction in capital requirements and operating costs for the utilities. Major economic benefits fall into three categories: reduced capital expenditures, reduced external financing requirements, and consumer savings. Tables 5 through 8 summarize the results, which are described briefly below.

Capital expenditures. Estimated average annual savings to the nation in capital requirements for new electric generating and transmission capacity over the period from 1976 to 1985 range from $2 billion a year in Case A to $5 billion a year in Case D. This means that without altering its rate of power consumption, the nation could spend from $2 billion to $5 billion less each year on new generating facilities. Over the period from 1976 to 1985, resources valued at $20 billion to $50 billion would be freed for uses in other parts of the economy. Thus, energy-industrial-center power generation would result in a significant increase in the productivity of the nation's resources.

External financing. Without implementation of the EIC proposals, investor-owned electric utilities will have to raise from external sources an average of $22.7 billion each year over the period from 1976 to 1985. In Case B this figure could fall to $18.6 billion, a reduction of $4.1 billion each year. With the dual-purpose central power stations (Case C), the electric utilities would have to raise from external sources an average of $15.4 billion a year on their own and $4.4 billion with their industrial partners—a total of $19.8 billion—a reduction of $2.9 billion in the amount they would have to raise on their own without implementation.

Consumer savings. As a result of the saving in capital-use cost, as well as in lower labor and fuel costs, customers of investor-owned electric utilities would pay less for electricity. Total consumer savings—residential, commercial, and industrial—from implementation would range from 2.9 percent to 6.0 percent for the several cases. Residential rates would be from 4.6 percent to 8.0 percent lower than they would be without implementation. The residential consumer's

Table 5

COMPARISON OF CAPITAL EXPENDITURES UNDER THE ALTERNATIVE CASES, 1976–85

($ millions)

	Selected Years			Average Annual Result, 1976–85
	1976	1980	1985	
BASE CASE:				
Utility	18,368	29,611	42,453	30,528
CASE A:				
Utility	16,195	24,418	39,918	26,966
Industry	—	4,146	866	1,420
Total	16,195	28,564	40,784	28,386
Total savings compared to base	2,173	1,047	1,669	2,142
Utilities' savings compared to base	2,173	5,193	2,535	3,562
CASE B:				
Utility	15,090	21,131	39,230	25,225
Industry	—	5,607	1,171	1,920
Total	15,090	26,738	40,301	27,145
Total savings compared to base	3,278	2,873	2,152	3,383
Utilities' savings compared to base	3,278	8,480	3,223	5,303
CASE C:				
Utility	17,273	16,196	20,972	17,488
Joint venture	—	5,914	17,122	8,732
Total	17,273	22,110	38,094	26,220
Total savings compared to base	1,095	7,501	4,359	4,308
Utilities' savings compared to base	1,095	13,415	21,481	13,040
CASE D:				
Utility	17,844	16,228	25,371	19,038
Joint venture	—	—	15,982	4,992
Industry	—	2,411	—	1,289
Total	17,844	18,639	41,353	25,319
Total savings compared to base	524	10,972	1,100	5,209
Utilities' savings compared to base	524	23,383	17,082	11,490

Source: *Energy Industrial Center Study,* p. 274.

Table 6

COMPARISON OF EXTERNAL FINANCING NEEDS UNDER THE ALTERNATIVE CASES, 1976–85

($ millions)

	Selected Years			Average Annual Result, 1976–85
	1976	1980	1985	
BASE CASE: Utility	15,581	23,203	28,464	22,732
CASE A:				
Utility	13,580	17,588	27,670	19,962
Industry [a]	—	3,110	650	1,065
Total	13,580	20,698	28,320	21,027
Total savings compared to base	2,001	2,505	144	1,705
Utilities' savings compared to base	2,001	5,615	794	2,770
CASE B:				
Utility	12,565	13,944	27,873	18,597
Industry	—	4,205	878	1,440
Total	12,565	18,149	28,751	20,037
Total savings compared to base	3,016	5,054	(287)	2,695
Utilities' savings compared to base	3,016	9,259	591	4,135
CASE C:				
Utility	14,593	15,497	18,820	15,426
Joint venture	—	2,957	8,561	4,366
Total	14,593	18,454	27,381	19,792
Total savings compared to base	988	4,749	1,083	2,940
Utilities' savings compared to base	988	7,706	9,644	7,306
CASE D:				
Utility	15,123	16,776	21,067	15,343
Joint venture	—	—	7,991	2,496
Industry	—	1,808	—	967
Total	15,123	18,584	29,058	18,806
Total savings compared to base	458	4,619	(594)	3,926
Utilities' savings compared to base	458	6,427	7,397	7,389

[a] Industry is assumed to finance externally the same proportions of capital expenditure as do utilities.

Source: *Energy Industrial Center Study,* p. 277.

electric bill could be an average of $2.60 a month or $31.20 a year lower than it would otherwise be over the period from 1976 to 1985.

On average, residential consumers will spend $44.9 billion a year for electricity with no implementation compared with $41.3 billion in the most optimistic of the cases above. That is, the most optimistic case would produce a savings of $3.6 billion per year. Without implementation, electric rates should remain more or less constant in real dollars between 1976 and 1985.[29]

These figures for consumer savings do not include the effect of the lower rates of return on capital likely to be required if external financial demands are in fact reduced. Generally speaking, the greater the quantity of capital a firm or industry demands in the capital markets, the greater the rate of return it must offer. Thus, reducing external capital demands would mean that overall rates of return for utilities, and hence consumer costs, would be somewhat lower than they would otherwise be. Moreover, at lower rates, consumers would presumably use more electricity and thereby derive still greater benefits. The consumer savings computed here reflect only one of the three sources of savings. Further research will be necessary before the contribution of lower rates of return and price elasticity to consumer savings can be quantified.

4. Legal and Regulatory Considerations

Federal, state, and local regulations governing the generation and sale of electric power affect every phase of utility operation and could interfere with industrial participation in power generation. Whatever degree of success utility regulations may have had in fulfilling their intended purposes, they might well prove to be an obstacle to the widespread implementation of a generation scheme never anticipated during the period in which they evolved.

In the short run, industrial firms and utilities would have to tread carefully in order to avoid running afoul of hidden regulatory pitfalls. Full implementation might require a major reform of the regulatory system, removing unintended obstacles and possibly adding calculated incentives. A survey of the existing legal and regulatory environment will suggest directions such reform might take.

For the purposes of this survey, it will be convenient to distinguish between the two approaches to EIC implementation by designating industrial power generation as Model 1 and dual-purpose

---

[29] Ibid., p. 287.

Table 7

COMPARISON OF UTILITY POWER RATES UNDER THE
ALTERNATIVE CASES, 1976–85

	Residential Rates				Commercial Rates			
	1976	1980	1985	Avg. Year	1976	1980	1985	Avg. Year
BASE CASE: ¢/kwh	3.62	4.79	6.21	5.03	3.49	4.70	6.16	4.84
1973 ¢/kwh	2.78	2.80	2.75	2.81	2.68	2.75	2.73	2.76
CASE A: ¢/kwh	3.61	4.60	6.09	4.80	3.47	4.50	6.03	4.71
1973 ¢/kwh	2.77	2.69	2.70	2.70	2.67	2.63	2.67	2.64
% change in nominal rates from base case	(0.2)	(4.0)	(1.9)	(4.6)	(0.6)	(4.2)	(2.1)	(2.7)
CASE B: ¢/kwh	3.60	4.46	5.93	4.69	3.47	4.35	5.85	4.58
1973 ¢/kwh	2.77	2.61	2.63	2.61	2.66	2.54	2.59	2.54
% change in nominal rates from base case	(0.5)	(6.9)	(4.5)	(6.8)	(0.6)	(7.4)	(5.0)	(5.4)
CASE C: ¢/kwh	3.59	4.60	5.51	4.63	3.52	4.49	5.37	4.52
1973 ¢/kwh	2.76	2.69	2.44	2.69	2.70	2.63	2.38	2.62
% change in nominal rates from base case	(0.8)	(4.0)	(11.3)	(8.0)	0.9	(4.5)	(12.8)	(6.6)
CASE D: ¢/kwh	3.59	4.60	5.51	4.63	3.52	4.49	5.44	4.54
1973 ¢/kwh	2.76	2.69	2.44	2.69	2.70	2.63	2.38	2.63
% change in nominal rates from base case	(0.8)	(4.0)	(11.3)	(8.0)	0.9	(4.5)	(11.7)	(6.2)

Source: *Energy Industrial Center Study*, p. 284.

central power stations as Model 2. Each of the two models raises its own questions, and the answers to these questions bear directly both on the desirability of the proposals and on the forms they might take. It is assumed here that the industrial participant would desire minimal federal and state regulation of its operations. For utility participants who are accustomed to the regulatory process, government regulation is less likely to be a deterrent to participation in such ventures.

The Federal Power Act (1920). This legislation established the Federal Power Commission (FPC) to regulate the operation of public utilities. Although the FPC would lack direct jurisdiction over industrial firms participating in EIC (either Model 1 or Model 2), it would still exercise indirect influence over the sale of industrial power to the

Industrial Rates				Other				Average Rates			
1976	1980	1985	Avg. Year	1976	1980	1985	Avg. Year	1976	1980	1985	Avg. Year
2.13	2.91	3.61	2.93	3.16	4.28	5.57	4.40	2.99	4.06	5.21	4.20
1.64	1.70	1.60	1.70	2.43	2.50	2.47	2.51	2.30	2.37	2.31	2.38
2.13	2.84	3.58	2.89	3.15	4.11	5.47	4.28	2.98	4.06	5.34	4.17
1.63	1.66	1.58	1.66	2.42	2.40	2.42	2.41	2.29	2.37	2.36	2.41
0	(2.4)	(0.8)	(1.4)	(0.3)	(4.0)	(1.8)	(2.7)	(0.3)	0	2.5	(0.7)
2.13	2.78	3.52	2.85	3.15	3.98	5.31	4.18	2.98	3.94	5.20	4.08
1.63	1.63	1.56	1.63	2.42	2.33	2.35	2.33	2.29	2.30	2.30	2.30
0	(4.5)	(2.5)	(2.7)	(0.3)	(7.0)	(4.7)	(5.0)	(0.3)	(3.0)	(0.2)	(2.9)
2.13	2.86	3.64	2.92	3.18	4.11	4.97	4.14	2.99	3.91	4.76	3.95
1.64	1.67	1.61	1.68	2.45	2.40	2.20	2.40	2.30	2.29	2.11	2.29
0	(1.7)	0.8	(0.3)	0.6	(4.0)	(10.8)	(5.9)	0	(3.7)	(8.6)	(6.0)
2.13	2.83	3.52	2.87	3.18	4.10	4.94	4.14	2.99	3.95	4.83	3.99
1.64	1.65	1.56	1.65	2.45	2.40	2.19	2.40	2.30	2.31	2.14	2.31
0	(6.2)	(2.5)	(2.0)	0.6	(4.2)	(11.3)	(5.9)	0	(7.6)	(7.3)	(5.0)

utility when it determined whether the cost of service claimed by the public utility, which would include the price it paid for power generated by industrial firms, was "just and reasonable." [30] The Federal Power Commission would disallow a portion of the contract price only if the cost were unreasonable compared with the cost of obtaining energy from alternative sources. The rate of return of the industrial firm would not be considered in this indirect FPC review.[31]

In the case of Model 2, the venture might be regarded as an integral facility of a public utility already subject to direct regulation by the FPC, and the FPC would have authority to review the reasonableness of the venture's profit as well as the price charged to the

[30] Ibid., p. 330.
[31] Ibid., p. 338.

Table 8

COMPARISON OF RESIDENTIAL POWER BILLS
UNDER THE ALTERNATIVE CASES, 1976–85

(dollars)

	Average Monthly Bill			
	1976	1980	1985	Average, 1976-85
BASE CASE	23.40	37.44	54.54	39.75
CASE A	23.32	35.97	53.52	38.70
Change from base case	(0.08)	(1.47)	(1.02)	(1.05)
Percentage change from base case	(0.3)	(3.9)	(1.9)	(2.6)[a]
CASE B	23.28	34.86	52.07	37.82
Change from base case	(0.12)	(2.58)	(2.47)	(1.93)
Percentage change from base case	(0.5)	(6.9)	(4.5)	(4.9)
CASE C	23.19	35.33	48.42	37.14
Change from base case	(0.21)	(1.51)	(6.12)	(2.61)
Percentage change from base case	(0.9)	(4.0)	(11.2)	(6.6)
CASE D	23.20	35.93	48.35	37.13
Change from base case	(0.20)	(1.51)	(6.19)	(2.62)
Percentage change from base case	(0.8)	(4.0)	(11.3)	(6.6)

[a] Because the growth pattern in the number of customers differs from the growth in residential demand, the case-to-case percentage change in average monthly residential bill shown here is not the same as the percentage change in average residential rates as given in Table 7.

Source: *Energy Industrial Center Study*, p. 285.

utility partner for energy acquired from the joint venture.[32] There is sufficient uncertainty as to FPC jurisdiction over the relationship created by the jointly owned central power station that if such joint ventures are to be encouraged as a matter of economic policy, the Federal Power Act should be amended to rule out direct FPC jurisdiction over such a venture. The FPC could still retain the right to review the utility partner's costs of energy acquired from the venture

---

[32] Ibid.

in determining whether utility charges for wholesale resales of that energy are "just and reasonable."

Although the only escalation provision expressly authorized by FPC regulations is a fuel cost adjustment clause, it would appear that a long-term power sale contract could contain a complete cost-of-service adjustment formula as long as it fairly reflected all costs of service.[33]

Public Utility Holding Company Act (1935). This act vests jurisdiction over all statutory public utility holding companies in the Securities and Exchange Commission. In the absence of a parent corporation or a 10 percent stockholder, the act will generally have no application where a participant in the venture operates the generating assets directly. If the industrial participant in Model 1 operates its generating facilities as a separate subsidiary, the industrial company might be a holding company, although it is likely under Model 1 that either the subsidiary or the parent company, or both, could qualify for certain exemptions from the jurisdiction of the act. For example, under the act the parent would not be a holding company if it were primarily engaged in other non-utility business and did not derive a material part of its income from a public utility subsidiary.[34]

It seems likely that the venture in Model 2 would be regarded as an electric utility under the act because a substantial portion of its business would be to provide one of its parents with electricity for distribution to the public. Both the industrial and public utility participants would then be holding companies, again with certain exemptions specified.

Although it seems likely that one or more exemptions from the Public Utility Holding Company Act should be available to both the industrial firms and the public utility, the establishment of such an exemption requires an application to, and approval from, the Securities and Exchange Commission. In light of the serious consequences of violating this complex statute and the disincentive effect of its mere presence, serious consideration should be given to establishing a clear exemption from its provisions for ventures of the type contemplated. Otherwise, the requirements of the act would produce serious constraints on the corporate structure of these ventures.

State Regulations. In general, state regulatory commissions would have no direct jurisdiction over the price of energy or the rate of

---

[33] Ibid., p. 339.
[34] Ibid., p. 350. Other exemptions are listed here.

251

return to the industrial participant in a Model 1 arrangement, because most states regulate only companies that own or operate facilities to supply electricity to the public or for the public use. However, in certain states (New York, for example) the mere ownership of an electric plant at which electricity generated for sale is sufficient to create public utility status. In such a case, a regulatory commission would have the authority to regulate the price that an industrial firm charged for by-product electricity sold under a long-term power sale contract. Similarly, all commissions would presumably regulate the price at which a subsidiary of a venture under Model 2 sold power to its parent corporations or to wholesale customers in intrastate commerce.

The fact that a utility entered into a long-term arrangement with an industrial company either under Model 1 or Model 2 would not seem to be a violation of the typical state statutory requirement that rates and service be nondiscriminatory. Although under either model the industrial participant might be an incidental beneficiary of the utility's desire to create an economical power source, this would probably not be construed as the adoption of an unlawful preferential practice or rate by the utility partner.

Application of Antitrust Laws. Neither Model 1 nor Model 2 appears to raise any unavoidable antitrust problems under the Sherman and Clayton acts. Neither form of the venture would appear to affect competition adversely, because the two participants would not be potential competitors within the meaning of current law. Moreover, contractual restrictions as to the parties that might acquire energy from the new generation facilities and the provisions for the participants' taking their own energy requirements in kind would seem acceptable, since they would serve a reasonable business purpose. Where power generation would be incidental to its primary, non-utility business, the industrial company would not normally be willing to undertake such an investment in generation facilities without a guaranteed purchaser of power. The utility, in turn, could not depend on the industrial company or the joint venture company as a source of electricity unless it were guaranteed a reasonably steady supply.

The long-term character of the proposed relationship would also seem reasonable given the necessity for the utility to plan for a stable supply of electricity for future public needs. However, there is some suggestion in the recent *Otter Tail* decision that where similar ventures cannot be formed by other parties, the participants might be ordered to wheel or to sell energy to parties unable to enter their own agreements independently.[35]

Arrangements under both models would have to avoid restrictions on the use that either party would make of the energy sold and on the territory in which either party could operate. Such restrictions, in any case, should not be essential to the feasibility or desirability of the proposed ventures. The arrangement under either model also seems unlikely to involve price discrimination prohibited by the Robinson-Patman Act.[36]

Tax Considerations. The Tax Reduction Act of 1975 increased the investment tax credit for utilities and other industries to 10 percent for a period of two years. For the utilities, the act raised from 50 percent to 100 percent the portion of tax liability that may be offset by the investment tax credit in 1975. This will decrease by 10 percent each year for five years beginning in 1975.

Under Model 1, the industrial firm would be the owner of the facility and would therefore be entitled to claim any available investment tax credit and depreciation deductions on the facility. The public utility would, of course, reduce operating revenues by the cost of purchased power in arriving at taxable federal income. Under Model 2 in the subsidiary corporation form, applicable investment tax credit and depreciation could probably be claimed only by the subsidiary corporation. This would have disadvantages since the subsidiary corporation would be unlikely to have sufficient income in the early years to make use of these tax benefits.

There are two possible refinements to these conclusions.[37] First, if either the industrial firm or the utility owned more than 80 percent of the subsidiary corporation, the subsidiary could join in consolidated returns filed by the predominant shareholder, thus making investment tax credit and depreciation deductions available to that shareholder. Second, it is conceivable (though currently unlikely) that a ruling might be received from the Internal Revenue Service treating the subsidiary corporation as analogous to the "cost companies" employed in mining ventures. This treatment would allow the subsidiary's income, deduction, and credits to be allocated to its shareholders. The Internal Revenue Service is not known to have approved the "cost company" concept in connection with non-mining ventures.

[35] Ibid., pp. 400-1.
[36] Ibid., pp. 405-7.
[37] See *EICS*, pp. 444-49 for more detailed background for these conclusions.

If a joint venture for the construction of a central generating station were entered into as an unincorporated joint venture or partnership, with the industrial firm and the utility partner each having an undivided interest in the venture and in the energy produced, the items of income deduction and credit of the unincorporated joint venture would be allocated between the ventures in accordance with the provisions of the joint venture agreement, so long as those provisions would have a business purpose and are not motivated by tax avoidance.

A more sophisticated version of the joint venture might take the form of a "leveraged lease" financing. In this form, a substantial part of the cost of the generating facility would be paid for through equity capital contributed by an investor (or group of investors) seeking the tax benefits generated by the facility. The remainder would be financed through long-term loans which would be nonrecourse for the equity investors. These investors would then lease the generating facility either to the industrial firm under Model 1 or to the subsidiary corporation or unincorporated joint venture under Model 2, with the residual value of the facility retained by the investors.

Concluding Note. Although this discussion has touched on only the most basic of the legal questions that would confront the prospective EIC participant, it may perhaps have provided an adequate outline of the jurisdictional landscape. If the advantages of EICs are as substantial as has been suggested here, there should be an effort to encourage such ventures, either by reform or by clarification of the regulatory system.

5. Policy Implications

Although the dramatic increases in fuel costs, capital costs, and other utility expenses—and the resulting rate increases—should provide a strong incentive for implementing the EIC concept, the level of existing or planned industrial participation in power generation remains low. In time, the favorable economics of the concept will probably prevail over regulatory and managerial inertia and will induce an increasing number of firms to enter the field of power generation. However, the urgency of the situation in the utility industry makes it imperative to consider an active government policy to promote implementation.

The policy implications of the concept could themselves be the subject of an entire study. However, the foregoing discussion does indicate where some of the obstacles to implementation may lie and thus implicitly suggests several preliminary proposals.

Preliminary Proposals. Although it is too early to give full endorsement to all of the suggestions that follow, a comprehensive study of these and other proposals would be the first step in a national implementation policy.

Statutory revision. Those provisions of the Federal Power Act and Public Utility Holding Company Act which have the greatest discentive effect on implementation of the ventures could be changed.

Regulatory encouragement. Regulatory commissions could refuse to allow utilities to include capital and construction expenses for new capacity in their rate base wherever industrially generated power is available at lower cost—adjusted for dependability. As more industrial power sources come on line, increased flexibility would make industrial power more nearly comparable in dependability to central-station power. Eventually, aggregate industrial capacity could serve as standby capacity during outages at individual industrial plants, and utilities could reduce or eliminate standby demand charges to EIC plants. This would further reduce the risks to the industrial plant that relied on self-generation. Until it becomes clear what effect business cycle fluctuations would have on industrial power generation, and as long as other areas of uncertainty remain, some allowance for the dependability requirements of utilities would have to be included in cost comparisons with industrially generated power.

Wheeling services. Utility transmission capacity could operate as a common carrier, with wheeling services accessible to all producers of electricity at a published tariff rate. This could pave the way for full integration of industrial generation into the national electrical system and permit the fullest possible degree of competition in the utility industry.

Tax incentives. Tax incentives might include a full pass-through of subsidiary income, deductions, and credits to parent industrial and utility corporations.

Fuel allocation priorities. Regulations issued by the Federal Energy Administration under the Emergency Petroleum Allocation Act of 1973 gave first priority in allocating residual fuel oil to agricultural uses, space heating, and utilities. Industrial uses were given second priority. Granting first priority status to industrial generation of power could provide additional stimulus to such ventures.

Environmental allowances. The generation and transmission of electricity can have an impact on the environment. Therefore, federal and state statutes on protection of air and water quality and on regulating land use will affect the location, design, and construction of generation transmission facilities under either Model 1 or Model 2. Because the overall environmental impact of EIC generation should be favorable, industrial firms and utilities that attempt an EIC venture could be granted exemption from the most burdensome air- and water-quality and land-use standards.

Conclusion. Under any circumstances a nation should take advantage of every opportunity to make more efficient use of its resources. Under present circumstances, failure to identify and capitalize on any opportunity could result in irreparable damage to the health of our economy. Fortunately, in unregulated competitive industries, market forces induce a preference for the most efficient organization and use of resources. In the case of the investor-owned electric utilities, an effort should be made to overcome the effects of a regulatory burden that has vitiated this natural impulse.

When so many other proposed energy solutions seem motivated primarily by a desire to punish the producers and consumers of power, and when even the best-intended strategies threaten to exacerbate the nation's economic problems, an idea that promises improvement through increased efficiency deserves full national attention.

ABOUT THE AUTHORS

EDWARD J. MITCHELL, Director of the American Enterprise Institute's National Energy Project, is professor of business economics at the University of Michigan's Graduate School of Business Administration.

PETER R..CHAFFETZ, formerly on the research staff at the American Enterprise Institute, is a student at the University of Chicago Law School.

PAUL W. MacAVOY is Henry R. Luce professor of public policy at M.I.T., and a member of the research staff of the M.I.T. Energy Laboratory.

RICHARD B. MANCKE is associate professor of international economic relations at the Fletcher School of Law and Diplomacy, Tufts University.

ROBERT S. PINDYCK is assistant professor of economics in the Sloan School of Management at M.I.T., and a member of the research staff of the M.I.T. Energy Laboratory.

ALTERNATIVE ENERGY STRATEGIES: Constraints and Opportunities
John Hagel, III

CHINA'S ENERGY: Achievements, Problems, Prospects
Vaclav Smil

THE ENERGY CRISIS AND U.S. FOREIGN POLICY*
edited by Joseph S. Szyliowicz and Bard E. O'Neill

THE SOVIET ENERGY BALANCE: Natural Gas, Other Fossil Fuels, and Alternative Power Sources
Iain F. Elliot

THE UNITED STATES AND INTERNATIONAL OIL: A Report for the Federal Energy Administration on U.S. Firms and Government Policy*
Robert B. Krueger

*Also available in paperback as a PSS Student Edition.